CHILDREN OF THE CITY

David Nasaw

CHILDREN OF THE CITY

At Work and At Play

Anchor Press/Doubleday
Garden City, New York
1985

To my mother, Beatrice Nasaw, and
the memory of my father, Joshua J. Nasaw

Library of Congress Cataloging in Publication Data

Nasaw, David.
  Children of the city.

  Includes index.
  1. Children of immigrants—United States—Case studies. 2. City children—United
States—Case studies. 3. United States—Social conditions—1865–1918. I. Title.
HQ792.U5N36 1985   305.2'3'0973   84-10142
ISBN 0-385-17164-1

Designed by Virginia M. Soulé

Library of Congress Cataloging in Publication Data

ISBN 0-385-17164-1

First Edition

Acknowledgments

I have received much assistance in the writing of this book. Rhoda Weyr's advice and encouragement were instrumental in the design of the project. Richard Drinnon carefully read and thoughtfully commented on the first draft. James Gilbert's critique of an early version helped me clarify my thoughts and focus my interpretation. Fred Binder and Daniel Coleman offered suggestions for improving the text. Herbert Leibowitz read and meticulously critiqued the final version.

Papers delivered at the Columbia University Faculty Seminar in American Civilization, the American Educational Research Association annual convention, the New York Institute for the Humanities, and Bucknell University offered an opportunity to share, clarify, and amend my thinking.

I am very grateful to Bill Leach for his help in the final stages of the project. Numerous discussions with him have helped me to sharpen and, I believe, buttress my arguments. Phil Pachoda has read several drafts of the manuscript and responded to each with valuable suggestions. Warren Susman has, almost from the first day, been generous with his time, energy, bibliographic resources, and analytic brilliance. He saw, at times before I did, the larger meaning of the story I was trying to tell.

I am thankful to Owen Laster for his ongoing support. Loretta Barrett's enthusiasm and editorial skills have been invaluable assets to the project. She has helped me to shape what was a mass of material into what I now hope is a coherent, structured whole. Felecia Abbadessa has, with grace and humor, shepherded the book through production. Viera Morse did a remarkable job of copy editing.

I am indebted to Dinitia Smith for her faith in me and my book. She has been my best reader, certainly my most critical one. I have profited immeasurably from her encouragement, her critical acumen, her editorial assistance, and her good humor.

I wish to acknowledge the financial support of the National Endowment for the Humanities.

Preface

This book is about children and the cities they grew up in, about children at play and children at work. The time is the first decades of this century, the period in which so many of our grandparents and great-grandparents emigrated to the cities and the era in which children were expected to work in their spare time after school, on weekends, and during holidays.

These were the years of our own social childhood: the years in which we first began to use the telephone, go to the movies, drive automobiles, ride on subways, eat fresh bananas and oranges, and survive—as best we could—by learning to play as hard as we worked. In all of this, the children were a step in front. Just as today children lead us into the computer age, seventy-five years ago they led the way into the twentieth century. In cities where the majority of adults had been raised in the countryside, it was the children who were the most comfortable, the most adaptable, the most competent. The city was, after all, the only world they knew; it was the place they called home.

This book does not take as its starting point the assumption that the city is, has been, and must be the worst possible environment for the young. City kids grew up without adequate air, light, and space to play and grow, but, compared to their rural counterparts locked inside mines, mills, and canneries or put out to work on sugar beet, cotton, and berry fields, they were privileged. The children of the city did not wither and die in the urban air but were able to carve out social space of their own. They converted streets, stoops, sidewalks, alleyways, and the city's wastelands into their playgrounds. As they reached the age of ten or eleven, they went to work in the downtown business, shopping, and entertainment districts where, every afternoon after school, they scavenged for junk, blacked boots, peddled gum, candy, and handkerchiefs, and hawked the latest editions of the afternoon dailies.

At play and at work, the children inhabited a social world in the midst of but distinct from the adult worlds around them. They organized their own space, regulated their own street trades, made and enforced their unwritten laws, protected their properties and their profits, and, when mistreated by the adults they worked with, established unions and went out on strike. In one such strike, in New York City in 1899, they astounded the public and the press by shutting down circulation of the New York *Evening Journal* and *Evening World*, forcing the two most powerful publishers in the nation, William Randolph Hearst and Joseph Pulitzer, to arrive at a compromise agreeable to employees too young to shave.

The children of the street worked hard—and then they played hard. Though they were expected to turn over all their earnings to their mothers, they held back enough to buy themselves a good time in the city. They were connoisseurs of the streets, devotees of the corner candy shops, the nickelodeons, penny arcades, amusement parks, vaudeville halls, cheap eateries, red-hot stands, and pushcart vendors. The money they earned magically transported them from the realm of dependent childhood to the world of consumption where money, not age, brought with it fun and freedom.

I have tried to write about the children of the street from their perspective, not that of parents, teachers, child labor reformers, settlement house workers, or juvenile justice authorities. I have approached them as sentient, intentional beings desirous and capable (within limits) of acting on and within their social environments. The children were subjects of history but like all historical beings they grew up in a social world they had not created. They were autonomous and free but within limits not of their own choosing. They claimed the street as their social center, playground, and workplace. It became "theirs" in a way that home, school, and settlement house could never be. Nonetheless, the street belonged to the city, not the children. And the city was ruled by adults. To paraphrase Jean-Paul Sartre, paraphrasing Friedrich Engels, the street made the children while the children made the street.

This study owes its life to the thousands of pages of primary source material generated, collected, assembled, and preserved by early twentieth-century settlement-house workers, educators, juvenile court officials, social workers, sociologists, law enforcement officials, and the thousands of men and women, amateurs and professionals, generically referred to as "reformers." These adults, like their muckraker journalist contemporaries, believed in the power of direct observation to crystallize truth which, communicated properly, would then lead to action. In the course of my research, I have examined hundreds of their reports: on newsboys in New York City, Buffalo, Syracuse, Albany, Yonkers, Mount Vernon, Boston, Philadelphia, Bennington and Burlington (Vermont), Newark and Jersey City, Cincinnati and Cleveland, Baltimore, Detroit, Des Moines, Milwaukee, Chicago, Seattle, St. Louis, Dallas, Kansas City, Birmingham, and other cities across the country; on "delinquents" in reformatories and "wayward" children in the children's courts; on the children's lives at work, at play, at school, and at home; on the foods they ate; the movies they watched; the games they played; the candy stores they frequented; the clothes they wore; the languages their parents spoke; and the homes they lived in.

These reports, some published, some unpublished, some never even completed, provided the base upon which I was able to construct my picture of urban childhood. Oral histories, autobiographies, and a few autobiographical novels offered a complementary but divergent perspective. While the reformers—to elicit action from public and politicians—painted their picture of urban youth in the most dismal tones, the narrative accounts and oral histories, with few exceptions, presented the subject in a very different light. They described the dirt and the dangers of urban life, but also the fun, the excitement, the hope for the future that the children experienced at the turn of the century.

Though, regrettably, by the time I began my research, the majority of my subjects were either deceased or at an age where they were not often able to remember their childhoods with clarity, I was able to utilize a number of oral history collections, published and unpublished, which included detailed first-person accounts of working-class childhood at the turn of the century.

An additional source of evidence used in the study were the photographs of children at work and at play taken by early twentieth-century photographers, reformers, and journalists. Though I had at first intended to use these pictures as "illustrations" for my text, I quickly discovered that they were primary source material as interesting and informative in their own right as the narrative accounts of life on the streets. A sample of the photographs consulted has been included in the book.

In the course of my research, I have read many biographies and autobiographies of novelists, educators, philosophers, gangsters, businessmen, housewives, textile workers, politicians, union organizers, musicians, diplomats, and even a heavyweight champion of the world. The most numerous and most valuable were the books by and about entertainers and celebrities. While many of these were written to settle scores, assail enemies, praise friends, and rescue or preserve reputations, the first twenty-five to seventy-five pages—where the authors speak of their childhood—were relatively free of cant, with few names dropped, grudges recalled, or actions defended. The authors seemed to enjoy recalling their childhood, finding in their past more than they realized was there and taking care to recreate it as vividly and accurately as possible.

The street children who grew up to become stars or make their mark in the entertainment world were not like all the others. Their ambition, drive, talent, and eventual success would put them into different social worlds when they grew up. As children, however, they lived the same daily lives as their friends, classmates, neighbors, or brothers and sisters (with a few exceptions like Milton Berle, who was whisked off the streets and onto the stage before he was six years old). Nobody knew they were going to be famous and nobody treated them any differently. They were kids, perhaps a bit louder, brasher, or funnier than the others, but still just kids who grew up on the same streets, doing the same things as their playmates. Their stories, critically evaluated, provide an invaluable source of information on the daily life and work of city kids in the first decades of this century.

Unlike my other sources of evidence, the celebrity autobiographies are biased toward Russian Jewish children who grew up in Manhattan and Brooklyn. In comparing their accounts of childhood with those presented in the reformers' investigative reports and the oral histories, I discovered—to no great surprise—that no matter what city or town the boys and girls grew up in, and no matter what their ethnic origin, the conditions they encountered on the streets and their response to those conditions were much the same. Working-class Irish kids in Toledo and Philadelphia, Jews in Youngstown and Syracuse, Poles in Chicago and Pittsburgh, Italians in Los Angeles and Cleveland, and "natives" in cities across the country earned their money after school by scavenging for the same kind of junk, selling afternoon papers, blacking boots, and peddling spearmint gum and chocolate bars to commuters, tourists, and people out for a good time on a Saturday night. Wherever they came from, they were expected to turn in their money to their parents. Wherever they came from, they were likely to hold some back to see the same kinds of movies in the nickelodeons and gorge themselves on the same kinds of treats from pushcart peddlers and corner candy stores. Though there were differences in the languages they spoke at home, the gods they worshipped, and the land their parents called "home," the developing twentieth-century urban culture transcended the particularities of ethnicity, geography, and population size to bind them together into one generation.

Contents

1

The City
They Called Home

The early twentieth-century city was among the wonders of the New World. Concentrated within it were the marvels of the age. Electric lights made night into day. Subways, streetcars, and the elevated sped commuters through the streets. Steel-girded skyscrapers and granite railroad stations expressed its solidity and its power. Lobster palaces, vaudeville palaces, movie palaces, and department store palaces of consumption recreated in the present the mythic splendors of the past.

American cities had expanded in all directions in the decades surrounding the turn of the century: up with the skyscrapers, down into the subway tunnels, outward across the bridges and tunnels to the new streetcar suburbs. The central business districts, once crowded with warehouses but not much else, had been enlarged and subdivided into financial, government, manufacturing, warehousing, shopping, and entertainment districts, each with its army of workers.[1]

Every morning swarms of commuters boarded their trolleys, trains, cable cars, elevateds, and subways for the ride to town. Three quarters of a million people flowed daily off the elevated into the Chicago Loop. They arrived in downtown Boston from Roxbury, West Roxbury, Dorchester, and the surrounding "streetcar suburbs." In Cincinnati, Columbus, and Pittsburgh, they took electric streetcars from the heights into the "flats" of the central city. In Manhattan, they trooped to work across the bridges, on the ferries, and by streetcar, elevated train, and subway.

Theodore Dreiser described the procession from his vantage point at the Williamsburg Bridge. "Already at six and six-thirty in the morning they have begun to trickle small streams of human beings Manhattan or cityward, and by seven and seven-fifteen these streams have become sizable affairs. By seven-thirty and eight they have changed into heavy, turbulent rivers and by eight-fifteen and eight-thirty and nine they are raging torrents, no less. They overflow all the streets and avenues and every available means of conveyance. They are pouring into all available doorways, shops, factories, office-buildings—those huge affairs towering so significantly above them. Here they stay all day long, causing those great hives and their adjacent streets to flush with a softness of color not indigenous to them, and then at night, between five and six, they are going again, pouring forth over the bridges and through the subways and across the ferries and out on the trains, until the last drop of them appears to have been exuded."[2]

Those who arrived in the central business districts came to work, but they stayed to be entertained and to shop. The city's palaces of consumption were as new, as exciting, and as spectacular as its skyscrapers and bridges. The downtown department stores, huge as factories, luxurious as the most opulent millionaire's mansions, and jammed full of goods were a relatively new phenomenon in the life of the city. Until the 1870s there had been no real downtown shopping streets. City folk did their shopping in neighborhood stores or from itinerant peddlers. Local shops were specialized: butcher, baker, and candlestick maker had their own establishments where they produced and sold their own goods.

The extension of the streetcar lines into the suburbs and the new concentration of white-collar workers downtown provided retailers with hundreds of thousands of customers. Old-fashioned dry goods stores were expanded into department stores and then relocated and rebuilt along the busiest streetcar and subway lines to make shopping as convenient as possible for suburban women, tourists, and downtown workers.

Visitors to the city joined the commuters and workers on the shopping streets where the department stores were located. In Manhattan, the first "Ladies' Mile" was situated along Broadway and Fifth and Sixth Avenues between Eighth and Twenty-third Streets. There was nothing like it anywhere in the world. Wanamaker's, a sixteen-story cast-iron giant, was at Eighth Street and Broadway, Hearn's was on Fourteenth Street, and Siegel-Cooper's on Sixth Avenue and Eighteenth Street with its main attraction, "The Fountain," a circular marble terrace surrounding a mammoth marble and brass statue of "The Republic" shooting jets of water, "illuminated by myriad colored lights." Across the street from the

Wilmington, Delaware, May 1910. "James Loquilla, newsboy, twelve years old. Selling newspapers three years. Average earnings 50¢ per week. Selling newspapers own choice. Earnings not needed at home. Don't smoke. Visits saloons. Works seven hours a day." Unlike the mythic street-urchin newsboy portrayed by Horatio Alger, the real-life model was apt to be well dressed, as this boy was, with a sturdy pair of shoes, high socks, knickers and a stylish cap. (*Lewis Hine, LC*)

Big Store was B. Altman's, a short walk away were Stern Brothers, Lord and Taylor, Arnold Constable, Best and Company, Bonwit Teller's, W. and J. Sloane, and Macy's.[3]

As the city moved northward so did the department stores. Macy's in 1901 broke ground on its new Herald Square store—with one million square feet of floor space. Within a decade all the other downtown stores had relocated on Fifth Avenue or close by.[4]

In Chicago, State Street was as grand a tourist attraction as New

York's Fifth Avenue. One could wander up and down the avenue for days without running out of stores to visit and windows to peer into. There was Marshall Field's with its forty acres of shopping and its forty-five plate glass windows; Carson, Pirie, Scott's in its new building designed by Louis Sullivan; Fair, Rothschild's, Siegel, Cooper and Company; the Boston Store; Mandel Brothers; and the Stevens Store— all within walking distance of one another.[5]

Every city had its own special stores, stores which had grown up with the downtown areas and, in the beginning, helped lure customers from the outskirts: Jordan Marsh's and Filene's in Boston, the original Wanamaker's and Gimbel's in Philadelphia, Kaufmann's in Pittsburgh, Abraham and Straus in Brooklyn, Rich's in Atlanta, Neiman-Marcus in Dallas, Goldwater's in Prescott and then in Phoenix, Arizona, I. Magnin's in San Francisco, Hudson's in Detroit, and Lazarus in Columbus.

The department stores were more than containers of goods or huge indoor markets. They were living encyclopedias of abundance designed to overwhelm the consumer with the variety of items available for purchase. The department stores brought together under one roof an unimaginable collection of commodities, catalogued by department, arranged by floor. Furniture, rugs, and bedding were on the upper floors; ready-to-wear clothing and shoes for women and children on the middle floors; bargain goods and groceries in the basement. The street-level floors displayed clothing and accessories for men, who it was feared would not take the time to ride to the higher floors; and for the women, dozens and dozens of alluring, lower-priced items: cosmetics, notions, gloves, stationery, hosiery.[6]

What overwhelmed was not simply the variety of goods, but the variety and abundance of luxury goods, "from silk dresses and chocolate-covered candies to bicycles, cigarettes, and pink popcorn, which consumers had not produced themselves and which they did not need."[7]

The department stores, by so artfully juxtaposing the necessary and the frivolous, redefined and intertwined needs with desires. There was so much there, at such a range of prices, it was difficult to know what to buy. Sister Carrie, recently arrived in the city from the countryside and looking for work, was directed by a policeman to "The Fair," one of Chicago's more massive and imposing stores. "Carrie passed along the busy aisles, much affected by the remarkable displays of trinkets, dress goods, stationery, and jewelry. Each separate counter was a showplace of dazzling interest and attraction. She could not help feeling the claim of each trinket and valuable upon her personally, and yet she did not stop. There was nothing there which she could not have used—nothing which she did not long to own. The dainty slippers and stockings, the

4

delicately frilled skirts and petticoats, the laces, ribbons, hair-combs, purses, all touched her with individual desire."[8]

One did not have to go inside to be touched by the magic of the stores. Plate-glass windows with superbly crafted displays highlighted by "the planned adoption of electrical lighting and of a new color technology, of drapery and mechanical props, of reflectors and wax mannequins, and even, occasionally of living models . . . consciously converted what had once been dull places stuffed with goods into focused *show* windows, 'gorgeous' little theatrical stage-sets, sculpted scenes, where *single* commodities might be presented in the best possible light." The banks of show windows opened up the street, extending the interior opulence of the palaces onto the sidewalks and inviting the passers-by to pause and dream of the splendors inside. Window-shopping, in essence no more than a dignified form of loafing, became a new and acceptable pastime.[9]

If shopping brought people downtown, entertainment establishments kept them there after dark or, to be more accurate, after the sun went down. There was, in reality, no more "dark" in the theater districts. Street lighting, first by kerosene and gas, then by electric arc and

---

New York City, 1908–15. A group of children studying the contents of a carefully arranged department store show window during the Christmas season. The window is probably Macy's. (*Bain Collection, LC*)

incandescent lights, extended day into night. Theater marquees, billboards, and restaurants with plate glass windows revealing and highlighting the gaiety within converted dark, deserted streets into well-lit thoroughfares of fun and fantasy. Broadway, the Great White Way, illuminated for two miles between Madison and Longacre Squares, was the prototype for the all-night entertainment district, but every city had its theaters, its restaurants, its hotels, its vaudeville palaces, and motion picture shows.[10]

Night life, once the province of lower-class characters and men who acted as if they were, had moved out from the tenderloin and vice districts into the lights of the new and expanded "Broadways." Every city had its cheap public dance halls, saloons, and whorehouses, but for those who wanted to be entertained without shame and guilt and in the company of respectable women, there were new and proper places to do it.[11]

The vaudeville theaters were the first establishments to, quite literally, clean up their acts. Once a men-only affair, with prostitutes cruising the aisles, profanity rampant, "girly shows" on stage, and the aroma of stale beer inescapable, vaudeville had, in the 1870s and 1880s, been transformed into acceptable, wholesome entertainment for the entire family. "Jeering, drinking, smoking, and soliciting were all but abolished by policing. Managers also clamped down on vulgar stage language and actions, creating a strict system of censorship that outlawed the uttered 'hell' and 'damn.' "[12] Animal acts, magicians, pantomimists, and ladies who played the "concertina, banjo, and xylophone" were brought in to replace the "blue" acts that had once been standard.[13]

Though vaudeville shows could be seen in every town, at country fairs, and at amusement parks, it was in the cities that the theaters attracted the largest number of customers. In New York City there were, by 1910, thirty-one different vaudeville houses. Chicago had twenty-two, Philadelphia thirty.[14]

Vaudeville brought the middle classes—in the thousands—downtown for the show. It was not, however, the only attraction of the entertainment districts. There were also the variety theaters and the music halls, where on any given night one could see operettas, new musical comedies like *Little Johnny Jones* and *George Washington Junior*, melodramas, or Shakespeare. Arnold Bennett, on his trip to the United States in 1912, was astounded to find "nearly twice as many first-class theaters in New York as in London."[15]

Within walking distance of the theaters were restaurants to wine, dine, and be seen in. Dining out, once the preserve of society people who could afford fancy hotel dining rooms and restaurants like Delmonico's and of working men who frequented taverns, chophouses, and rathskellers, had become an acceptable—and accessible—form of entertainment for middle-class men and women. In New York City, the dozens of new "Broadway" restaurants which opened their doors between 1899 and 1912 "helped make the life of conspicuous consumption available to a wider portion of the city and the nation."[16]

Patrons were not only wined and dined but also treated like kings and queens on holiday. Restauranteurs created sumptuous new interior decors to bedazzle their customers with a taste of luxury. "In Murray's [on Broadway in New York City], patrons entered the main dining room through a black and gold mosaic-lined foyer. The main dining room was built to resemble the atrium of a Roman home, complete with an open court with colonnades on each side. Surrounded by trees and statues and gazing out on an ancient barge fronting a terraced fountain crowned by a classical temple rising clear to the ceiling, diners enjoyed the illusion of being in ancient Rome or at a villa in Pompeii. . . . The classical porticos and temples provided a sense of restful magnificence, while the enormous height of the room and open space suggested the lofty opulence and power of the diner."[17]

Entering the room was only the beginning of the treat. Eating in a lobster palace, like shopping in a department store, was an adventure, an excitement, an event to be savored. The beginning to a proper meal in hotel dining room or lobster palace was oysters (when not in season, clams could be substituted), followed by soup, hors d'oeuvres, fish, the entrée, the main course (usually a roast), the game dish, and dessert and coffee.[18]

For those who preferred to keep the good time rolling late into the night, there were cabarets and nightclubs, another early twentieth century addition to city night life. Fast dancing, once practiced only in the cheap dance halls and bawdy houses, was a major attraction in the new clubs. And when people danced, they danced—not waltzes or two-steps—but the turkey trot and the grizzly bear to the syncopated ragtime beat of black musicians who, had they not been playing in the band, would never have been allowed in such respectable downtown establishments.[19]

As Lloyd Morris has noted, it was just three miles from Rector's on Broadway, where twenty dollars would buy a dinner for five with two bottles of champagne, to the lower end of Orchard Street, where another restaurant "served a dinner of soup, meat stew, bread, pickles, pie, and a 'schooner' of beer for thirteen cents."[20]

In New York City, as in Chicago, Boston, Cincinnati, Columbus, and almost every other city in the nation, the "other half" lived close by and a world away from the downtown business, shopping, and entertainment districts. H. G. Wells noticed during his visit in 1905 that there were "moments when I could have imagined there were no immigrants at all" in American cities. "One goes about the wide streets of Boston, one meets all sorts of Boston people, one visits the State-House; it's all the authentic English-speaking America. Fifth Avenue, too, is America without a touch of foreign-born." And yet, Wells recognized, the America of the immigrant and the working class, though out of sight, was just around the corner, just down the street, just over the hill, "a hundred yards south of the pretty Boston Common," "a block or so east of Fifth Avenue," an elevated stop from the Loop in Chicago.[21]

The two urban worlds did not mingle or mix. Each recognized the presence of the other, but neither went out of its way to cross over into the other's workplace or neighborhood. As Robert Shackleton noted in Chicago, the sellers and customers in the department stores were almost all "Americans." "The great foreign population of the city lives and does its shopping mainly in its own districts."[22]

Most residents of the working-class city had no reason to travel downtown. Why leave the neighborhood where goods were cheaper and shopkeepers spoke your own language? Why go elsewhere to be entertained when you had little free time and the local streets provided all you needed in friends, family, neighbors, social clubs, saloons, and coffee houses?

Working men and women stayed behind in their own neighborhood because they were comfortable there. While the neighborhoods were not ethnically homogeneous, there were always enough "landsmen" clustered to establish and sustain churches, lodges, patriotic groups, food shops, bakers, butchers, restaurants, theaters, banks, and newspapers.

Settlement-house workers at the turn of the century and historians, more recently, who portray the working-class immigrants as helpless, hopeless, uprooted victims misread the historical record.[23] On the downtown business, shopping, and entertainment streets the Italian, Polish, and Russian Jewish immigrants wearing dirty overalls and speaking foreign tongues might have been out of place. But in their own communities, they were at home.

The two cities, though geographically distinct, shared the same congested, polluted urban space. There were many constants in city life. No matter where you lived or worked, you were assaulted daily by the smoke, soot, and dust in the air; the noise of clattering cobblestones, cable cars, trolleys, and the elevated; the smell of horse dung on the streets. In the working-class and immigrant residential districts, these annoyances were intensified a hundredfold. It was in the city of the "other half" that the sewers were always clogged and the streets and alleyways filled with garbage. It was here that dead horses lay for days, bloated and decaying, children poking at their eyes and pulling out their hair to weave into rings. It was here that cats roamed at will through the streets, alleyways, backyards, roofs, and interior hallways, alley cats with gaping wounds, flesh hung loosely on starving bodies, wide frightened eyes, and the look, smell, and howl of starvation. It was here that tuberculosis raged and babies died of exposure or cold or heat or spoiled milk, that pushcarts, streetcars, and horse-drawn wagons fought for space, and children were crushed to death in the duel.

The residents of the working-class districts lived in a variety of dwellings: multistory tenements, converted single-family row houses, double-deckers, triple-deckers, wooden shacks and shanties. Wherever they lived, they were likely to live piled together, several families in space designed for one, several persons to a room.

New York City, 1908–15. There is no way of knowing how long this horse has been lying here. During the warm spells of summer, dozens of horses dropped dead on city streets and lay rotting for days on end. Motorcar enthusiasts claimed that the "horseless" buggy was the only solution to this particular pollution problem. (*Bain Collection, LC*)

Families made the best possible use of their limited space, re-arranging their flats every evening to provide maximum sleeping room for children, relatives, and boarders. On his first evening in the New World, Marcus Ravage, future historian and author of *An American in the Making,* looked on in amazement as his relatives transformed their apartment into a "camp." "The sofas opened up and revealed their true character. The bureau lengthened out shamelessly, careless of its daylight pretensions. Even the wash-tubs, it turned out, were a miserable sham. The carved dining-room chairs arranged themselves into two rows that faced each other like dancers in a cotillion. . . . The two young ladies' room was not, I learned, a young ladies' room at all; it was a female dormitory. The sofa in the parlor alone held four sleepers, of whom I was one. We were ranged broadside, with the rocking-chairs at the foot to insure the proper length. And the floor was by no means exempt. I counted no fewer than nine male inmates in that parlor alone one night. Mrs. Segal with one baby slept on the washtubs, while the rest of the youngsters held the kitchen floor. The pretended children's room was occupied by a man and his family of four."[24]

As the population and land values in the central cities increased, working people and the poor were forced to live in spaces that should have remained uninhabited. In Washington, D.C., and Baltimore, Maryland, cities within the city were built in the alleyways. In Pittsburgh and Chicago, investigators discovered hundreds of families living below street level in cellars, basements, and dark, dreary, "cave-like" dwellings. In Chicago, where landlords had increased their profits—and the congestion—by building on every inch of land they owned, "rear tenements" and wooden shacks facing on alleyways were built in the back of long, slender lots.[25]

Cities with massive, multistory tenements had the worst congestion. In New York City, where a higher percentage of residents lived in tenements than anywhere else in the country, the congestion inside and out was beyond belief. Theodore Dreiser, among those visitors to the Lower East Side overwhelmed by the sight, reported having seen "block after block of four-story and five-story buildings, "all painted a dull red, and nearly all . . . divided in the most unsanitary manner. Originally they were built five rooms deep, with two flats on a floor, but now the single flats have been subdivided and two or three, occasionally four or five, families live and toil in the space which was originally intended for one."[26]

Light, air, and privacy were at a premium for the working-class and immigrant residents of the early twentieth-century cities. In the typical New York City tenement, with fourteen rooms on each floor, only four—

two in front and two in back—"received direct light and air from the street or from the small yard at the back of the building."[27] A housing inspector testified that the inner kitchens and bedrooms on the lower floors of the tenements he visited "were so dark that the lights are kept burning in the kitchen during the daytime. The bedrooms may be used for sleeping at any time within the twenty-four hours, as they exceed the Arctic Zone in having night 365 days in the year."[28]

Lack of windows meant lack of ventilation. The front and rear windows let in a bit of air—along with the noise and stench of street and alleyway. The interior rooms had windows, but because they opened onto airshafts and courtyards stuffed with rotting garbage, most residents kept them permanently closed.

The flats were dark, the hallways darker. In most tenements, the only light in the halls came from the front door when that was opened. A tenement house inspector testified that, in his experience, "the most barbarous parts of [tenement] buildings are the halls. A person coming in from the sunlight outside, plunges into these halls just like a car filled with men plunges and disappears in the black mouth of a mine shaft. If he is fortunate in not running against anybody, he stumbles along, finding his way with his feet. . . . [H]e hurries forward as rapidly as possible and rushes out upon the roof or into some open room, because the air is so dense and stifling [in the hallway] that he wishes to escape quickly."[29]

Privacy was as treasured and rare in the working-class districts as fresh air and light. High rents forced families to economize on space and sublet rooms and parts of rooms to boarders. City dwellers shared their flats, their rooms, even their beds and their toilets with virtual strangers. In many tenements, the water closet was located in the hall or the backyard, where it was used by several families and their boarders and relatives. In Chicago, for example, a turn-of-the-century study found that only 43 percent of families had toilets in their flats, 30 percent had to use the water closet in the yard, 10 percent had a toilet in the basement or cellar, and another 17 percent shared a hall toilet with their neighbors on the floor.[30]

Unventilated, overused water closets and backyard privies were bound to and did overflow continually, seeping waste through the floorboards and into the yards. The odor of human excrement joined that of horse dung from the streets and stables and of garbage rotting in the airshafts, inner courtyards, streets, and alleyways.

If we were to be moved backward in time to the early twentieth-century city, we would probably be most repelled not by the lack of privacy, or toilets, or space, air, and light, but by this stench. Without proper ventilation, the interior halls and rooms of the tenements retained their odors indefinitely. Inside and out, the air was not just heavy and fetid but, at times, unbearable. Cities like Chicago, Cincinnati, and Kansas City, with their slaughterhouses, packing plants, and streets clogged with hogs, sheep, and cattle smelled the worst, but no city was free of what we today would consider an overpowering stench.

The residents of the central cities struggled as best they could to find a breath of air, cool, fresh, clean air. Men, women, and children herded themselves into streetcars and subways for interminable Sunday excursions to the parks and beaches, looking for grass to walk on and air to breathe. In the summertime, when the air was so heavy and hot "it was painful to draw one's breath," entire families—abandoning their last grasp at privacy—relocated on the docks, in the parks, at the stoops, the fire escapes or up on the roofs. As Mike Gold put it in *Jews Without Money*, "People went exploring for sleep as for a treasure."[31] "Like rats scrambling on deck from the hold of a burning ship, that's how we poured on the roof at night to sleep. What a mélange in the starlight! Mothers, graybeards, lively young girls, exhausted sweatshop fathers, young consumptive coughers and spitters, all of us snored and groaned there side by side, on newspapers or mattresses. We slept in pants and undershirt, heaped like corpses. The city reared about us."[32]

Light, air, and privacy were scarce commodities in the working-class districts of the cities. But to paint too grim a picture of life in the early twentieth century, to speak only of scarcity, to emphasize only poverty is to caricature the conditions of daily life for many. The city was no golden land, but it was also no desert. There was plenty mixed with the poverty, abundance interspersed with scarcity. The city was many things at the same time to the same people.

Marcus Ravage, who arrived in New York City from his native Vaslui, Rumania, at the turn of the century, tried hard to organize his perceptions of this new land. He could not resolve the contradictions. He was disappointed on his arrival, "bitterly disappointed" at the "littered streets, with the rows of pushcarts lining the sidewalks and the centers of the thoroughfares, the ill-smelling merchandise, and the deafening noise," at the congestion inside the homes, and the boarders crowded into too little space, stuffed into too few beds. (In Vaslui, he remembered, only the "very lowest of people kept roomers.") And yet, at the very same time, he was astonished at the material abundance displayed amidst the poverty. His landlady scrubbed the floor, not with sand, but with a "pretty white powder out of a metal can." "Moreover, she kept the light burning all the time we were in the kitchen, which was criminal wastefulness even if the room was a bit dark." There was "eggplant in midwinter, and tomatoes, and yellow fruit which had the shape of a cucumber and the taste of a muskmelon." There was meat in the middle of the day and "twists instead of plain rye bread, to say nothing of rice-and-raisins . . . and liver paste and black radish." And then, as if he had not seen enough such wonders in his first day in the country, the young men calling on his Cousin Rose arrived that evening "with beer in a pitcher from the corner saloon." Common people—with beer in a pitcher—at home.[33]

The city—not just New York City, but every early twentieth-century city—overwhelmed with its abundance. There were enough goods to go around town and back again. The department stores and specialty shops got the best of the lot, but the working-class districts, according to Harry Roskolenko, a poet and journalist who grew up on the Lower East Side, were stocked with their own "massive supplies of shoddy goods . . . leftovers from other years and seasons; things that could not be sold"

New York City, 1908–15. An East Side "pushcart market." Migrants from rural areas on both sides of the Atlantic marveled at the abundance and the variety of produce sold on the streets of the city. (*Bain Collection, LC*)

elsewhere; and goods produced especially for sale to "the peddlers and the peasants and the proletarians jamming the sidewalks and gutters."[34]

The pushcarts overflowed, the shops were littered with items for sale: umbrellas, stockings, boys' sailor suits with whistles attached, suspenders, gabardine overcoats, handkerchiefs, laces and ribbons and shoes and long underwear. There were carts filled with oranges and others loaded with bananas, herring came in barrels, milk was ladled out of forty-quart cans, potatoes dug out of fifty-pound sacks. Food, drink, and sweets could be purchased from peddlers and pushcarts, from stands, butchers, bakers, and grocers who sold it in cans, in boxes, in jars, in bottles, in packages, in bags.[35]

Newcomers might have assumed that city markets had always displayed such variety and abundance, but many of the items now prominently displayed were as new to the city as the electric streetcars and lobster palaces. The banana, for example, among the most proletarian of fruits, had until the 1880s been almost entirely absent from the working-class shops and shopping streets. On arrival in New Orleans, "each fruit was wrapped individually in tinfoil and like a rare and precious object rushed to New York or New England, where, if it survived the journey, a single banana was worth a dollar."[36]

Oranges were also a luxury item until the 1890s when, with the completion of the Florida East Coast Railway, they could be shipped north by rail instead of being imported from the Mediterranean.[37]

Grapefruits were entirely new to the city. The old pear-shaped fruit, distinguished by its lack of juice, coarse rind, and expensive price tag had been redesigned by Florida growers who shipped them north in refrigerated boxcars. Between 1909 and 1920, annual consumption of the new pink fruit jumped from under a pound to over five pounds per capita.[38]

The immigrants who arrived in American cities in the early twentieth century were astounded by the number of foods for sale and the variety of ways in which they could be purchased. Fruits, vegetables, soups, meats, even baby food, were sold fresh *and* in cans and tins. Propelled into the marketplace by new food companies alert to the advantages of national distribution, advertising, and brand name promotions, Campbell's soups, Heinz's fifty-seven varieties, and Libby's canned goods became part of the city's daily diet. Between 1909 and 1920, annual per capita consumption of canned fruits increased from under three pounds to over nine, canned soups from less than a third of a pound to two, and baby food from less than a tenth of a pound to over two.[39]

The addition of fresh and canned fruits and vegetables to a diet that had once consisted of little more than bread, potatoes, crackers, and various forms of salted and preserved meats was no doubt beneficial. From a social standpoint, the availability of food in cans meant even more. Here was yet another item once exclusively the preserve of the wealthy (and of military expeditions which could survive on no other form of food) that had become part of the common folks' daily diet.[40] The family that could now for the first time eat peas for dinner was certainly more pleased by the new addition to its diet than it was distressed by the nutritional loss suffered in the canning process.

Of all the foods entering the diet of the working people, none were as enticing, as aristocratic, as luxurious, and as plentiful as the sweets. One by one, luxuries like refined white sugar and chocolate and homemade delights like fresh ice cream were mass-produced, distributed, and marketed in the cities. Candy consumption increased from 2.2 pounds per capita in 1880 to 5.6 in 1914 and 13.1 in 1919; ice cream from 1.5 pounds in 1909 to 7.5 in 1920. To wash it all down, there was Coca-Cola, invented as a "remedy for headaches and hangovers" by an Atlanta dentist in 1886.[41]

The new sweets further broadened and "democratized" the urban diet. Luxuries became commonplaces available for pennies from neighborhood shops and pushcart peddlers. And yet, there remained significant differences between the diet of the downtown gentleman and the factory worker's family. Both ate sweets and vegetables and meat. But the sirloin and spring lamb served in the lobster palaces was a far cry from the meat soup "made up of leftovers and ends and bones which the butcher sold for six cents a pound instead of throwing it away."[42] Bananas and oranges and grapefruits were, for the first time, available downtown and in the slums, but only for the few who had the money to pay for them. For the rest, they remained as inaccessible as they had been in the days before refrigerated boats and boxcars carried them north.

In the midst of plenty, poverty and hunger remained. Within sight of the carts and shops filled with enough food to feed armies, parents struggled to provide for their families. Children grew up with what actress Ruth Gordon has called "the dark brown taste of being poor."[43] Hy Kraft, later a successful Broadway playwright, never forgot what it was like to grow up poor. "A boy stands in front of a candy store—in front, mind you. He sees a hundred varieties of sweets, but he doesn't have a penny, one cent. Or he's in the street; a vendor pushes his cart, calling 'Icacrim sendwich, pennyapiss.' Other kids holler up to their mamas, 'Mama, t'row me down a penny' and the mama wraps the penny in paper and 't'rows' it down. This kid doesn't have a penny—one cent. And there's no mama upstairs; she's in the back of the basement."[44]

Poverty was not unique to the metropolis, but nowhere else did it coexist with such splendor and spectacle. As Charles Zueblin, an authority on American cities, noted in the preface to his widely read volume on *American Municipal Progress,* "There is poverty in the country, sordid and ugly. But city poverty is under the shadow of wealth. Luxury flaunts itself in the city."[45]

The city was suffused with contrasts: between the electrically illuminated magnificence of the downtown shopping and entertainment districts and the grayish squalor of the slums, between the abundance of goods offered for sale on the streets and the paucity of resources available to pay for them. Poverty and plenty lived side by side, in the same city, on the same block, in the same tenement flat. The contradictions that assailed Marcus Ravage on his first day in the city were inescapable. Wise men peddled suspenders on the streets while fools lived like millionaires. People slept crowded one on top of another, but they ate meat several times a week. Families shared toilets with complete strangers, but they were able to purchase shoes, stockings, and underwear for everyone—even for the children. It made no sense and yet it was real. It was the city.

2

At Play in the City

The central city districts were deprived of space, privacy, light, and air. But they were, as Theodore Dreiser found on his visit to the Lower East Side, "rich . . . in those quickly withering flowers of flesh and blood, the boys and girls of the city."[1]

In the mornings, after 3 P.M. when school let out, and after dinner, the tenements poured forth their armies of children: through the darkened halls, out the front door, down the stoop, into the street they walked, ran, skipped, and jumped.

The children were everywhere: in the streets and alleyways, on the stoops and sidewalks, hanging from fire escapes and out of windows. Henry James on his visit to the Lower East Side was overwhelmed by "the sense . . . of a great swarming, a swarming that had begun to thicken, infinitely." It was "the children [who] swarmed above all." "Here was multiplication with a vengeance." Theodore Dreiser counted "thousands" running the thoroughfare. Robert Woods, a Boston settlement-house worker, describing the South End, noted that "sometimes in a little side street you will see a hundred . . . at play."[2]

The children played on the streets because there was nowhere else for them. Urban space was a commodity, an item bought and sold like any other. As the population of the cities expanded, land became more and more valuable.[3] The logic of urban progress was inexorable. Undeveloped land was wasted land. With space at a premium, even the backyards were too valuable to be given over to the children. They were

New York City. While their older brothers left the block to sell papers and black boots, the little ones stayed behind. The children used all the space on the block. There was, as you can see from this photograph, no strict boundary between sidewalk and street, nor did there have to be. On streets such as this, where the traffic was light, the children could play their games without undue interference. To the right of the photograph are two "little mothers" watching over their younger siblings. (LC)

quickly filled up by the adults: with goats or chickens, herb and vegetable gardens, or some combination of "outhouses, sheds, fences, clothes lines, trash heaps, and even garbage piles."[4]

Inflated land prices led to congestion inside as well as out. There was no room for children to play in tiny tenement flats and subdivided one-family houses stuffed full with aunts, uncles, grandparents, parents, babies, and boarders. The best rooms in the flat, the front and rear ones, were reserved for parents or boarders willing to pay extra for the privilege. The little ones slept in the living room or kitchen or with their parents or, if in rooms of their own, interior ones without windows, light, or air.

18

The children not only lacked rooms of their own; they didn't even have their own beds. In his oral history, Frank Broska, a Chicago factory worker who grew up in a house heated only by a stove in the kitchen, remembered warmly being bundled up in bed with big feather ticks piled on top, heated house bricks wrapped in towels at his feet, and brothers and sisters on either side of him.[5]

It was much easier for a family to make space for the children to sleep than it was to find room for them to play. The little ones could be tied to chairs or put in makeshift playpens in a corner of the kitchen. The bigger ones, if they sat quietly at the kitchen table doing their homework, were allowed to stay indoors. Otherwise, they were free to gaze out the window, sit on the fire escape, or leave altogether. Indoors was for adults; children only got in the way: of mother and her chores, of father trying to relax after a long day at work, of boarders who worked the night shift and had to sleep during the day.[6] Catharine Brody, a journalist who grew up on a city block in Manhattan, remembered in a 1928 article for *The American Mercury* that when she was a girl "there was no such thing as gathering or playing in the house." The children required no special encouragement to go outside to play. That was where they belonged. "The streets," as Catharine Brody put it, "were the true homes of the [city's] small Italians, Irish, and Jews."[7]

The children shared these "homes" with others. The street was their playground, but it was also a marketplace, meeting ground, social club,

---

New York City, 1908–15. Three city kids intent on some sort of game, involving a hoop, a stick, and an empty can. While these children appear to be "alone" in the street, their mothers in the tenements overhead, older sisters along the sidewalks and on the stoops, and local shopkeepers kept watch over them. (*Bain Collection, LC*)

place of assignation, political forum, sports arena, parade grounds, open-air tavern, coffeehouse, and thoroughfare. The life on the street was the life of the city. While the children played, the policemen walked their beat, prostitutes solicited "johns," peddlers shouted their wares, delivery wagons squeezed down the block to neighborhood shops, and men and women clustered in small groups on the corners, in front of the shops, at the threshold of the saloons, and on their front stoops.

The presence of adults in the street—and in the tenements over-head—protected the children at play. There was always someone within shouting distance should trouble appear. When Joey Cohen was lured into a tenement hallway by the "scarecrow" who offered him a nickel and then tried to pull down his pants, the boy's shout for help brought assistance at once. The apple peddler down the street, a man "in flannel shirt and cap," "two Italian laborers who [had] been digging a sewer nearby," and a crowd of peddlers, children, and housewives appeared from nowhere. According to Mike Gold, who witnessed the scene and wrote about it years later, "If a cop had not arrived," the crowd would have "torn . . . the pervert . . . into little bleeding hunks."[8]

The presence of adults on their play streets was not an unmixed blessing for the children. They shared their space, but only grudgingly. As Peter and Iona Opie reported in their magnificent study of *Children's Games in Street and Playground*, adults and children have fought over the public space they share since the Middle Ages. While the older generation has tried to get the children off the street and out from under foot, the children have exacerbated tensions by appearing "deliberately to attract attention to themselves, screaming, scribbling on the pavements, smashing milk bottles, banging on doors, and getting in people's way." In the words of Colin Ward, author of *The Child in the City*, "one of the things that play is about, intermingled with all the others, is conflict with the adult world."[9] This was certainly true for the children who grew up in the turn-of-the-century American cities. Their play communities were defined not only by their commitment to their own rules but by their disregard for those laid down by adults. City kids, "good" city kids, appeared to take special delight in disobeying the "No Swimming" signs in front of the city's concrete fountains, climbing the poles that held up the clothes lines, playing tag on the roofs and "hide and seek" on the stairways, bouncing their balls off front doors and occupied stoops, teasing the ice man's horse, and stealing whatever they could from the trucks and pushcarts that invaded their territory.

The children fought with the adults, not simply because they were perverse, obstinate, and unruly, but because they resented the intrusion of others into their play world. As Johan Huizinga has written, "All play

20

Hester Street in New York City, early 1890s. Jacob Riis, who took this photograph, captioned it "the school children's only playground." (*Jacob Riis Collection, LC*)

moves and has its being within a playground marked off beforehand either materially or ideally, deliberately or as a matter of course. . . . All [playgrounds] are temporary worlds within the ordinary world, dedicated to the performance of an act apart."[10] The children, in establishing their playground on the street, had to exclude from it adults and their activities. Through sheer force of numbers, raw energy (released in a torrent after a day in the classroom), and a bit of ingenuity, they converted public space into their community playground, pushing aside the ordinary adult world of peddlers and pushcarts, policemen and delivery wagons. The intensity with which the children threw themselves into their games startled middle-class observers. But this intensity was just the outward manifestation of their capacity for putting the adult world at a distance.

Except on the busier thoroughfares where streetcars or cablecars ran regularly, the children were able to exclude or incorporate into their games the wagons, bicyclists, automobiles, and individuals who might otherwise have interfered. When delivery wagons parked for too long on the block, they could be incorporated into the game. Beer trucks outside the saloon became the home run fence for the ballplayers. Ice trucks provided a test of strength, speed, and daring for the boys who competed in stealing a block without getting caught. Open-bed wagons offered free rides for those courageous enough to hitch onto the back and hold on tight.

Horse-drawn carts, trucks, and wagons could be a lot of fun. But they also killed children who failed to get out of the way in time. Harry Roskolenko's sister "was killed by a truck at the age of fifteen." Mike Gold's friend Joey Cohen was run over by a horsecar. "He had stolen a ride, and in jumping, fell under the wheels. The people around saw the flash of his body, and then heard a last scream of pain. The car rolled on. The people rushed to the tracks and picked up the broken body of my playmate."[11]

It was dangers such as these that prompted settlement-house workers and reformers to campaign in the newspapers, magazines, city halls, and legislative lobbies for parks, playgrounds, and after-school programs. The reformers were, no doubt, hoping to use such supervised play programs as vehicles for socialization and Americanization, but they were also genuinely concerned for the future of children who had no place but the street to play.

The street was not the perfect playground, but it was the best the children had. "Where children are is where they play," the Opies have written. "The street in front of their home is seemingly theirs, more theirs sometimes than the family living-rooms."[12] The children made good use of the available space, the streets and sidewalks as well as the doorways, gutters, stoops, and inside stairways. The boundaries that marked off public and private space were ignored. The "block" belonged to those who took possession of it.

The children, as we have seen, dealt in their own way with the adults and vehicles that trespassed on their space. Only the police were beyond reason, humoring, teasing, or incorporating into the game. There were, of course, policemen who could be expected to look the other way as the children took over the street, but there were more who took seriously their "responsibility" to clear the thoroughfare of its child impediments. Why, Mike Gold wondered in his autobiographical novel, *Jews Without Money*, were the police always in the way? "Why . . . did they adopt such an attitude of stern virtue toward the small boys? They broke up our baseball games, confiscated our bats. They beat us for splashing under the fire hydrant. They cursed us, growled and chased us for any reason. They hated to see us having fun."[13]

Harpo Marx had the same experience but could not profess the same degree of hurt innocence. "There was no such character as 'the kindly cop on the beat' in New York in those days. The cops were sworn enemies. By the same token we, the street kids, were the biggest source of trouble for the police. Individually and in gangs we accounted for most of the petty thievery and destruction of property on the upper East Side. And since we couldn't afford to pay off the cops in the proper, respectable Tammany manner, they hounded us, harassed us, chased us, and every chance they got, happily beat the hell out of us."[14]

Mike Gold and Harpo Marx were Jewish in a city where the majority of police were not, but this was not the reason they found themselves at odds with the law. The People's Institute, in its 1913 study of juvenile arrests on the Middle West Side, an Irish and German neighborhood, discovered that there too the police harassed children at play and work on the streets. More than 50 percent of the arrests made in the district were for noncrimes like "begging, bonfires, fighting, gambling, jumping on [street]cars, kicking the garbage can, loitering, playing football on the streets, pitching pennies, playing [base]ball, playing shinney, playing with water pistol, putting out lights, selling papers, shooting craps, snowballing, subway disturbances, and throwing stones."[15]

New York City was not the only place where children were arrested and punished for activities that, in the case of adults, would not have been considered criminal. Jane Addams, after studying the records of the Chicago Juvenile Court, concluded that dozens of children had been arrested for "deeds of adventure": stealing, junking, harassing railroad employees, "calling a neighbor a 'scab,' breaking down a fence, flipping cars [jumping on and off while they were moving], picking up coal from railroad tracks, loafing on the docks, 'sleeping out' nights, getting 'wandering spells,' and refusing to get off the fender of a streetcar."[16]

There appeared to be little rhyme or reason in the causes for arrest. Some of the children's crimes involved junking, petty thievery, and playing with or on private property, but there were many more that were victimless. Gambling, for example, the most common cause for arrest, was, from the children's perspective, just another street game. What difference could it possibly make to the police if a group of boys wanted to shoot craps with their own money? They weren't harming anybody, stealing anything, or causing any trouble. And yet the police seemed to take a special delight in breaking up their games. According to Jan Peerce, the opera singer, "the police who patrolled the Lower East Side on the lookout for crime seemed to take most seriously kids congregated in a backyard—or even a little circle on the street—to shoot craps. Not that the stakes were high. In the whole circle there possibly wasn't more than a couple of dollars."[17]

Mike Gold and his gang thought they knew the reason for the police obsession with kiddie gambling. They figured that the police were on their tail because they enjoyed "pocketing" the "small change" the players left behind when they scrambled for cover. "It was one of our grievances. We often suspected them of being moralists for the sake of this petty graft."[18]

The children were a subject population liable to be scolded, chased, or arrested without warning. Still, the threat was more potential than real. Though the kids all knew of instances where innocent youngsters had been unfairly dealt with, most survived childhood without arrest records. As long as you kept a lookout and remembered that the police were not ordinary citizens but far more unpredictable and dangerous, you could expect to stay out of trouble.

The children at play inhabited a world that was encased in but separate from the ordinary adult world that surrounded them. For children who had spent a long day in school and would, at dusk, be called inside their parents' homes, there was something liberating in this temporary separation from supervising adults. On the streets they could play as they pleased and say what they wanted. They did not have to seek approval or permission to play their games. Teachers disappeared from their lives at three o'clock. Parents exercised more constant authority, but that authority reached into the streets only in the most attenuated form. As long as the children did not disgrace themselves or their families, get into trouble with the police, abandon younger brothers or sisters, or get hurt, their parents left them alone. Though Eddie Cantor's grandmother on the Lower East Side and Charles Angoff's father in Boston were both convinced that playing ball was an activity fit only for bums, they did not forbid their children to hit their balls with wooden sticks. Parents had far more important things to do than watch their children play in the streets.[19]

All children learn from one another. But the scope, style, form, and content of this learning are affected by their relationship—as a group—with adults. Children who are under the thumb of adults from morning to night obviously have less opportunity to learn from one another than those who are free of adult supervision for long stretches of time. The children of the early twentieth-century city were blessed or cursed—depending on your perspective—with more unstructured and unsupervised free time than the generations that preceded or followed them. Unlike their nineteenth-century predecessors, they did not have to work all day alongside adults in factory, shop, mine, or mill. Unlike their mid-twentieth-century counterparts, they did not spend their afternoons, weekends, and summers in umpired and regulated Little League,

Boston. Playing baseball in a tenement alley. (*Lewis Hine Collection, International Museum of Photography at George Eastman House, Rochester, N.Y.*)

scouting, after-school, and summer camp programs. The children of the street were, it is true, watched like hawks in school and at home, but out of school and out of the home, they were on their own or, to be more precise, immersed in a community defined by the absence of adults.

The children learned a lot from one another about life in the city: too much, according to reformers who were concerned that the lessons of the street were more easily assimilated than those of school and classroom. Philip Davis, who worked directly with children as Boston's Commissioner of Street Trades, compared the two sources of learning in *Street-land*, his classic study of Boston's children. "We fail to recognize that school education very frequently finds but surface roots in the minds of children and, therefore, gets wrenched out of place under the least storm or strain; whereas the roots of street education run deep." Robert Woods, the Boston settlement-house worker and author, agreed entirely. "The streets," he noted, "educate with fatal precision." The classrooms did not.[20]

Urban public and parochial schoolteachers were not as a rule

25

interested in teaching skills or providing information that would be of immediate assistance in the children's daily lives. Their task was to prepare them for the future: to educate, socialize, and Americanize them, catechize them in the duties of citizenship, instruct them in manners and morals, and, most important, teach them to read, write, recite, and do sums. The school's goal was to take the children from the streets and the streets from the children. The children, unfortunately, were not yet ready to abandon the streets. As we have seen, they had no place else to call their own.

Harpo Marx, who was abruptly tossed out of school in second grade by two Irish kids who hoisted him out the classroom window when Miss Flatto turned her back, never regretted the abrupt end of his formal schooling. Unlike his brother Groucho, who was a dedicated and able student, Harpo never found anything worth learning in the classroom. "School was all wrong," he recalled in his autobiography. "It didn't teach anybody how to exist from day to day, which was how the poor had to live." Teachers had a lot to say "about holidays you could never afford to celebrate, like Thanksgiving and Christmas, [but nothing] about the real holidays like St. Patrick's Day, when you could watch a parade for free, or Election Day, when you could make a giant bonfire in the middle of the street and the cops wouldn't stop you. School didn't teach you what to do when you were stopped by an enemy gang—when to run and when to stand your ground. School didn't teach you how to collect tennis balls, build a scooter, ride the El trains and trolleys, hitch onto delivery wagons, own a dog, go for a swim, get a chunk of ice or a piece of fruit— all without paying a cent. School didn't teach you which hockshops would give you dough without asking where you got your merchandise . . . or where to sell junk or how to find sleeping room in a bed with four other brothers. School simply didn't teach you how to be poor and live from day to day."[21]

Harpo was, of course, an exceptional child. How many others "dropped out" of school in second grade never again to return? Still, the discontinuity that he experienced between the world presented in the classroom and the one outside was common to other city kids. For Samuel Ornitz and his gang, the daily trip from "the strict rarefied public school world" to the boys' "street existence, our sweet lawless, personal, high colored life" was like "traveling from planet to planet."[22]

The street was a separate world with its own standards of right and wrong, its own code of ethics. The children learned in school—and probably at home as well—that gambling was wasteful and sinful, stealing was a crime, money was for saving, and citizens owed allegiance to the law and the officials sworn to enforce it. On the streets, however, they observed that lots of kids shot craps or pitched pennies, that stealing

New York City, 1907. Minnie Fiske, an actress, had this photograph taken for use "as an aid in designing sets, etc." for "Salvation Nell," a play she was to star in. (*Minnie Fiske Collection, LC*)

from the railroads was as common an afternoon's occupation as stickball, that money was for spending, and that your primary duty was to friends, family and fellow gang members—not the police or the laws they claimed to enforce. The adults the children came in contact with, especially their teachers, tried to wean the children from the street and its laws. But they could not succeed. Not even the threat of corporal punishment would make children inform on one another. In case after case, reported Frederick Thrasher, children preferred to "take a beating than 'stool' on their associates."[23]

The children took care of one another. They managed their own space and their own games—according to their own rules. They laid out their ball fields and decided what was fair, foul, and a home run. They chalked their potsie squares and watched the lines. They decided the proper punishment for the kid who refused to follow the leader down into the basement to make faces at the Chinese laundryman.

The children's play community of the street, like all other play

27

New York City. "East Side Children" playing on the sidewalk. (*Bain Collection, LC*)

communities, was founded on a bedrock of rules. Every game had its own particular rules: the children as a group might alter or adapt them to their own circumstances, but they could not ignore or dispense with them.[24]

It was the task of the older, more experienced street kids to teach the greenies, newcomers, and little ones how to run the bases, shoot dice, swing a broom handle bat, and jump rope in rhyme. There were always new kids on the block. Some were recent immigrants, some were just shifting neighborhoods—perhaps so their parents could take advantage of a landlord's offer of a few months' free rent; others were for the first time being permitted to leave the protective grasp of their sisters on the stoops. What was constant was the community, not the individuals who comprised it.

Each child was initiated into the larger play community and a smaller subgroup defined by age and gender. Each subgroup had its space on the block, its separate games, and its responsibilities to others. The girls looked after the babies and toddlers; the bigger boys—in their gangs—guarded the block from "other streeters"; all kept a special eye out for younger siblings and relatives.

The block—that totality of street, gutter, sidewalk, stoop, and doorways—was informally divided to provide each group with the space it needed and a bit of distance from the others. Children of every ethnic, religious, racial, and language group played together. But girls did not always play with boys. Nor were the little ones allowed in the bigger ones' games.

The girls occupied the stoops, where they met each afternoon to spend what author Kate Simon of the Bronx remembered in her autobiography as "long, chattering, comfortable" hours watching their little brothers and sisters, embroidering their French knots and pink roses on bits of cloth clamped onto small hoops, and hearing from their more experienced friends about the forbidden subjects: the monthlies, where babies came from, and what "shooting scum" really meant. They also played potsies on the sidewalks, jumped rope to complicated nonsense rhymes, and bounced their balls. Periodically they joined the boys for a game of prisoner's base, ring-a-levio, or a race around the block.[25]

The center of the street belonged to the boys. It was there that they played their thousand and one variations on a theme with ball and bat, kicked the can, lit and tended fires, played marbles—always for keeps— and leapfrogged milk cans, fire pumps, and one another.

Though the older boys (ten and up) often joined in the ball games, much of their time was spent on the corners. With their backs to the street, huddled in a semicircle, they shielded their crap games, pitched

Cincinnati, 1908. Shooting craps on the sidewalk. (*Lewis Hine, NCLC*)

pennies, and did the grown-up things big boys do while waiting for something more exciting to happen.[26]

City kids made do with what they had. "You know," George Burns remembers in his sometimes serious autobiography, *The Third Time Around,* "when I look back on those days on Rivington Street it makes me realize how lucky kids are today. They've got organized playgrounds, Little League, field trips, and in the summer they all get on buses and go to summer camps where they have swimming pools, basketball courts, baseball diamonds, and even a counselor to hand them a Kleenex in case they sneeze. When I was a kid we had none of those things. Our playground was the middle of Rivington Street. We only played games that needed very little equipment, games like kick-the-can, hopscotch, hide-and-go-seek, follow-the-leader. When we played baseball we used a broom handle and a rubber ball. A manhole cover was home plate, a fire hydrant was first base, second base was a lamp post, and Mr. Gitletz, who used to bring a kitchen chair down to sit and watch us play, was third base. One time I slid into Mr. Gitletz; he caught the ball and tagged me out."[27]

Children had to scrounge for their equipment and then some. Garbage pail lids were made into sleds, bicycle wheels into hoops, discarded cans and used bags into footballs; baby carriages were transformed into pushcarts and wagons, and scraps of wood too insignificant to be used for kindling at home were burned in bonfires in discarded lunch pails.

For the younger kids, the streets provided constant fun, games, and companions. There was always something to do or watch. Just when it was getting a bit dull, a horse might drop dead in the gutter, fire engines and ambulances appear from nowhere, teamsters and pushcarts do battle for the right-of-way, a stray cat creep out of the basement to be tortured.[28] What made the spectacles even more fun was that you never had to watch them alone. As George Burns remembers, "There was never any problem finding someone to play with because the streets were loaded with kids. . . . In our building alone there were sixteen families, and each family had between eight and ten kids. When we were all playing together in the street there were so many of us we'd get mixed up and forget which family we belonged to. At nine o'clock in the evening my mother would holler out the window, 'Come on up, children, it's time to go to bed!' We'd all rush up, and my mother would stand there with the door open. When the house was full she'd close it. Sometimes I made it, sometimes I slept in the hall."[29]

The children found their playmates in the same way that they found their equipment: they made use of what was there. They played with the kids who lived in their building and the other buildings on the block.

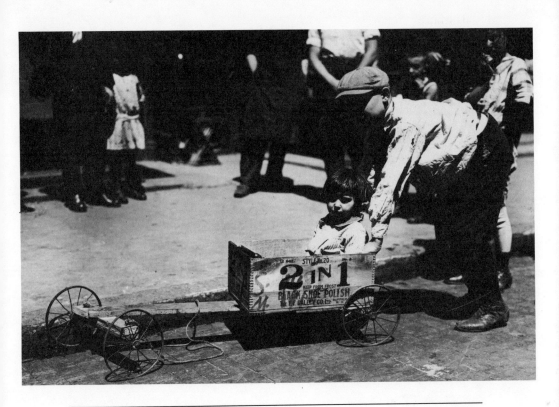

New York City, 1912. Taking a ride in a homemade pushcart. The child pushing may well have been an older brother taking care of a younger sibling after school. (*Bain Collection, LC*)

When the block was ethnically homogeneous, their playmates were likely to be "landsmen." When, as was more often the case, the block was a mixed one, they played with kids who at home spoke different languages, ate different foods, and worshipped different gods. Kids whose parents would not have dreamed of socializing became the best of friends. In her article on "A New York Childhood," journalist Catharine Brody recalled that there were "innumerable obstacles of caste and race" which prevented friends from visiting each other's homes. On the streets, however, all "met on fairly equal terms." Celia Blazek, a Chicago woman whose oral history is found in the Oral History Archives of Chicago-Polonia, played with the three "colored" girls, Ethel, Mabel, and Corrine, who lived across the street from her. Jerre Mangione, the writer, who grew up in Rochester, New York, played with Tony Long, whose mother spoke only Polish, Abe Rappaport, a Jew, and Robert di Nella, who claimed to be a real Italian, not some "lousy Siciliano" like Mangione. In the Bronx, Milton Berle, the future comedian, and his brother Jack tagged along

31

with a "Catholic kid" named McDermott who lived in their building. Jimmy Cagney, the future actor, spent so much time with his Jewish pals from the block that he learned to speak Yiddish.[30]

The block was the basic unit of social organization for city kids. Play groups and gangs were organized exclusively by geography. Frederick Thrasher, in his exhaustive and exhausting study of Chicago's eight hundred and eighty gangs, found that geography, not ethnicity or religion, determined membership. "In the more crowded sections of the city, the geographical basis of a gang is both sides of the same street for a distance of two blocks." The boys who lived on these blocks became gang members, no matter what language their parents spoke at home. Thrasher quoted approvingly one of his gang contacts: "Aw, we never ask what nationality dey are. . . . If dey are good guys, dey get in our gang. Dat's all we want."[31]

When children moved away from the block, they were forced to leave their friends—and gang—behind. Without access to transportation, they had no way of returning to play with their old buddies on the block. The only solution was to make new friends and join a new gang.[32] William Gropper, whose family moved constantly to get the month's free rent landlords offered to new tenants, was never settled long enough to feel comfortable. "No sooner did I get acquainted in this [new] street" than

"Cleveland Boy Gang." April 8, 1911. A boy gang at the foot of a hill it had claimed for itself. Like most "gangs," this one had members of different ages. The third boy from the right in the second row was probably five or six years older than the child sitting cross-legged in front of him. (*Bain Collection, LC*)

it was time to move again. Every time he moved he'd "be initiated into different gangs, but they'd remember, 'Oh, you were in the other street,' and give [him] a hard time."[33]

The cities were divided by block and gang. Gang fighting to protect turf or extend it into the vacant lot next door was commonplace and often ferocious. Kids fought with paving stones, bottles, bricks, and garbage can lids as shields until one side, bloodied and bowed, was forced to retreat.[34] The wars appeared to outsiders to be ethnically inspired, especially when the combatants called each other Sheeny, Christ-killer, Dago, and Mickie. But it was space, not ethnicity or religion they fought over. Territory was everything to the children. It was, indeed, the only thing they could call their own.[35]

Kids who ventured off the block were likely to get in trouble. If the foreign block was occupied by a rival gang, the trouble was compounded. The children of the city, all of them, grew up with street maps etched into their brains. Harpo Marx, who spent a good part of his childhood on the streets, survived by learning precisely who lived where for blocks in every direction. When he had to leave the block, he made sure to carry "some kind of boodle in my pocket—a dead tennis ball, an empty spool, a penny, anything. It didn't cost much to buy your freedom; the gesture was the important thing."[36]

Springfield, Massachusetts, June 27, 1916. "Street gang—corner Margaret and Water Streets—4:30." (*Lewis Hine Collection, LC*)

All city kids faced the same consequences should they be caught on foreign blocks. If they had suitable ransom—like Harpo—they would be released. If not, they would be chased out of the neighborhood with sticks, stones, and fists. For black boys in "transitional" white neighborhoods and Jewish boys caught on Gentile blocks, there were added dangers. Though the Jews did not risk serious bodily injury as some of the blacks did, each knew what was in store should he be trapped off the block. Harry Golden recalls his first "brush with anti-Semitism [at age ten]. I ventured a block or two beyond our slum into the Irish slum. Some Irish kids chased me. A year later, three of these Irish buckoes caught me when I dared a similar venture. They 'cockalized' me. There are hundreds of men in their sixties who know what it is to be cockalized. Indeed, cockalization was universal. . . . The enemy kids threw the Jew to the ground, opened his pants, and spat and urinated on his circumcised penis while they shouted, 'Christ killer.' "[37]

In his autobiography Golden recalls this incident without bitterness or resentment. Harpo Marx and George Burns remembered their battles with the same matter-of-fact tone. Getting threatened or ambushed in enemy territory was as American as apple pie. It hurt at the time and might leave scars for years to come, but it was unavoidable, part of the price one paid in growing up.[38]

It was, of course, possible to avoid such dangers by staying on your home block, as the smaller kids did. The bigger ones, however, as they approached their teens found the block too confining and the lure of foreign adventure too strong. In small groups or with their gangs, they searched the city for open space. When the weather grew warm, they traveled to the lakes, the rivers, and the ponds for a swim. It mattered little whether the water was on private or public land or how polluted it might appear. If there was enough room to swim and no adults to get in the way, it would do. On a hot July day in Cleveland, investigators found groups of boys bathing all along the lakefront, from East Sixteenth to Gordon Park, "most of them without suits." In New York City, the boys' swimming hole was the East River, where they used a modified dog paddle to push the garbage out of their way. "It was," Samuel Chotzinoff, pianist and music critic, remembered, "perfectly legal to dive off the docks provided one wore one's underwear."[39]

The geography of the city was kinder to some children than others. Those who lived near "swimming holes" or within walking distance of the undeveloped parts of town and the urban wastelands had little trouble locating areas to explore and play in. In Cleveland, the children who lived near the lakefront played in the gullies. They constructed "dens, dug-outs, and shanties," listened to the hoboes' stories, built bonfires

34

in the sand, and with food "copped" from the freight trains, cooked themselves feasts.[40]

The children were not without their allies in the search for usable play areas. Though, as David Macleod has shown in his insightful and comprehensive book, *Building Character in the American Boy,* many middle-class "boys' workers" devoted their energies to saving boys of their own class, there were others who took up the rescue of lower-class children.[41] The reformers' first priority was to remove these children from the contaminating effect of life on the city streets. Boys and girls who escaped being run over by wagons, trucks, and horsecars remained subject to the debilitating influence of the bad elements with whom they shared public space. As Simon Patten observed in his 1905 lectures on "The New Basis of Civilization," the respectable poor in the early twentieth-century city had no choice but to share their living quarters "with the vicious, the depraved, and the chronic paupers."[42]

From the 1880s on, a loosely connected coalition of settlement-house workers, educators, Protestant clergy, crusading journalists, and full-time "child-savers" and "boys' workers" campaigned for playgrounds and supervised play spaces large enough to accommodate the thousands of children who had no place but the street to call their own. While they

New York City. The old swimming hole, New York City style. (*Bain Collection, LC*)

were successful in building dozens of new playgrounds, in opening up some schoolyards for after-school activities, and in establishing scores of boys' clubs in cities across the country, they had neither the energy nor the resources nor the volunteers to serve all the children of the city.

The child-savers' problems were compounded by the children's reluctance to follow their lead. The boys' clubs set up expressly for "street" and working boys fought a never-ending battle to keep their young charges in attendance and in line. Though their ultimate goal was to teach the boys to play properly, submit their "individual wills to the welfare of the team," follow orders, obey preestablished rules, practice self-control, and experience the exhilaration of "fighting shoulder to shoulder for the honor of the team," they found that most of their efforts were devoted to building a stable membership.[43] No matter how many different and exciting activities, sports, and games they offered as inducements, the boys continued to drop in only sporadically rather than committing themselves full-time to the club.[44] The reformers found the same difficulty in attracting children to their after-school centers and playgrounds. While neighborhood kids enjoyed using the equipment provided, they did not relish the adult "supervision" that came along with it. Roy Rosenzweig, in his marvelous study of "workers and leisure in an industrial city," quotes from what are purported to be interviews with Worcester (Massachusetts) children who had used the city's playgrounds. In all cases, the children expressed disdain for the adult efforts to teach them how to play, and many said that they either no longer paid attention to the play leaders or had stopped attending the playgrounds altogether. 'I can't go to the playgrounds now,' complained one eleven-year-old . . . 'They get on me nerves with so many men and women around telling you what to do.'"[44]

The reformers were stymied as well by the children's highly developed sense of turf. Most children would only consider playing at playgrounds near enough to their homes to "belong" to them. They would not, no matter what the apparent benefits, venture onto someone else's playground. Roy Rosenzweig found that in Worcester "82% of the children who attended a particular playground lived within a quarter mile of it." In Chicago, Henry S. Curtis reported in 1910 that "little children below six will not come regularly to a playground that is more than two blocks [from their home], the children under nine or ten will not come over one-quarter of a mile, and even the older children will not come regularly over a half mile." Even had the children been willing to travel greater distances, it is doubtful that their mothers would have let them leave their home blocks for such distant locations.[45]

There was no simple way to solve this problem. Though legislators,

New York City, August 1911. A photograph taken at the Carnegie Playground on Fifth Avenue in New York City. The attraction here was the real basketball court and ball. Unfortunately, children who wanted to use the court had to submit to the supervision of the adult standing to the left. (*Bain Collection, LC*)

mayors, school officials, and progressive-minded philanthropists agreed in principle that more playgrounds had to be built to accommodate more city kids, they did not have or did not want to provide the funds necessary to buy and clear the land, construct the playgrounds, and staff them with qualified supervisors. A number of cities, Chicago and Pittsburgh most prominently, embarked on ambitious building campaigns, but none came close to providing sufficient play space for all the children who needed it.[46]

Studies of child's play in New York City (1913), Milwaukee (1914), and Cleveland (1920) confirmed what was obvious from the window of any tenement. The children—and their mothers—preferred the streets as playgrounds to the supervised parks and after-school settlement house programs. In Milwaukee, where such facilities were within walking distance of 20 percent of the city's children, less than 4 percent used them. The figures from Cleveland were almost identical: only 4 percent of the school-age children played in city and school playgrounds. In New York City, 95 percent of the children played on the streets.[47] The children, though aware of the dangers posed by traffic and the bad elements, felt safer on their home blocks than anywhere else. This was *their* space—with its mud, horse dung, bums, and prostitutes. There was something reassuring about the clutter, the noise, the turmoil, the congestion. The dangers were known and visible by mothers from the front room window. Should the worst happen, help was only a shout away.

The play communities of the streets existed only for those children still young enough to be allowed to spend their free time on the block. As working-class city kids reached the ages of eleven or twelve, their days of leisure came to an end. One after the other, they were called away from the block to help out at home or earn money downtown.

Those who traveled downtown to earn some money did not, on that account, join the adult community. They remained members of a children's community of the streets which, like the earlier play communities, defined itself by its difference from and, at times, opposition to the ordinary adult world. At work—as at play—the children would remain, in Huizinga's words, "apart-together"[48] in the midst of but separate from the adult world.

Child Labor and Laborers

This is a book about children, but not about all children or even all city children. I have chosen to write about a particular group of city kids. These were children born to working-class parents who owned little or no property, had received little or no formal education, and worked for wages or piece rates at skilled or unskilled jobs.

The children of the city were immigrant and native-born, of Jewish, Italian, Polish, German, Irish, or native-born American parents. They grew up in cities across the country. What united them as a group—and what distinguished them from their more prosperous middle-class contemporaries—was the size, shape, and reach of their families' incomes.

As the numerous "family budget" studies demonstrated at the time, most working-class families made do by stretching every possible resource as far as it would go. Seldom if ever could the heads of households earn enough to support their families by themselves. In the stockyards district of Chicago, in New York City and Buffalo, New York, in Springfield, Illinois, and almost everywhere else investigators studied working-class budgets, they found families spending more each month than the primary wage earners brought home.[1] In Springfield, Illinois, in 1916, only nineteen of the one hundred families studied (80 percent of which were headed by native-born white fathers) lived on the father's salary. In the Chicago stockyards community, a 1914 study found that while the average father's salary was $503, the average yearly family income was $854.[2] Wages were low and work was irregular. Men who worked outdoors,

Cincinnati. A Lewis Hine photograph of "Marie Costa, Basket Seller, 605 Elm Street. Sister and friend help her." (*Lewis Hine Collection, LC*)

skilled craftsmen like bricklayers, stonecutters, and ironworkers, and unskilled laborers, drivers, longshoremen, and street and sewer workers, lost their jobs when the weather turned bad.[3]

In other industries employment was seasonal because management found it profitable to lay off workers during slack times and speed them up during booms. In dressmaking, employees could count on only about eight months of guaranteed work a year. From May through July, there was plenty of work—and overtime—preparing next winter's garments. August and September were slack times, with less work and shorter work weeks. In October, it was back to full time to produce spring and summer wear. By February, the work had given out and the slack times returned.[4] In meat-packing, there was less work in summer as demand fell off and short weeks in winter as management rushed animals from the pens to the packinghouses and sped them down the disassembly line early in the week so that by Thursday they could begin sending workers home with less than a full week's wages.[5]

There was no escaping the recurrent layoffs and short weeks. Families responded as best they could by fortifying their income to diminish reliance on the father's wages. Though most wives with children at home did not go out to work, they contributed to the family income by cooking or doing laundry for single men or taking in industrial homework or boarders. There were variations in the strategies employed by different ethnic and racial groups. Black women were more likely than white to take in homework, Poles to take in boarders.[6] What was common to all, however, was the need to make use of every potential source of income. Boarders were squeezed into front rooms, kitchens converted into work areas for industrial homework, and everyone put to work—including the children.

There was nothing new or extraordinary about asking children to go to work. Only recently has childhood become—almost by definition—an

Roxbury, Massachusetts, August 1912. "Family of Mrs. Donovan, 293½ Highland Street, Roxbury, Massachusetts, tying tags for Dennison Company. This is the family that has worked on tags for seven years and makes an average from that work of $30 a month. One month they made $42 a month. . . . All the children aged 13, 9, 11 and the twins, 4½ years, help the mother. They often have to work late at night to get done." (*Lewis Hine Collection, LC*)

age of irresponsibility. In the eighteenth and nineteenth centuries, rural and preindustrial parents routinely sent their children off to work. Large families with many mouths to feed could not afford to keep the kids at home until they were ready to start their own households. Nor could most of them find work for the children at home. The solution was to ship them off to households which could make use of them. Ten- and eleven-year-old boys and girls were placed out as maids, servants, plowboys, and helpers of every description.

Only the coming of industrialization—here and in Europe—altered this pattern. With the expansion of factory cities—with their thousands of jobs for children—working-class families discovered that they could find work for their youngsters within walking distance of home.[7] Child labor kept working-class families solvent and together, but it did so by sacrificing the children who were sent into the mines, mills, and factories. As observed in England by commentators as diverse as Charles Dickens, Friedrich Engels, and Benjamin Disraeli, child laborers in industry were so brutally exploited that many did not survive to become adults.

Across the Atlantic, Americans with their characteristic optimism saw what was happening in England and declared that they could do better. Child labor might pose a problem to society, but as American commentators observed with growing distaste and suspicion, so too did the increase in the number and visibility of the idle urchins, orphans, runaways, and "ragged outcasts" who were found in such quantities on the streets of the larger cities.[8]

Charles Loring Brace, founder of the Children's Aid Society, proposed sending the urchins out of the city to live, work, and be properly raised on small family farms. Unfortunately, as he soon discovered, there was an overabundance of urchins and only a limited supply of farm families prepared to take them in. An alternate solution to the problem was to remove the children from the streets by sending them to work. Though Brace was no doubt aware of the English industrial experience, he was confident that conditions in this country would be different. If manufacturing could put idle teenagers to work, it could only benefit them and their city. From the 1860s on, the Society, while continuing to place children on family farms, devoted more and more of its funds to lodging houses and industrial schools designed to protect and prepare the city's "ragged outcasts" for productive labor in manufacturing establishments.[9]

This vision of the future—with middle-class reformers sweeping idle teenagers off the streets into industrial schools and from there into factories—may have been a comforting one and, in the 1870s, not entirely unrealistic. Regrettably, industrial society was not to progress along these

Children at work in a stringbean cannery. (*Lewis Hine Collection, NCLC*)

paths. Although employment possibilities for teenagers expanded through the last decades of the nineteenth century, manufacturing jobs did not. Children who found work found it in dead-end positions: as helpers, errand boys, messengers, maids, and unskilled laborers. By the turn of the century, even these jobs were disappearing. Children, once a major component of the work force in factories, shops, and department stores, were being pushed back onto the streets.[10]

The decrease in the number of child laborers was most dramatic in the department stores, those paragons of modernity. During their nineteenth-century infancy, the stores had employed thousands of children, most of them as "cash" boys and girls. When sales were made, the children were called on to carry the item sold, the customer's money, and the sales slip to an inspector who checked the price and wrapped the merchandise. From the inspector the children hurried to the cashier, then back to the customer with wrapped package and change.

In the 1870s, one third of Macy's employees had worked in this capacity. By the turn of the century they were gone, all of them. The pneumatic tube, followed swiftly by cash registers at each sales counter, made the children superfluous. Some were kept on as messengers, but only until the stores installed telephones on the sales floor. By the early decades of the century, the only children still at work in the stores were those hidden below in the packing rooms and warehouses and those sent out on deliveries.[11]

Automation not only eliminated the department store employees, it took away the jobs of many of the children who had packed candies, pulled bastings, folded paper boxes, pasted labels on cans, and assisted glassblowers at the glassworks. In the nineteenth century and into the early years of the twentieth, boys had been as much a part of the glassmaking process as the huge furnaces which melted the glass. In 1892, according to Robert and Helen Lynd, 42 percent of the employees in the Middletown glass plant had been "boys." The "take-out boys" and "snapper-ups" carried the blown glass in tongs from the blowers to the finishers; the "carry-in boys" picked it up from the finishers and placed it in the cooling ovens to harden.

As long as the glassworks remained organized on craft lines, there was plenty of work for the boys. When the manufacturers automated their plants, the boys' usefulness came to an end. They and the skilled blowers and finishers they had assisted were replaced by machines and machine tenders, most of them recent immigrants from southern and eastern Europe.[12]

The manufacturers, though they fought like hell to keep the child labor reformers from tampering with their infant work force, were not sorry to see the children go. While cheap, the boys and girls had never been the most productive of laborers. They were sloppy, unsteady, prone to falling asleep and forever taking unauthorized vacations or quitting without notice.[13] They were also no longer needed. Though there remained thousands upon thousands of unskilled, menial tasks to be performed in the nation's mines, mills, factories, and workshops, adult immigrants arriving daily from eastern and southern Europe were available to perform them as cheaply as the children had, and more efficiently.

The substitution of immigrant adults for children and the automation of many of their specialized jobs did not mean an end to child labor. Those employers (e.g., southern textile mills) who had not yet automated their plants or were unable to secure a large enough supply of unskilled adult immigrant laborers continued to hire children by the thousands. In the South and in rural areas throughout the country, children continued to sort coal, pick berries, can fruit, shuck oysters, and tend machines in textile mills.[14]

In urban areas as well, though the larger commercial and manufacturing establishments no longer needed child laborers, families who could

Picking cotton. (*Lewis Hine Collection, NCLC*)

not have survived without the young ones' help could still find places for them. Children no more than ten or eleven were hidden away in sweatshops, back rooms, and their own tenement flats where for hours on end they assisted their parents and other adults at menial tasks that had not yet been automated or moved into factory buildings. Day after day they pulled bastings and assembled artificial flowers. Day after day, the same tasks, from early in the morning until the light grew too dim to see what lay before them.

It was these working children—in countryside and city—who aroused the sympathy of the reform community and motivated the early twentieth-century crusade against child labor. Though their numbers—and their suffering—remained worthy of the reformers' attention, these children were a minority—and a diminishing one. In urban areas especially, the decline in child laborers accelerated through the first years of the new century. By 1920, the proportion of ten-to-fourteen-year-olds in non-agricultural pursuits was less than one third what it had been twenty

Bowling Green, Kentucky, November 1916. "The Howell Family 'stripping tobacco'; the 8 and 10 year old boys 'tie up waste.' There are two children (12 and 14 years old) not in the photo who are regular strippers. All lost much schooling on account of farm work." (*Lewis Hine Collection, NCLC*)

years before.[15] As the Lynds discovered in Muncie, children were beginning work "from two to five years later" than they had in the 1890s.[16] Reformers and educators—with their improved laws and enforcement—took full credit for the decreases in child labor and the accompanying increases in school enrollments.* But the children and their parents were also responsible for the changes. As it was perceived that the more schooling students received, the better their chances for landing preferred white-collar jobs, families who could afford to kept their children in school and out of full-time work as long as possible.

* From 1910 to 1920, school enrollments for seven-to-thirteen- and fourteen-to-fifteen- and fourteen-to-seventeen-year-olds increased for native-born, foreign-born, and second-generation immigrant children. By 1920, the number of fourteen-to-seventeen-year-olds in high school was 600 percent what it had been just thirty years before. Of Chicago's fourteen- and fifteen-year-olds, 73 percent were in school. Comparable figures were, for Baltimore, 69 percent; New England, 75 percent; the Middle Atlantic region, 79 percent; and the Middle West, 84 percent.[17]

Fortunately for the children—and their families—earning money and going to school were not mutually exclusive activities in the early twentieth century. There might have been a shortage of decent full-time positions for children in their teens, but there were more than enough part-time, after-school jobs. For the children of the city, schooling was a major activity, but not a full-time, all-inclusive one. Not for a moment did their parents consider the possibility that attending school should exempt ten- to sixteen-year-olds from helping out at home.

The children who are the subject of this book were a privileged group of youngsters, privileged at play and at work. Not only were they spared the deadly tedium of full-time menial labor, but they were freed from the pressures that had accompanied such work for their nineteenth-century counterparts and the minority of their peers who were still at work. Children who worked full-time did so because their parents—or parent—had no way of making ends meet without their weekly wages. Children who worked part-time, on the contrary, knew that their income was extra, that their little brothers and sisters would not go hungry if they brought home less this week than they had the week before.

Work for the part-time child laborers of the early twentieth-century city was far from the routinized hell that had destroyed generations of working children. It was, on the contrary, almost a pleasant interlude between a day's confinement in school and an evening in cramped quarters at home.

4

The Littlest Hustlers

City kids who worked part-time after school, on weekends, and during vacations were blessed with abundant job opportunities. The early twentieth-century cities, it appeared, survived on the part-time work of their children. The children did the work that would, in later years, be taken over by adults, alleviated by labor-saving appliances, or automated out of existence. They provided city workers and residents with their afternoon and Sunday papers, their gum, candy, pencils, and shiny shoes. They helped out at home with the cooking, cleaning, and laundry. They ran errands and made deliveries for neighborhood tradesmen, carried messages for downtown businessmen who could not yet rely on their customers to have telephones, and did odd jobs for shopkeepers and local manufacturers. In summer, their part-time jobs were extended into full-time positions. There was more than enough work to go around—so much, indeed, that children could quit or get fired, knowing that they would soon find other work. Jan Peerce, the future opera singer, worked one summer in a metal-spinning factory as a nine-dollar-a-week errand boy. The following summer he had three different jobs. He began the season delivering cotton trimmings, canvas, and white binding tape in a wheelbarrow. When he was fired after two weeks, he found a second job on Houston Street under a "Boy Wanted" sign. "It was a pants factory . . . My job was to turn the trousers inside out." A month later, Peerce, fired again, landed his third and "best job

Probably Washington, D.C., April 1912. "At Center Market, eleven year old celery vendor, Gus Straleges, 212 Jackson Hole Alley. He sold until 11 P.M. and was out again Sunday morning selling papers and gum. Has been in this country only a year and a half." (*Lewis Hine Collection, NCLC*)

yet" at the Breakstone Dairy, where he recorded "the gallons of milk delivered by farmers."[1]

Harry Golden, who sold papers during the winter, got delivery jobs in summertime. One summer, he landed the ideal job for a city boy on vacation. "I delivered pretzels to the Polo Grounds for Bock and Company. Mr. Bock gave me two big bags of pretzels, two nickels for carfare, and a dime for myself. I took the pretzels to the Stevens concession on the mezzanine and had to be there by ten A.M. Then I could hang around the ball park until the game started that afternoon."[2]

Not many children were as fortunate as Golden when it came to finding work for the summer. Hy Kraft had a job "working for the

49

National Cloak and Suit Company, a mail-order house. I had the very responsible job of hanging suits on hangers and then hanging the hangers on racks that were wheeled away to some mysterious burial ground. I did that for eight hours a day for a month and gave up."[3]

While most of the eleven- to fifteen-year-olds left the immediate neighborhood to earn their money, a significant number stayed closer to home. In those days before the widespread residential use of the telephone, there were plenty of errands to run—and children to pay for running them. The neighborhood children and the local shopkeepers were made for one another. The baker, the butcher, the grocer, and the delicatessen owner, all in need of help but unable to afford full-time assistants, hired boys by the week, the day, or the hour. Theodore Waterman, described by an investigator from the New York Child Labor Committee as a "West Indian Negro," worked after school for the butcher on his Harlem block. He got a dollar a week for himself and a piece of meat to take home to his family every evening. Milton Berle and Eddie Cantor both claimed in their autobiographies that they earned their first money making deliveries for local delis. Berle got paid in tips, raspberry soda, and halvah; Cantor in salami sandwiches.[4]

Most of the work the children did in the neighborhood was too ill-paid to be offered to adults. There was a separate kiddie labor market with jobs set aside for them to do after school. Author Harry Roskolenko tells us in his memoirs that he "rolled empty milk cans for Breakstone & Levine, then starting out in business. . . . For a nickel an hour we got the containers into the freezers in the back, taking a little cheese away with us for home use." James Cagney and his brothers worked at the library, where they "picked up books left on the table." George Burns and his friends had an after-school job in the basement of Rosenzweig's candy store. "The four of us each got five cents a day mixing the syrup that Rosenzweig put in his ice cream sodas. And as a fringe benefit we got all the sodas we could drink. By the end of the first week we could have opened a pimple factory."[5]

Though running errands, making deliveries, and doing odd jobs in the neighborhood could pay off handsomely in sweets and salami, these were not the children's favorite jobs. Many of the children who ran errands for local tradesmen did so not out of choice but because they were forbidden to work elsewhere. Antonio Giordano, a Lower East Side "wood carver," explained to an investigator from the New York Child Labor Committee that he forced his son Nicholas to take "a place at errands for a baker after school." The boy had wanted to sell papers downtown but his father forbade it, convinced that "paper selling makes boys gamblers and bums."[6]

Whether paper-selling made boys "gamblers and bums" was not precisely the issue. What the father objected to and the boy desired was the relative freedom offered the street traders. Errand boys had bosses and worked regular hours in a fixed location. From the moment they left school until the time they arrived home for dinner, they were watched over by responsible adults. They had no free time to play with the gang, gamble, or get into trouble. Street traders, on the contrary, had neither bosses or supervisors nor regular hours. They were on their own from the sound of the dismissal bell until dinnertime.

Parents like Antonio Giordano were concerned that their boys and girls would, if allowed downtown to work, get in with the wrong crowd. Their fears were misguided but understandable. Children who traded away from the neighborhood were swept up in a children's community of the streets. Out of school, off the block, away from home, they looked to one another for advice, guidance, and support. Aside from a minority who worked with their parents, like the Italian children Edward Clopper found selling baskets, fruit, and flowers in Cincinnati, most street traders were on their own.[7] They learned what they had to know on the streets, not from parents at home or teachers in school.

Max Ravage began his career as a street trader peddling chocolates at Fourteenth Street and Fifth Avenue in Manhattan, an "American" shopping street located within walking distance of his Lower East Side flat. On his first day as a trader, he was taken in hand by the lace peddler who set up beside him. Americans, he was informed, had no sense of value. They were so rich they didn't need any. Ravage had started off selling his chocolates for a penny a piece. At that price, the peddler warned him, customers would be sure to pass him by, convinced that he was selling trash—which he was. If he raised the price, however, and advertised sufficiently, he just might be able to convince them that his chocolates were quality merchandise.

He had to advertise, shout, gesticulate. Americans were aggressive, brash, forever on the make. If he, Max Ravage, wanted to succeed, he had to do as they did. "Move along, elbow your way through the crowds in front of the stores. Seek out the women with kids; shove your tray into their faces. Don't be timid. America likes the nervy ones. This is the land where modesty starves. And yell, never stop yelling. Advertising sells the goods. Here is a formula to begin on: 'Candy, ladies! Finest in America. Only a nickel, a half-a-dime, five cents!' Go on, now; try it."

"Reluctantly and with some misgiving," Ravage followed the advice. He was astonished to find that it worked. The more he shouted, the more he lied, the more he shoved and pushed, the cruder his salesmanship, the more chocolates he sold. "Incredible as it seemed, these people actually paid five cents for every piece that cost me less than two-thirds of one cent."[8]

Ravage, a recent émigré from Rumania, had been thrown into street trading at the advanced age of sixteen. He had had to learn from the lace peddler what the street traders who had grown up in the city took for granted. America was the land of the huckster, and the early twentieth century the era of "salesmanship," defined by the Detroit *Free Press* as the art of selling a dress shirt to the customer who came into the store looking for a celluloid collar.[9]

The children of the city grew up listening to the peddlers cry their wares in the street. They were watching when the pots-and-pans merchant paraded his utensils across the kitchen table; they listened to the insurance man and the undertaker as they sold their goods and services; they stood by as their mothers haggled with the vegetable man and their fathers bargained with the tailor over the price of a new suit—with an extra pair of pants thrown in. The huckster and his sales pitch were as much a part of their culture as baseball and movie stars. They grew up with the newspaper advertisements and the movie posters and billboards and the barkers' spiel at the amusement park. They learned how to sell and, just as important, that it was the salesman's job to pitch and the customer's to resist. All was fair in the marketplace. Whether buyer or seller, you had to look out for yourself. No one else was going to watch out for you.

The children who earned their money as street traders peddled whatever they could buy cheaply, fit into their pockets or the canvas bag slung over their shoulders, and sell for a profit. Bessie Turner Kriesberg, a Russian émigré whose oral history translated from the Yiddish is found in the YIVO archives, was astounded on her arrival in Chicago by the number of boys on the streets—and the variety of items they sold. "She enjoyed watching the young boys acting as businessmen. They were shouting out the merchandise they had for sale. One was selling newspapers, one chewing gum, one peanuts, one theater tickets, and the youngest carried on his shoulder a small wooden box with tools to clean shoes for people."[10]

Many children sold more than one item at a time. The newsies in particular were always adopting "side lines" to hawk with their papers.

Twenty-third Street and Fourth Avenue, New York City. A Lewis Hine photograph of two peddlers waiting outside a subway station. The older boy carries the display box that the gum came in, advertising "Wrigley's Spearmint: The flavor lasts." (*Lewis Hine Collection, LC*)

Hy Kraft, the future Broadway playwright, who claimed to have held more jobs as a child "than there are categories in the Yellow Pages of the phone book," sold newspapers with his brother Willie "at the corner of 116th Street and Lenox Avenue, in front of the pool parlor next to the subway kiosk, defying the onrush of bicycles and streetcars. We almost got ourselves killed, but we never got rich. So we took on a side line— Spearmint gum. We had the same deal as we had on the newspapers— two for a penny and sold them for a penny a slice, when we sold them. Packages were two for a nickel; we sold them at a nickel a pack. A 100 percent profit."[11]

George Burns claims in his autobiography that he sold so many different items he "became sort of a one-man conglomerate. And that was before I became a man, or before I knew what conglomerate meant. . . . One of my many big business ventures lasted exactly two hours and twenty minutes. I thought there was money to be made by selling vanilla crackers. I'd go into a grocery store and buy a bunch of vanilla crackers at ten for a penny. Then on the street I'd sell them eight for a penny. . . . The problem here was by the time I sold eight crackers I'd eaten two crackers. It didn't take me long to realize that this was the wrong business for a kid who was hooked on vanilla crackers."[12]

Al Jolson and his brother Harry sold newspapers in Washington, D.C. In the summer, they went into the watermelon business. "We could buy watermelons at the wharves at a wholesale price, three for a nickel. Sometimes we could get four for a nickel. We had a patched and battered wagon, for which we had traded. We would load it with melons, and haul them to a promising section of town for resale. Here our voices . . . became part of our stock-in-trade. We made up a little song which Al and I [Harry] would sing in tones that carried far:

> Wa---------a-termelons
> Red to da rind
> Five cents a piece
> And you eat 'em all da time."[13]

As the Jolsons and the other young hustlers quickly discovered, their youth was their greatest selling point. There was something

---

Boston, October 1909. Selling suspenders in the street. (*Lewis Hine Collection, NCLC*)

irresistible about innocent-looking children trying so hard to earn money. The incongruity between their size and their salesmanship attracted customers. In their own neighborhoods, the children were helped out by working-class and immigrant adults who had children of their own. Downtown, they were patronized by prosperous Americans who found the little hustlers too cute to pass by.

All the street traders had to perform for their customers. One needed a bit of bravado and an immunity from embarrassment to survive on the streets. Children with a surfeit of each—and a bit of talent—went a step further. The streets of the city were filled with young hustlers who clowned, pantomimed, sang, and danced, some for the sheer sport of it, others for the change they hoped to collect from bystanders. The Jewish neighborhoods in particular were, as Irving Howe has written, the training grounds for future generations of comics, dancers, and singers. "There are the famous or once-famous names: Al Jolson, George Jessel, Eddie Cantor, Sophie Tucker, Fanny Brice, Ben Blue, Jack Benny, George Burns, George Sidney, Milton Berle, Ted Lewis, Bennie Fields, and others. And there are the hundreds who played the small towns, the ratty theaters, the Orpheum circuit, the Catskills, the smelly houses in Brooklyn and the Bronx."[14]

The children of the streets observed from the outside the great panorama of urban life, taking it all in, and then, if they had the talent, representing it in comic or melodramatic form from the stage (and later on the screen, over the radio, on television). They learned to mimic the dialects, the dialogues, the patter of peddlers, policemen, and "the hoity-toity Irish teacher who recited Browning in high school."[15] They began by entertaining each other. Only later would they begin charging for it.

At the age of six, Eddie Cantor began keeping "late hours . . . with a band of boys two and three times [his] age who spent their nights in a revelry of song. For the East Side at night is not only menaced by the caterwauling of cats, but by gangs of youngsters who sit on the stoops and the corner stands, singing all the popular songs with all their might at an age when their voices are changing."[16] The Jolson brothers, George Burns, and Fanny Brice began their careers in similar fashion, singing or clowning on street corners and in backyards and alleyways with their friends. When they discovered that adults were willing to throw pennies their way, they quickly abandoned their amateur status. Fanny Brice roamed with her gang through backyards until they found "a likely-looking tenement" to perform for. The children sang all the popular songs of the day and, when they were lucky, were rewarded with a "brief, scattered shower of pennies."[17] When the Jolson brothers and their gang in Washington, D.C., "found that grown people would stop

55

Indianapolis, August 1908. "American District Telegraph messengers: the night shift." (*Lewis Hine Collection, NCLC*)

to listen" and even throw coins at them, they moved away from the street corners they had been gathering on to well-situated sidewalks where they were sure to meet adults with change in their pockets. "Our favorite stage was the sidewalk in front of the Hotel Raleigh. In those days, congressmen, high government officials, and even Supreme Court Justices would sit on chairs on the sidewalks during spring and summer evenings, just as people did in small towns. They not only appreciated our singing, but they became an unusual source of income for us. We sang all the popular songs, such as: Sweet Marie, The Sidewalks of New York, Who Threw the Overalls in Mrs. Murphy's Chowder, Daisy Bell, and Say Au Revoir But Not Goodbye. We soon learned that statesmen and jurists preferred the songs that carried them into the romantic past, the songs of Stephen Foster, and Listen to the Mocking Bird, Come Where My Love Lies Dreaming, and When You and I Were Young, Maggie. Songs such as these brought a shower of nickels, dimes, and even quarters."[18]

For children whose songs or clowning met with applause, laughter, and pennies, there was no turning back. George Burns and the three friends who mixed syrup with him in Rosenzweig's basement began work as the Peewee Quartet after school one afternoon "at the corner of Columbia and Houston." "We stood there and sang from three-thirty to six, and made exactly four cents." The boys did not give up. They continued to sing—in saloons until they were thrown out, on the Staten Island ferry until "Mortzy" got seasick, and in backyards where they were greeted by rotten fruit and occasional pennies.[19]

Though future show business characters tell the best stories about performing on the streets, they were by no means the only children who tried to make some money this way. Of the four friends who made up the Peewee Quartet, only George Burns went into show business. Two others went into the taxi business; the third became an insurance broker. Similarly, the dozens of children who sang in groups with Eddie Cantor on the Lower East Side, Fanny Brice in Brooklyn, and the Jolson brothers in Washington, D.C., had neither the talent nor the inclination to go into show business.[20]

Children with imagination put it all to use, coming up with special ways to make money. Because they were their own bosses, they could conjure up and follow their own leads. If they failed, they could start all over again tomorrow. Fanny Brice made twenty cents an afternoon by charging the kids in the neighborhood a penny a piece to attend her variety show in the shed behind her Brooklyn tenement.[21] Children with a less theatrical bent were every bit as enterprising and inventive. In the Berlinger family (Milton would later change the family name to Berle), it was the older boy, Jack, who came up with the big ideas while little brother Milton was off plugging songs in his Buster Brown haircut and kiddie tuxedo. The Berlingers lived "about ten blocks from the Hunt's Point railroad stop [where they had discovered] an open spring that flowed down the railroad embankment. It was July, and hot as hell, and Jack and a kid named McDermott, who was the janitor's son in [their] building, found two big jugs, like the kind they use in water coolers today. . . . Jack and McDermott went around the building asking if anyone wanted fresh cold spring water. A lady said she'd take the two jugs and pay them a nickel, which seemed like pretty good money.

"I was allowed to tag along when they went to fill the order. The empty jugs were heavy enough going to Hunt's Point. They were murder coming back filled. And then, because it was Saturday and McDermott was a Catholic, we had to stop by the church while he went in to confession."

When the boys got back to their tenement, they hoisted the jug into their customer's apartment and then waited to collect their nickel. "We waited and waited for the nickel to come down. Finally McDermott rang her bell again. 'What?' the lady shouted down.

" 'Where's our nickel, lady?'

" 'A nickel you want? The police you could get! You call that hot stuff spring water? You filled it from the tap.'

"Jack shouted up, 'We went all the way to the Hunt's Point spring. It's hot outside, lady.'

" 'Get away from there, you liars, or I swear, I'll call the police. I'm counting to five!'

"We ran."

This was, of course, neither the first nor the last of Jack Berlinger's "big ideas." Like other city kids (most of them without younger brothers to tell their stories in show business autobiographies), Jack had different hustles for different kinds of weather. When it rained, he took his umbrella to the IRT subway station near the Berlinger's home. "Jack would get there when the people were coming home from work. Jack would run after anybody without an umbrella. 'Take you home, mister? Take you home, lady? Only a nickel.' . . . It was a small-time Hertz operation. When I [Milton] got a little older, I tried it once. I got pneumonia."[22]

With one eye on their potential customers and another on the bottom line, the children stood ready to take advantage of whatever came their way. Because they were on their own, they could change locations and goods at will, add to or subtract from their wares, and adjust their practices to the demands of the marketplace. When, in the early months of World War I, fifty thousand soldiers moved into Camp Greene, the children who lived in Charlotte, North Carolina, hitched rides or walked the two miles to the camp to hustle food, candy, and soft drinks after school. According to a National Child Labor Committee study published in 1918, 35 percent of the students in Charlotte's "white schools [were] selling at camp."[23]

The children had few scruples when it came to making money from adults. Adults were old enough and experienced enough to watch out for themselves. If they got taken by a bunch of children, it was their own fault. The children were too busy trying to earn some money to watch out for their customers. Some of the children's schemes were slightly deceptive, others were clearly fraudulent. Two of the "little twelve year old merchants" who did business with the Camp Greene soldiers boosted their profits by buying leftover pies, warming them up, and selling them as fresh.[24]

The street traders knew that their adult customers, even the soldiers, had more money than they had. The children who worked in the downtown business and entertainment districts had seen firsthand the wealth of the city. They read the newspaper and Sunday supplement stories about the idle rich and their yachts, ocean liners, Twentieth Century expresses, million-dollar hotels, charity balls, and Newport "fête champêtre," and watched them as they ate in their restaurants, shopped in their department stores, and rode in their fancy cars through the city streets. There was more than enough wealth to go around. The children wanted their share. And they were willing to work days and stay up nights figuring out some way to get it.

In the Marx household on Manhattan's Upper East Side (then an immigrant and working-class neighborhood), Leonard taught his little brother Adolph how to make money on the streets. "You don't earn mazuma," he explained, "you hustle it."

In later years, long after Adolph had become Harpo and Leonard Chico, the little brother recounted one of their most imaginative hustles, "The Great Cuckoo Clock Bonanza of 1902." Chico had found cuckooless cuckoo clocks on sale at "a novelty shop on 86th Street" near the boys' home. "These cuckoo clocks had no working cuckoos (the birds were painted on) but they had the genuine Black Forest look, they kept time, and they were on sale for only twenty cents apiece . . . Chico bought a clock. We got fifty cents for it in a hockshop down at Third and 63rd. Thirty cents profit. We went back and bought two clocks, pawned them for four bits apiece. [Business was now so good that the boys branched out. Chico continued to cover the hockshops, Harpo was detailed to]

Rochester, 1912. (*Lewis Hine Collection, NCLC*)

work on people up in the neighborhood. Early the next morning, I took a clock and gathered up my courage and went to the office of the ice works on Third Avenue. The manager there was a friendly guy, who winked whenever the loader chipped off wedges of ice for us kids. He seemed like an ideal customer.

"'Cuckoo clock for sale,' I said to the manager, trying to sound self-assured, like Chico. 'Good bargain. Guaranteed.' . . . The ice works manager wanted to know how long the clock was guaranteed to run on a winding. Whereupon I heard myself saying, as I began to sweat, 'Eight hours.'

"'All right,' he said, 'Wind 'er up. If she's still running eight hours from now I'll buy her.'

"I pulled the chain that wound the clock. I stood in a corner of the office, out of the way, holding the clock, waiting and praying. It was a torturous battle of nerves. Every time the manager turned his back, I gave the chain the little pull to keep the clock wound tight. Along about lunch time, he suspected what I was doing, and caught me with my hand on the chain with a swift, unexpected look. He took the clock and hung it on the wall, without a word.

"At two-thirty, the clock ran down and died. . . . Those were the most grueling six hours I had ever spent and my net profit was, in round figures, zero."[25]

Most of Chico's prospects ended that way. So did most of the other children's. There was some hidden flaw in every "big idea." But that didn't stop the children from thinking up new ones.

The street traders were a creative bunch and a restless one, never satisfied with what they had, always on the lookout for better jobs, hustles, selling locations, and merchandise. They were exhilarated by what their money could buy but at the same time driven by the need to make more. There was so much wealth in the city, it was not unreasonable to want more than you had—and expect that you might get it.

The children were barely adolescents, but they had learned on the streets to put their faith in the American dream, Horatio Alger style. The way to riches was through what Alger called "luck and pluck," being in the right place at the right time. The boys were avid Alger fans because he told them what they wanted to hear.[26] No poor but deserving boy ever stayed that way in his magical urban landscapes. Each got the opportunity he deserved.

The children were not fools or dreamers. They knew that the Alger stories were just that, stories. They did not expect to strike it rich. But neither did they expect to live their lives as their parents lived theirs. They would not be trapped in tenement flats or squeezed into the back rooms of heavily mortgaged houses; they would not work all day and then, in the evening, fall asleep exhausted after dinner; they would not allow themselves to be marooned by fear and by debt in slums and ghettos while the life of the city swirled on around them.

The children did not blame their parents for their poverty. They knew how hard their parents worked and how they were exploited on the job. But their own lives on the street offered them a view of a very different world, a world where one could live by one's wits, where hustle counted, where work was rewarded. The social relations of the marketplace, as the children experienced them, were not particularly onerous or exploitative. Because they didn't have to support their families—or themselves—the pennies they earned stretched a long, long way to give them a false sense of the value of their labor. They worked hard each afternoon but were, they believed, amply rewarded for that labor. And they were only children. When they grew up, they would work harder, earn more, and with those earnings buy even more fun on the streets of the city.

5

The Newsies

There were dozens and dozens of ways for enterprising eleven- to fifteen-year-olds to make money in the early twentieth-century cities. Of them all, the most accessible and most fun was selling newspapers.

Newsies were as old and established an aspect of the urban landscape as the "dailies" they hawked in the streets. There was, nonetheless, something quite different about the twentieth-century boys, something that set them off from their nineteenth-century counterparts. Though every bit as streetwise, tough, and cunning as the street urchins immortalized by Horatio Alger, the newsies who peddled their papers in the turn-of-the-century cities were neither orphans nor streets waifs; nor were they the sole support of ailing mothers and infant siblings. They slept at home, not in alleyways or flophouses, and ate at the dinner table, not at free lunch counters in cheap saloons. As the superintendent of a "newsboy's lodging house" explained to Jacob Riis in 1912, "The newsboy of to-day is another kind of chap, who has a home and folks." The picturesque little ragamuffins Riis had earlier written about had been replaced by "the commercial little chap who lives at home and sells papers after school-hours."[1]

The new generation of newsies was a product of the boom in afternoon circulation that had been building through the 1880s and 1890s but took off during the Spanish-American War. The morning papers that had been the mainstay of the industry had, by the turn of the century, been eclipsed by the late editions. "By 1890, two-thirds of American dailies were published in the afternoon." By 1900, "evening papers, bought on the way home from work, outnumbered morning papers . . . about three to one."[2]

The new metropolis had spawned the new newspaper. With the expansion of the cities outward into the urban fringes and suburbs came a new population of workers, many of whom could be enticed to buy an afternoon paper to occupy them during the commute home by ferry, streetcar, subway, or train.[3] Better illumination on the streets and at home meant that readers had more time to read, advertisers more time to advertise, and publishers a new market of "homebound shoppers and workers and downtown evening crowds" to sell their late editions to. Technological advances in news-gathering, printing, and transportation made it possible to put out "late" editions timed to greet these new readers with "new" news and advertisements.[4]

The newsies were reborn with the expansion of the afternoon editions. Nineteenth-century street urchins had sold the morning editions all day long. Twentieth-century newsies could sell enough papers after school to make up for what they might have lost in the morning. Hawking papers was transformed from a full-time to a part-time job, one that began, most conveniently, at four in the afternoon and extended through the evening rush hours.

Because of the timing of the editions and the hundreds of thousands of customers anxious to get their papers on their way home from work, no newspaper ever had enough newsies. As every circulation manager, city editor, advertising director, and publisher knew, the boys were the last and most vital link in the business chain. Without large numbers out on the streets, crying their wares, advertising their papers, exciting and interesting the public in the latest news and the latest edition, the newspaper business would have been in serious trouble.[5]

In most cities the circulation managers, their assistants, and routemen welcomed the children at the downtown offices and distribution centers. Those who wanted to work steadily, every day after school and on weekends and holidays, were most welcome. But no one was turned away. Children who only wanted to sell the Sunday papers on Saturday nights or the baseball editions with the latest scores during the warm weather were free to do so. So were those who hawked the news only when they were in dire need of extra money, when they lost other jobs, or when the "news" was so hot and the headlines so bold the papers sold themselves.

In cities with more than one afternoon paper (and before World

Cincinnati, 1908. While Edward Clopper reported that black newsies in Cincinnati had been hired by one newspaper to intimidate and disrupt the activities of the boys who sold for a rival paper, it appears from this photograph that black and white newsies were well integrated, at least in the ranks of the Cincinnati *Post*'s hustlers. The younger barefoot boys in the front of the picture were probably not regular newsies, but youngsters enlisted to pose for Hine's photograph. (*Lewis Hine Collection, NCLC*)

War I that included most cities),[6] the circulation managers fought with one another to build up their stock of boys. The more boys on the street, the more papers would be available to customers. Because the profit margin on every paper was the same, the slightest incentive (negative or positive) could shift vendors from one paper to the next or give them a reason to hawk one more enthusiastically then its competitors. An editorial in *Editor and Publisher* reminded circulation managers of the dangers of alienating the boys and the benefits of treating them well. "As the newsboys can increase street sales or can, by refusing to handle a paper, cut them down, their good will and support are considered a valuable asset. Boys are humans, like grown-ups, but are much more appreciative and respond quicker to their impulses. Treat them well, that is, entertain them, give them help when they need it, and invite them to Thanksgiving and Christmas dinners and they will show their gratitude by selling your papers in preference of all others."[7]

Publishers competing for newsies did what they could to curry the boys' favor. In Philadelphia, the *Telegram* treated twelve hundred newsies to see " 'Lover's Lane' at the Park Theater with Miss Millie James in the role of 'Simplicity Johnson.' It was the first time a majority of the boys ever had a seat below the top gallery and they appreciated the honor."[8] In Cincinnati, the dailies competed with one another by spending between three and four thousand dollars each for theater parties, baseball leagues, and furnished recreation rooms.[9] In Detroit, St. Paul, Baltimore, Ogden (Utah), Spokane, Fort Worth, San Antonio, Austin, Buffalo, Schenectady, Boston, Lawrence and Lynn (Massachusetts), New Orleans, Dayton, and Butte (Montana), publishers provided newsies with furnished clubhouses, tickets to ball games, trips to summer camps and free turkeys on holidays.[10]

The publishers did it all, not for humanitarian or public relations considerations, but—as the editor of the Grand Rapids *Press* reminded his fellow editors—for pure "selfish interest."[11]

Turkeys and theater tickets were the preferred weapons in the newspapers' war for the newsies, but there were other strategies as well. Some publishers used intimidation and violence instead of or in combination with their "welfare work." Circulation managers could, if they chose, hire thugs, arm their delivery men, and make it clear to the boys on the street that anyone not pushing their papers was headed for serious trouble. In Cincinnati, according to Edward Clopper (a reliable if somewhat histrionic reporter), the agents for two afternoon papers that were engaged in a circulation battle hired bullies "to follow the newsboys who sell the opposition paper and threaten and harass them if they are found trying to sell more than a specified number of copies." In one instance, Clopper watched as a "small band of young men . . . instead of entering into fair competition with the boys [hawking the rival newspaper], deliberately got in front of them and harassed them wherever they went, to prevent their making sales." When questioned by Clopper, the circulation manager admitted hiring five of the "bullies," but claimed to have done it in self-defense.[12]

In Cincinnati, at least, the circulation managers used children, not adults, as strong-arms, and the violence was sporadic and short-lived. When Maurice Hexter did his study of newsboy life in Cincinnati in 1917, almost ten years after Clopper's investigation, he found no hint of such tactics. The circulation managers were instead bidding for the boys' favor with baseball leagues and theater parties.[13] In Chicago, on the other hand, circulation battles were real battles fought by adult hoodlums hired specifically for the occasion. When William Randolph Hearst moved into the Chicago market at the turn of the century, many newsstands and newsies, bowing to pressure from the already established papers, refused to carry his papers. Hearst and the Annenberg brothers, his circulation managers, armed their delivery men and hired adult thugs to force the dealers and newsies to carry the *American* and the *Examiner*. Full-scale war broke out when Hearst's rivals enlisted their own street armies to protect the vendors still loyal to them. The newsboys were caught in the middle—and remained there for years—while the war raged through the streets. Some took advantage of the situation to sign on as "sluggers" with one of the publishers. Others made their peace as best they could and continued to sell their papers on the street.[14]

Chicago was the only city where it took the publishers so long to discover that street battles were bad for business. Elsewhere, when violence was used, it was used selectively—to get newspapers onto the streets or temporarily scare away the competition. Circulation managers like the Annenbergs, with their arsenal of weapons, were the exception, not the rule. Their counterparts in most cities did not own guns or employ hoodlums. They were new-style managers who saw their mission as boosting circulation through efficiency and better management principles, not violence and intimidation.[15]

In most cities and towns, the relations between circulation managers and newsies were cool but stable. The boys did not expect theater tickets or armed thugs as inducements to help them do their job. An unwritten contract existed between the boys and the adults who sold them their papers. As long as the adults honored the contract—and did nothing to cut into the boys' profit margin or disturb their laws of the street—the newsies would cooperate with them. They would push each paper with equal fervor and keep on pushing until the edition was sold out.

The children's relationship with their adult suppliers and circulation managers was a business one. The street traders were given no special consideration because of age or size. The adults they did business with treated them only as fairly as they had to. It was the children's informal organization and the conditions of street trading that protected their interests, not adult benevolence.

The street traders who hustled newspapers were blessed by circumstances not of their own making. At this point in the history of the city and of the newspapers, the publishers depended on the children for 50 percent or more of their afternoon sales. The thousands upon thousands of city workers who bought their papers on the way home from work could only have been served by a part-time work force that began work in mid-afternoon. Within a mere twenty years, there would be adults and new distribution companies to get the afternoon dailies to their

St. Louis (1910?). A group of newsies, probably in front of the distribution office where they picked up their afternoon editions. (*Lewis Hine Collection, NCLC*)

customers. For the first two decades of the century, however, the newspapers had no choice but to rely on the children.

City kids who hustled papers inhabited a work world in which the pressure of self-interest was often sufficient to protect each side of the labor contract. The newspapers needed the children as much as the children needed the newspapers. The children's situation was almost unique. Their first encounter with the workplace was as workers without bosses. As independent contractors they did not have to accept management control of the workplace or work routines. They were free to set their own schedules, establish their own pace, and work when and where they chose. They, in fact, experienced more autonomy at work than in school or at home. In school, they were watched over, tested, and disciplined by teachers. At home, they were subject to the authority of parents, adult relatives, and older siblings. On the street, there were no parents, teachers, bosses, managers, or foremen to tell them what to do or how to do it. The harder and longer they hustled, the more papers they sold. The more time they took for themselves, the less they would have to bring home and to spend. In either case, the choice was theirs. When business was slow because of bad weather or dull headlines, they had no one to blame—not themselves and certainly not the publishers or suppliers. It was bad luck and bad luck alone that came between them and their profits. And today's bad luck, they knew, could easily turn better tomorrow.

Regrettably, this situation could not—and did not—last forever. The littlest hustlers would grow up and leave the streets behind. They would, however, carry with them the memory of the work world they had encountered as children and the notion that work in America need not be exploitative or unpleasant.

The newsies came from every ethnic group, in numbers roughly proportional to the adult working-class population. In New York City, three quarters of the boys were Russian-Jewish or Italian. In Chicago, over two thirds were "American," "Negro," German, or Irish. In Baltimore, more than 40 percent were "American whites." In Cincinnati, 29 percent were "American, colored." In Dallas, 80 percent were "American" or northern European.[16]

What defined the newsie population was not ethnicity as much as class. A July 1917 study of eight hundred and six New York City newsies found that, with the exception of four contractors and builders, five grocers, twenty-three clerks, seven salesmen, and a handful of other white-collar workers, the vast majority of the newsboys' fathers worked as laborers, tailors, drivers, peddlers, porters, pressers, longshoremen, bootblacks, skilled craftsmen, and factory hands. A 1910 St. Louis study similarly found that only 9.6 percent of newsboys' fathers were "independent business men" and 3.1 percent "public officials"; all the rest were skilled or unskilled workers.[17]

The newsies were no exotic breed of city child. The historical record suggests that selling papers on the streets was a common children's occupation. Hundreds of thousands of boys who grew up in American cities in the first decades of this century sold papers, if not regularly, then when they or their families were most in need of cash. The number of special investigative reports on "newsboy conditions" prepared by child labor reformers testifies to the widespread nature of the practice (see Appendix), as do the many biographies and autobiographies of boys who came of age in the early twentieth-century city. Louis Armstrong,

Cincinnati, 1908. (*Lewis Hine Collection, NCLC*)

Irving Berlin, Joe E. Brown, George Burns, Ralph Bunche, Eddie Cantor, Frank Capra, Morris Raphael Cohen, Leonard Covello, Jack Dempsey, William O. Douglas, Harry Golden, Joseph Hirschhorn, the Jolson brothers, Mervyn LeRoy, Jerre Mangione, the Marx brothers, David Sarnoff, Spyros Skouras, the Warner brothers, Earl Warren, and Bertram Wolfe, to mention a few, sold papers as boys.

Unfortunately for the historian, no accurate quantitative data are available on the number of children who hawked papers on the streets. The census figures are virtually useless, as the Bureau itself admitted in its 1924 report on *Children in Gainful Occupations:* "The characteristics of the occupations of newsboys are such that accurate enumeration of the workers is extremely difficult."[18]

The parents and children who were the only potentially reliable sources of information on the subject could not be counted on to tell the truth—and for good reasons. By 1915, some seventeen states, the District of Columbia, and several cities had passed laws restricting children from trading on the streets.[19] The children, more often than not, simply ignored the laws. When asked if they worked on the streets, many simply answered in the negative rather than provide some investigator with incriminating information. Their parents were as circumspect in their conversation with census takers and child labor investigators.

The best information we have on the percentage of city boys who sold papers comes from the local studies which used school teachers or licensing bureaus as informants. A 1911 Chicago study reported that 65 percent of fifth-graders (eleven-to-twelve-year-olds) and 35 percent of fourth-graders in a particular school were street traders. Unfortunately for our purposes, the study is suspect. It was undertaken to dramatize the plight of the child laborer for the Chicago Child Welfare Exhibit which probably chose for its survey the one school in Chicago with the greatest number of working children.[20]

A 1909 Cincinnati study is a bit more reliable. It found that the two thousand boys, aged ten to thirteen, licensed to sell papers in the city constituted 15 percent of their age group.[21] Had the study included newsboys who sold without licenses, the 15 percent figure would have climbed somewhat. A second Cincinnati study (1917) attempted to correct for this factor by including the unlicensed newsies but compromised its usefulness by computing the percentage of newsboys in the ten-to-sixteen age group.[22] Since most were over eleven and under fifteen, the conclusion that 12 percent of ten- to sixteen-year-olds sold papers is less meaningful than might appear.

Anna Reed's 1916 Seattle study did not include figures on the percentage of youth who sold papers. Extrapolating from her data, however, we find that 12 percent of sixth-graders, 11 percent of seventh-graders, and 14 percent of eighth-graders regularly sold on the streets. Here, too, the figures probably under-represent the percentage of boys selling, since they exclude those who worked occasionally or were not working the day of the survey and those who, for their own reasons, preferred not to answer in the affirmative when asked if they sold papers after school.[23]

Of the dozens of newsboy studies, these were the only ones that attempted to figure out the percentage of city boys who sold papers. The others were more concerned with collecting data to reinforce their contention that street trading led directly to juvenile delinquency. To provide themselves with evidence establishing the connection, child labor reformers scoured the juvenile courts, jails, asylums, houses of refuge, and reformatories for ex-newsies. They found what they were looking for. A 1911 memo from the secretary of the New York Child Labor Committee summarized the findings that would be used again and again to prove the connection between street work and juvenile crime:

"New York Juvenile Asylum (1911), 31% were newsboys.

Rochester, N.Y., Industrial School (1903), 75% were newsboys. (Buffalo boys only counted.)

Hart's Island, N.Y.C. (1906), 63% were newsboys.

Catholic Protectory, N.Y.C. (1911), 50% were newsboys.

House of Refuge, at Randall's Island, N.Y.C. (1911), 32% were newsboys.

Glen Mills, Pennsylvania (1910), 77% were newsboys. (Philadelphia boys only counted.)"[24]

The data were impressive, but they proved nothing. What the reformers either did not understand or conveniently ignored was that most city boys, delinquent or not, sold papers on the street. As Justice Harvey Baker of the Boston Juvenile Court reported to a New York Child Labor Committee investigator, it was "very difficult to determine what part, if any, the selling of papers plays in the delinquency of the boys who come before this court. Since most of the Jewish boys . . . sell papers, if we are to have any delinquent Jewish boys at all, we are bound to get a large number of newspaper sellers among them."[25] The judge's remarks could have been generalized to other city boys. Since most had, at one time or another, sold papers, most of those in trouble would have had a history of paper-selling.

The children who hawked their papers on the street enjoyed their work. The excitement, the noise, the ever-changing aspects of street life provided a needed antidote to a day spent in a crowded, stuffy classroom. Watching children from his post as superintendent of the United Jewish Charities of Cincinnati and chief investigator of a study of newsboys in that city, Maurice Hexter found few children who preferred their hours in the classroom to those spent working on the street. "The school represents a task: street work is an enjoyment."[26]

The street was the ideal workplace: it was outdoors, alive with activity, and away from the prying eyes of teachers and parents. When, in 1918, a University of Chicago graduate student asked 378 newsies if they enjoyed their work, 87 percent responded that they did. Other investigators, employing less scientific methodologies, came to the same conclusion.[27]

The children who worked after school were serious about earning money, but they were not ready to leave their childhood behind. Though they now had responsibilities—to their families and to themselves—these responsibilities did not prevent them from having fun whenever and wherever they could. "Children" could play all afternoon. "Adults" had to work all day. But eleven- to fifteen-year-olds, suspended somewhere in between, needed to squeeze their work and their play into the hours they had to themselves between the end of school and the moment they had to be home for dinner.

The gap between dismissal time at school—three o'clock—and working people's quitting time—after five, generally—was to the street traders' advantage. It gave them time to play before their customers hit the streets for the trip home. Unfortunately their play time, circumscribed as it was by work schedules, was too abbreviated to allow them to travel far from the streets where they would begin work later in the afternoon. Their "playgrounds" would necessarily have to be located near their workplaces.

The children who worked together came together to play before and after the rush hours. With an intensity that startled the investigators sent

Denver, 1910–20. "Newsboys Alley—Waiting for the paper to issue." A photograph of the "alley" where the newsies congregated in the afternoons to await delivery of their papers. The smallest of the children were probably just hanging around to play with the bigger ones. The two men (right and center) were probably assistant circulation managers. (*Mrs. Ben Lindsey Collection, LC*)

to observe their habits, they converted the public space they shared with adults into their "playgrounds" and proceeded to "kick the can," match pennies, and play ball—oblivious to the adults who got in their way. In midtown Manhattan, groups of newsies played in the Times Square subway station that served as the distribution point of the afternoon papers they would soon have to sell. When they were bored with "rough-housing" underground, they "went upstairs to the Square, secured a couple of tin cans, and, in the midst of the heavy traffic of Broadway between 42nd and 43rd Street, engaged themselves in a mad and aimless competition in kicking the can." An investigator from the New York Child Labor Committee looked on in amazement as the boys dashed after the can in and out of traffic, dodging automobiles and streetcars. "More than once did it seem that one or the other of them would be run over, and many a [street]car and automobile stopped in its own tracks in the middle of the block to avoid running over them. There were frequent collisions with people on the sidewalk, men and women, who might just as well not have been there for all the attention the boys paid them."

The game continued until the boys' attention was distracted by a wind-blown hat. Almost magically, they sensed its presence, halted their game, and turned "as one to pursue" it, knowing that whoever caught it was in line for a nice tip from the owner. The hat retrieved and returned, and the tip pocketed, the boys went back to the game, which continued for a time, interrupted only momentarily by the argument that broke out when the can hit Bull Head Gus in his bull head.[28]

In Birmingham, Alabama, according to a local observer, the newsies "congregate[d]" in front of the newspaper office downtown, where they spent the "hour or so before the papers came off the press . . . matching pennies, rolling dice, fighting, using foul and profane language and creating bedlam in general."[29]

In Chicago, where most of the action was concentrated at the Loop, the boys who sold newspapers picked them up in the alleys behind the publishers' offices. The newspapers did their best to provide the children with all the entertainment they needed—right there in the alleys. The closer the boys were kept to the presses, the sooner they could be sprung on the city with the latest editions. The *American* offered the newsies free lunches. The *Daily News* invited vendors to set up stands inside the alley. "Almost at the entrance is a small booth where 'red-hots' and ice cream are sold for a penny a-piece, and 'pop' for two cents a bottle. Just beyond this is a restaurant where cheap lunches are on sale. On one side of the alley is a man sitting under an umbrella selling ice cream from a freezer. Upstairs . . . is a penny lunch stand. . . . Just at the west entrance of the alley is a store where dime novels, dice, cards, cigarette papers and tobacco are kept on sale and prominently displayed in the window." If the reformers who visited the alleys are to be believed (and in this they probably are), the boys spent their afternoons shooting craps, pitching pennies, trading dirty stories among themselves and with the older vagrants who took shelter there, and stuffing themselves with "trash."[30] The newsies had no time to waste. They had to squeeze a full day's play into the brief interval that separated the end of school from the start of the rush hour.

The street traders lived a dual existence on the downtown streets of the city. The street was their background, but it was their workplace as well. Though outsiders might have been confused by the sudden switch from child at play to little merchant at work, the children themselves knew precisely what they were doing. They played as long as they could and then, as the rush hour began in earnest, put away their dice, their red-hots, their baseballs, and their gossip to go to work. Like Superman emerging from the phone booth, industrious little hustlers appeared where carefree children had stood moments before. Alexander Fleisher, visiting a newspaper distribution center in Milwaukee, was amazed at the transformation worked by the arrival of the papers. "When the edition comes from the press, the boys line up before the grating and receive their papers and rush out. . . . The place takes on a business-like air and everything goes with snap and order."[31]

The children worked such miracles without the prompting of adults. The afternoon was too short to waste. Once their papers were ready and their customers about to hit the streets, they set to work. Schedule and pace were determined by the rhythm of the rush hour. As it began to build, they eased their way into their trading. By the time it had reached its peak, they were all business. Arms and legs in perpetual motion, they chased customers up and down the block, shouting their wares at the top of their lungs.

The children stationed themselves along the streets with the heaviest pedestrian traffic. Their own neighborhoods were crowded with people but not always the right kind. The newsies needed customers with change in their pockets. They did not have to travel far to find them. Streetcars and trolleys cost a nickel each way, a considerable sum for part-time child workers. Fortunately the residential areas where most of their families lived were not far from the downtown shopping, business, and entertainment districts. In New York City, the Lower East Side children traveled to the City Hall area or to the East River bridges to sell their wares; the Upper East Side and West Side children walked into midtown to do their peddling and newspaper hawking.

The children set up shop outside the department store exits, in front

74

of the subway stations and elevated stops, and at the entrances to the bridges, ferry terminals, and train stations, wherever they could be sure of meeting up with homebound workers. In Mount Vernon, the boys crowded "about the [trolley] cars that deposit passengers at the corner of Fourth Avenue and First street. . . . Every passenger who alights is immediately besieged, and the boys tumble over each other in order to make the first sale. . . . A similar situation may be witnessed at the New Haven Railroad Station at the time the evening trains come in."[32] In Newark, the boys gathered at the Delaware, Lackawanna, and Western depot and the Pennsylvania Railroad station. The Hoboken and Jersey City boys sold their wares outside the entrance to the "tubes" and the ferry station.[33]

In the smaller cities, where the business, entertainment, and shopping streets were concentrated in a circumscribed area, boys hawked their papers along the main business streets. In Yonkers, they gathered along Main Street and in Getty Square.[34] In Rutland, Vermont, a "busy town of 15,000 persons" visited by Lewis Hine for the National Child Labor Committee, the entire population of fifteen newsies worked the "principal streets from 4:30 to 6:30 every afternoon."[35]

Hawking papers was fun, but it was also work that required physical exertion and no small amount of careful planning. Children who expected to earn decent money on the streets had to apply themselves to mastering the economics of their trade.

Newsies needed a "stake" to get started. Some borrowed money from their mothers, many got it from friends. Their "stake" bought them their first batch of papers. From that point on, they would hold back enough from each day's sales to buy tomorrow's papers from the circulation manager.

The newsies had to decide for themselves how many papers to purchase each afternoon and on Sundays. That was no easy task. Newspapers, unlike Spearmint gum, Hershey's chocolate with almonds, pencils, and handkerchiefs, went bad if not sold immediately. Every paper purchased from the circulation manager had to be unloaded before the next edition came out.

If the children bought too many papers, they would have to swallow the loss on the unsold copies or stay out all night to sell them—and that became progressively more difficult as it got later and the street traffic thinned. If, on the other hand, they bought too few, they stood in danger of losing customers. Adults were creatures of habit and creatures in a hurry. They would buy from the same boy at the same spot as long as

Philadelphia, 1910. (*Lewis Hine Collection, NCLC*)

he guaranteed them the latest edition. If he ran short once, they would cross the street to another newsie—and probably continue to do so until he too ran short.[36]

The children could expect no help from the circulation managers they worked with. The newspapermen were entirely untrustworthy. They cared only about boosting circulation and to do so would regularly pressure the boys to buy more papers than they could sell.[37] The newsies had to figure out what their probable sales would be—and buy just that amount of papers. To arrive at an accurate figure, they had to sift and sort a number of diverse factors: the time of day the papers were ready for distribution, the weather, the day of the week, the season of the year, the number of papers sold the day before, the number and importance of the sports scores, and, most crucially, the size and content of the headlines.

Afternoon circulations were never as constant as morning ones, which were more likely to be sold by subscription. While many readers considered the morning paper a necessity, few thought the same of the afternoon editions. Customers might forego the late papers altogether or, on big news days, buy several editions of several different papers. It was the headlines that made the difference.

The children lived for the great headlines, the red-faced, bold-type banner catastrophes that sold out editions. Murder, mayhem, riot, war, natural disaster: this was the stuff their dreams were made of. A half century after he had left the streets of Toledo, Ohio, Joe E. Brown, the comedian, still remembered vividly that "the biggest week I had in the newspaper business was the week following President McKinley's assassination. He lived for a week after he was shot at the Exposition in Buffalo and throughout that week interest in the news was at fever pitch." Brown sold more Toledo *Bees* and *Blades* than he had ever dreamed possible.[38]

Banner headlines, no matter how dramatic, did not sell themselves. It was the boys' job to create the excitement that brought customers running. The children had no time for digesting the significance of the headlines, feeling sorrow at the tragedies, or mourning the dead. They devoted all their energy and ingenuity to communicating to the public in a language it could understand.

Harry Golden, the writer, sold papers on the Lower East Side and was on the streets the day Leo Frank was lynched for the murder of fourteen-year-old Mary Phagan. His first thought when he saw the headline of Frank's death in red ink was that "the word 'lynched' would have little meaning for Jewish immigrants." He translated it to "murder" and ran through the streets shouting the news.[39]

When the *Titanic* sank, when the Triangle Shirtwaist Factory burst out in flames, or during the Spanish-American War, the Mexican War scare, and World War I, the newsies did their best to excite and incite the public into buying their papers. The children of the city were adept at converting disaster into profit. They played the newspapers' game as well as the city editors and reporters did. Their news as they presented it was always current, always exciting, always provocative. They took what the headline writers gave them and added the appropriate emphasis and detail. When the news was dull, they cheated a bit. George Burns jokingly recalls making up catastrophes on slow news days. "Sometimes I'd have eight or nine papers left over, and to get rid of them I'd run through the streets hollering things like 'Extra! Extra! Ferry Boat sinks in East River!!' or 'Big Gun Battle in Sharkey's Restaurant!!' One day when I was stuck with eleven papers I took off down the street yelling, 'Extra! Extra! Huber's Museum Goes Down in Flames!!!' Well, I was selling newspapers like hotcakes, when all of a sudden I felt a hand on my shoulder. It turned out to be a disgruntled customer. He held the paper in front of my face and said, 'What are you pulling, kid? There's nothing in this newspaper about a fire at Huber's Museum!'

"For a split second I didn't know what to say. Then I blurted out, 'I know, that's such an early edition the fire hasn't started yet!' and ran."[40]

Burns was not the only newsie who embellished the news to sell more papers. During the Great War there was a virtual epidemic of false headlines. In Cleveland, according to a story in *Editor and Publisher*, city officials were so disturbed by the boys' blatant distortion of the news that they threatened to prosecute those who shouted "false and amazing statements. . . . In extreme cases . . . offenders may be prosecuted under the Espionage Act." In New York City, where it was claimed the boys hollered louder than anywhere else in the world, the problem was even greater. In October 1917, a New York *Times* article, headed "Police Move to Stop Noise of Newsboys: Public Annoyed by Shouting of War Calamities for Which There is No Basis," reported that the police department had received scores of complaints about newsboys making up the news. "Knowing the people to be keenly interested in European events, the newsboys, to stimulate sales, often take advantage of popular concern by converting occurrences of no significance in Paris, London or Petrograd into stupendous disasters. This practice has unnerved men and women who have relatives in the service and to whom the war is of vital and personal concern. Not only in the city but in the suburbs newsboys have aroused neighborhoods late at night with their fictitious sensations." Police Commissioner Woods promised to do his best "to stop this nuisance" but made it clear that there were no specific laws forbidding the practice. Only when the citizens took the time to swear out complaints against the newsboys would the problem be solved.[41]

In Philadelphia, the police and courts, undeterred by lack of legislation, started their own campaign to rid the streets of the newsboy menace. For "agitating and frightening mothers and others who have relatives in the war, several Philadelphia newsboys [were] fined, or given the alternative of spending a term in jail."[42]

In those helter-skelter days of journalism between the Spanish-American War and World War I, the newsies shouting the headlines were as much a part of the urban street scene as the lampposts on every corner. Informing the world of the latest calamities, they broadcast the news with an immediacy and enthusiasm no other medium could approach. Not all city residents, however, appreciated the service. The boys, to be sure, made a lot of noise. They also shouted their headlines in immigrant and working-class accents that grated on the ears of those

78

in the high-priced neighborhoods and hotel districts who preferred to spend their evenings in total isolation from the raucous elements of urban life. As one disturbed resident of New York City wrote to the New York *Times* in the summer of 1912, the boys had become "an unmitigated nuisance in the neighborhoods they invade" and a serious health hazard to those "who are sick or nervous. . . . Doctors will testify that the chances of recovery for their patients are sometimes seriously impaired by the raucous shouts portentous of calamity."[43]

Had the boys been more quiet, refined, and middle-class in their manners and accent, they might have offended fewer people. An Atlanta judge, recognizing the class bias inherent in the city ordinance forbidding the boys to hawk their papers after eight in the evening, threw it out of court, claiming that the boys had every right to "cry their papers on the streets so long as they do not block traffic or disturb the sick. . . . The sidewalks are for the newsboys as well as the millionaires."[44] In New York City, Mayor Gaynor firmly but politely rebuffed a series of New York *Times* letter writers who complained about the "young foreigners" and their "offensive" pronunciation and voices. "They do not disturb me any," declared the Mayor. The newsies of El Paso and Seattle were not as lucky. In these cities, ordinances were passed forbidding the boys to shout after hours or within certain areas of the city.[45]

The newsies made a lot of noise because it was fun, part of their public service as unofficial town criers, and the only way they knew to advertise their wares. When the news was a bit stale, tame, or just plain dull, it was the newsie who sold the paper by creating the excitement the headline lacked. Regrettably there were days, weeks, even months when the news was so slow and the headlines so tame that not even the most imaginative and energetic hustlers could sell out the edition. The worst times were those following extended periods of crisis. In his poem "Post-Bellum," Dean Collins, a Portland (Oregon) newsie, described the boys' plight in the days following the close of World War I:

> A newsboy with his papers sat sighing on the street,
> For the cruel war was over and the foe had met defeat.
> And the scare-heads in the dailies, they had vanished
>   like a spell,
> And the liveliest thing the newsie had was market heads
>   to yell.
> "O, maybe Sherman had it right," said he, "but wars must
>   cease—
> And Sherman never tried to peddle papers when 'twas peace."
>
> "They used to saw an extra off each half hour by the clock.

And we used to wake the echoes when we whooped 'em
    down the block.
War may be just what Sherman said it was, but just the same,
If Sherman were a newsie, O, I wonder what he'd think
Of peddling papers after peace had put things on the blink?"

"How can I jar the people loose to buy the sheet and read,
If I start yelling 'bout the rise in price of clover seed?
When they are used to war and smoke and sulphur burning
    blue,
Will they warm up to read about the W.C.T.U.?
O, Maybe Sherman had it right on war—but wars must cease—
And Sherman never tried to peddle papers after peace."[46]

What is most remarkable about the poem is its candor. The poem
was printed in a newspaper put out by the boys to raise money for their
club, clubhouse, and organized activities. They used the publication to
emphasize their patriotism and their promise as future citizens. And yet,
no one at the paper, neither the poet nor his editors or publishers, saw
fit to exclude or at least tone down the sentiments expressed. While the
rest of the nation celebrated the cessation of hostilities, the newsboys
published a poem mourning the Great War's untimely conclusion.

The newsies had been so corrupted by their business that they no
longer knew when to keep quiet. They had learned to worship the bottom
line. What mattered was the number of papers sold. If war, catastrophe,
and tragedy sold the most, then they would gladly parade them through
the streets. Modesty, humility, honesty—it was clear—won no prizes
and sold no papers. The boys who shouted the loudest and twisted the
headlines most creatively earned the most. All was fair on the streets.
What counted was that you got the change, not how you got it.

The children, as we shall see, could be quite scrupulous in their
dealings with one another. Their customers were another story.

The newsies had two sources of income: sales and tips. To sell their
papers, they advertised their headlines, stretching the truth to make the
news more exciting. To secure their tips, they employed all the tricks
they knew. Tips didn't just happen. They had to be coaxed out of the
customers' pockets.

Since most afternoon papers cost a penny, customers with a nickel
had to either wait for their four pennies in change or leave a 400 percent
tip. The more frantic the customers, the more time the newsies took
fishing the change out of their pockets. Early in the afternoon, they
might claim to be out of change and suggest that if the customer just
waited a moment, they would scurry round the corner to get it from the

candy store. In such cases, the boys stood a good chance—as they knew—of being told to keep the change. Alexander Fleisher, who kept track of such things, estimated that in up to 33 percent of street sales, newsies without change or slow to make it ended up with "a larger coin than the sale call[ed] for."[47]

Next to dashing commuters, drunks were the softest touch for newsies on the prowl. The reformers feared that the boys hung out at saloons because they wanted free drinks. The truth was different. The boys knew that the drunker the customer, the easier it was to shortchange or coax a tip out of him. Harry Bremer, in his unpublished study of New York City newsies, recorded the following conversations with a twelve-year-old who claimed to specialize in squeezing tips from drunks outside saloons.

" 'A man'll give yer a quarter, and yer'll say yer ain't got change and he'll tell yer to go get some and yer'll go and won't come back.'

" 'And leave him standing on the curb?'

" 'Sure! He'll wait for yer. Last Saturday a man gave me $5, and I didn't have change—so he told me to get some. I tried one store and

Syracuse, New York, February 1910. "Group of Italian newsies on South Avenue, selling in saloons and stores. Had just come out of saloon in front of which they are standing. Behind them are two typical saloon-patrons who insist on being in the picture. 10 P.M. Cold. Snowing." (*Lewis Hine Collection, NCLC*)

they didn't have it—and I went to another and they didn't have it—and I went back and saw the man standing on the corner and I went around the other way!'

" 'What did you do with it?'

" 'Gave it to my mother.'

" 'All of it?'

" 'No, I kept half for myself and spent it.' "[48]

Prostitutes were also big tippers. Harry Golden, who "hawked papers from the corner of Delancey and Norfolk," made regular trips to Allen Street, the Lower East Side's red-light district, where he earned his tips by running "occasional errands for the whores who lived there. They always gave me an extra nickel for delivering the paper and another nickel for running to the grocery store or the soft-drink stand." In Chicago, investigators for the Vice Commission were startled and upset by similar business arrangements between prostitutes and the children who ran their errands and delivered their newspapers.[49]

Some children stole their tips, some chased them, others performed for them, preying on the sympathy of the "Americans" who felt sorry for the poor children peddling their papers. The evenings, especially Saturday nights during the cold weather months, were the best times to perform for tips. The children dressed for the occasion and chose their locations with care. In Syracuse, Mrs. W. J. Norton, a member of the city's Social Service Club, found a "small boy of eleven" standing outside a saloon for three quarters of an hour "weeping in a most realistic fashion as a possible customer approached. Again and again he had spasms of weeping at the opportune time. His paper bag was soon empty." Florence Kelley, at the time Secretary of the National Consumers' League, reported having seen in New York City "a little boy, a very ill-fed, wretched, shabby little boy, offering papers for sale at a quarter to twelve o'clock, midnight, at the door of the women's hotel, the Martha Washington Hotel. He seemed to be speculating on the pity of women who might be coming home late from theater or opera to that hotel."[50]

The Saturday night newsies were a mixed group. Some were regulars who sold every night of the week, others hustled the Sunday papers only. The Sunday papers, a recent publishing innovation, had become a necessary source of information and entertainment for city and suburban residents.[51] The first editions arrived on the streets late Saturday night, in time to reach the downtown crowds on their way home from the movie palaces, music halls, and restaurants.

The boys followed the crowds through the streets from the entertainment districts to the after-hours clubs and eating places and then to their train stations and ferry terminals. Saturday night was a good time for sales and tips. The streets were crowded with people who, after an evening of fun, had more trouble than usual resisting the importunings of the young merchants. Myers Diamond, who hustled Hershey's chocolate bars with almonds in front of the Lyric Theater on Market Street in Newark, sold four times more bars on Saturday nights than on weeknights. According to Scott Nearing, the Philadelphia newsies made as much on Saturday nights and Sunday mornings as "during the remainder of the week."[52]

The newsies who sold the Sunday papers stayed up with the downtown crowds, then got up again on Sunday mornings to sell their papers to the rest of the city. Some remained downtown all night, sleeping between editions in the newspaper offices or nearby. Their work schedules were determined by the newspapers' publishing schedule. In Baltimore, the boys began the evening hawking the Philadelphia papers, which arrived about 10:00 P.M. At 1:30 A.M. they moved on to the local Baltimore editions. In Chicago, at the Loop, the boys sold from midnight, when the first edition appeared, until the early morning hours. In New York City, they could be found in the Times Square area, papers in hand, from early in the evening to well after midnight. Jersey City newsies sold from 12:30 to 2:30 A.M., then slept a few hours "under the car shed at the ferry" or in the ferry house so they'd be up and ready for their Sunday morning customers. Business was so good in Jersey City and Elizabeth that the boys took the ferry into New York City to get the papers on Saturday night rather than wait for the regular delivery later in the morning.[53]

The newsies on the town on a Saturday night tried their best to behave as the "Americans" believed they should: with charm and servility. The newsie who tipped his cap, opened restaurant and car doors, and exhibited his respect for his betters had a good chance at a sizable tip.

According to child labor reformers, tips were so plentiful that many boys carried papers only as a front. Their real money was made begging tips. In this age of conspicuous consumers, the most conspicuous of all were the big spenders who lavished tips on doormen, waiters, cabbies, and newsies. The children went out of their way to encourage the practice. Scott Nearing, at the time Secretary of the Pennsylvania Child Labor Committee, was particularly bothered by the boys' shameless behavior in embarrassing tips out of customers who could not afford them. "A bashful young man, taking his best girl to the theater for the first time, is particularly 'easy,' and the newsboys 'spot' him at once and are sure that if they do not sell a paper, they will at least get a nickel for their pains."[54]

Though most newsies could not have resisted teasing a tip out of a "bashful young man," they were on the lookout for bigger game. Harry Bremer, who made several outings to Times Square in his capacity as special investigator for the National Child Labor Committee, described in his own dispassionate prose the Saturday evening he spent "following two boys, one not more than eleven years old, and the other about thirteen," as they canvassed the area in search of fine-looking ladies and gentlemen with change in their pockets. Bremer trailed after the boys "from the Criterion Theatre on 44th Street, through this street to the Hudson and Belasco theatres, then on to the Hippodrome, back across 42nd Street to Broadway and down to the Knickerbocker Theatre at 38th Street. By this time it was about 11:45 and the crowd had thinned, so the boys started west across 39th Street for home. At each theatre and in the crowd on 42nd Street they thrust lighted matches at cigar ends and waited for tips, and in some cases went right up to people and asked for money. One case of this kind is worthy of note. At the Hudson a middle aged gentleman was standing with two ladies. There was nothing about him to suggest any service to be rendered yet the little fellow stepped up to him, and in a few seconds I saw the man hand the boys some change, pennies and a white coin that might have been a nickel or a dime."[55]

As the evening wore on, the children grew bolder. Taking advantage of the late hour and adult compassion for children who should have been home in bed, the newsies practiced what the reformers called the "last paper ploy." Feigning exhaustion, cold, hunger, or all three, the children begged passers-by to buy their last papers so they could go home. As Edward Clopper, reformer and author, observed, "A kind-hearted person readily falls a victim to this ruse, and as soon as he has passed by, the newsboy draws another copy from his hidden supply and repeats his importuning."[56]

In Chicago, Elsa Wertheim, special officer of the Juvenile Protective Association, found a pair of brothers working this hustle. "Johnnie [seven years old] accosted the passer-by with his 'last paper,' while Harry [thirteen] concealed himself in a doorway with all the rest of their stock, and pocketed the money as soon as the customer's back was turned." On his Saturday night tour of Times Square, Harry Bremer saw the trick worked to perfection. "In front of the Republic Theatre on West 42nd Street, I saw three boys between the ages of eleven and thirteen. One had two papers, another had one, and the third had none. I bought the paper from the boy who had only one and in answer to my question he said he would now go home. . . . A half hour later, at 11:15 P.M. I returned to this spot and mixed with the crowd leaving the theatre. As I had anticipated the three boys were on the job dodging in and out of

Hartford, March 1909. "A common case of teamwork. Joseph, the smaller boy goes into the saloon and sells his 'last paper.' When he comes out his brother gives him more. Joseph said, 'Drunks are my best customers. I sell more'n me brudder does. Day buy me out so I kin go home.' He sells every afternoon and night, and extra late on Saturday. At 6 A.M. Sunday he is at it again." (*Lewis Hine Collection, NCLC*)

the crowd looking for opportunities to do something that would procure tips. The boy from whom I had bought the last paper, and who said he would go home, had procured another 'last' paper."[57]

The newsies were shameless when it came to soliciting sales and tips. Far from home and family, farther yet from school and teachers, they accepted the ethics of the street huckster as their own. If a bit of chicanery, an ounce of deception, a little playacting brought more sales, so be it. "Let the Buyer Beware." They, the sellers, were doing nothing illegal. They were merely performing for their public, extending and enlarging the truth like the headlines they shouted through the streets, cultivating an image like the ads in the papers they hawked. Why not, if it would add to their earnings, accentuate their poverty? Why not parade the fact that they were cold and poorly clad and in need of the change their customers carried in their pockets? Why not put on a show?

Such business practices, though not illegal, were roundly condemned by the reformers, who urged the public not to leave tips or buy "last papers." Adults who rewarded child duplicity, they suggested, were being taken for fools and, along the way, contributing to the delinquency of minors.[58]

It is easy to ridicule the reformers for their fears. Twelve-year-old newsies who pulled the "last paper ploy" were not in training for careers as pickpockets and hoodlums. They were, however, as the reformers understood, being swiftly corrupted by their success. The children were learning that there was no such thing as morality in the marketplace. Whatever sold goods and elicited tips was fine with them. They had absorbed the very worst lessons the business world had to offer: how to cheat, lie, and swindle customers. Eleven- to fifteen-year-olds who should have been getting their moral instruction from school, church, and, if they were fortunate, home, were growing up on the streets with the morals and values of sideshow barkers and snake oil salesmen.

The reformers broadcast their fears—and their warnings—in public meetings, pamphlets, and scores of press releases reprinted in the daily papers. Adults who should have known better ignored their pleas. They were not fooled by the child "hams" who wept for their tips. Most of them probably had a good idea what was going on, but continued, nonetheless, to buy papers and leave tips.

The more prosperous Americans, on their way home from business or pleasure, saw what they wanted to see in the city left behind. The children of the street were not, to their eyes, the exploited, deprived children the reformers had described, but a band of little merchants selling their wares. Some were dirty, some ragged; some scowled, some whimpered; but they were all on the streets for a noble cause: to make money for their families—and themselves. Here were scores of children who had adopted the American credo, who believed in hard work, hustle, and long hours, who were on their way up the ladder to success. With the help of kindly benefactors who bought their goods and left tips, these children would raise themselves from poverty to prosperity.

The children offered their customers an image of themselves that was but partially false. Their customers grabbed at it. They saw before them not simply a small army of children working hard for their pennies, but a flesh-and-blood enactment of the quintessential American morality play, a real-life Horatio Alger story on every street corner—Ragged Dick, Mark the Match Boy, Nelson the Newsboy, and Paul the Peddler, rough and ready, frank and fearless, struggling upward, bound to rise in a new world. [59]

The image was a reassuring one to those concerned with the picture of urban crime and destitution presented by spectacle-seeking newspapers and muckraking magazines. The turn-of-the-century city was a city divided by class and geography. Only the chroniclers of life "for the other half" and the street trading children bridged the two metropolitan worlds. The reformers and journalists painted lurid pictures of the working-class, immigrant city while the children reached out across the boundaries of class and ethnicity with their papers, shoeshine boxes, and candy bars.

While the reformers watched—with anger and alarm—the children and their customers cemented a symbiotic relationship. Each gave the other what was needed: the children got their tips, and their customers the reassurance that this remained the land of opportunity, if not for the poor and downtrodden, then at least for their hardworking children.

6

Junkers, Scavengers, and Petty Thieves

For eleven-year-old Francie Nolan, the heroine of *A Tree Grows in Brooklyn*, Betty Smith's autobiographical novel of working-class life before the first World War, "Saturday started with a trip to the junkie. She and her brother Neeley, like other Brooklyn kids, collected rags, paper, metal, rubber, and other junk and hoarded it in locked cellar bins or in boxes hidden under the bed." On Saturday mornings, they hauled it out and sold it to the junkman, after considerable haggling over quality, weight, and price.[1]

The working-class children of the early twentieth-century city were expert and experienced junkers, salvagers, ragpickers, and scavengers. Children too young to leave the block collected their junk in the streets, the backyards, the alleyways; older boys and girls ranged farther away, some on a regular basis, others when they were in special need of ready cash.

Boys and girls, five years old and fifteen years old, recognized at a glance the value of the junk adults had left behind. They scoured the back lots, dumps, railroad tracks, construction sites, and urban wastelands for discarded items to sell to the junkman or rehabilitate for use at home. Everything had its price: in Brooklyn, in 1912, according to Betty Smith, papers were worth "a penny for ten pounds. Rags brought two cents a pound and iron, four. Copper was good—ten cents a pound."[2]

For the children of the street, junking was as common a pastime as playing baseball or jumping rope. According to his biographer, Louis B. Mayer, the film producer, spent his young years "out on the street ragpicking and collecting scraps at all hours when not in school." Mayer gave his junk to his father, who was in the business.[3] Other children utilized the services of the junkmen, ragpickers, and pawnbrokers who could be found on every city block. No kid with junk to sell had any trouble selling it. Junking was a neighborhood business—and a big one. In 1916 alone, according to a U. S. Department of Commerce report, over five thousand tons of wastepaper (one quarter of the total consumed in a year) and $265 million worth of scrap metals were retrieved from junk, a good deal of it by children.[4] Massachusetts Child Labor Committee investigators found that more than 40 percent of the children in one Boston school district regularly scavenged wood to burn at home or sell to the junkman.[5] Had the investigators asked how many kids went junking—for iron or coal on the railroad tracks; for old clothing, furniture, and machine parts at the dump; for bones, rags, and bottles in the alleys;

Boston, probably from 1909. A group of boys hauling home their loot from an afternoon of scavenging. Though the wood in the cart probably came from the railroad tracks, construction sites, or other places the boys did not belong, none of the adults on the street appear to pay the scavengers any attention. This must have been a common scene on this particular Boston street. (*Lewis Hine Collection, LC*)

for faucets and lead pipe at vacant houses; for food at the produce markets; or just about anything in boxcars at the railroad yards—they would have found an even greater proportion of junkers among the children of the city.

There was plenty of valuable "stuff" lying around waiting for children to rescue and recycle it. (According to the Massachusetts Child Labor Committee, "stuff" was the "technical name of the material" the children gathered.) American cities were the waste capitals of the world, generating over 860 pounds per capita (an average taken from surveys of fourteen cities between 1888 and 1913), almost twice as much as was produced in English cities and almost three times more than in Germany. The waste came in several varieties: garbage—the name given the wet, organic materials; dry refuse, trash, litter, and rubbish; ashes from coal and wood stoves; street sweepings; and night soil, the contents of privies and chamber pots.

Year by year the mountains of garbage, ashes, and dry refuse grew. Between 1903 and 1907 alone, "Pittsburgh's garbage increased from 47,000 to 82,498 tons," Milwaukee's from thirty to forty thousand, Cincinnati's from twenty-two to thirty-one thousand tons. "As Luther E. Lovejoy, secretary of the Detroit Housing Commission, fatalistically concluded, 'The accumulation of garbage and rubbish is one of the penalties human society inevitably pays for the luxury of civilization.' "[6]

City governments, reform groups, and business/civic associations did their best to find solutions to the growing waste problem. They organized and reorganized health and sanitation departments; hired new street-cleaning squads, and, to boost their morale, dressed them in white from head to foot; lectured school children on sanitation and enlisted them in Juvenile Street Cleaning Leagues; held widely publicized clean-up-week campaigns; and purchased expensive machinery that did not always work: incinerators and reduction plants from Europe and automatic street sweepers like "The Sanitary Street Flushing Machine," which "flushes—not merely wets—but scrubs, washes, scours, cleans, rids the street of all health menacing unsanitary conditions."[7]

Many cities required residents to separate their wet garbage from ashes and dry refuse, though from that point on there was little agreement on what to do with it. The sanitary experts and engineers wanted to turn the "waste into wealth"or, at the very least, get rid of it as cheaply as possible. Indoor plumbing connected to sewers was beginning to carry away the "night soil," but something had to be done about the wet organic garbage, which decayed rapidly, attracted rats and flies, smelled bad, and looked worse. In some cities, the sanitation departments only collected the wet stuff, leaving householders and private scavengers to dispose of the ashes and refuse. A surprisingly large number of cities collected the organic garbage and fed it to hogs; others reduced it to grease; a few simply dumped it as far from downtown as possible.[8]

The dry refuse was less of a problem. It could be burned—or dumped. European cities, with less land for dumps, had to rely on incinerators. Americans, with more trash *and* more land, had an alternative. As the new century wore on and the cities piled up more and more trash, authorities found it simpler and cheaper to dump it than burn it. By 1909, 102 of the 180 "crematories" built in the 1880s and 1890s had been "abandoned or dismantled."[9]

The sanitarians' loss was the scavengers' gain. Had the incinerators proved more economical, there would have been less to scavenge. The junk would have been carted away and burned before the children had the opportunity to pick through it.

The children were also aided by the cities' efforts at waste separation. Because collecting and disposing of the wet organic garbage was the first concern, dry refuse was often left standing on the streets or in backyards for days. When collected, it was removed to nearby dumps where the scavengers could examine it and haul away what they wanted.

Every city had its dumps, and working-class kids knew precisely

Boston, October 1909. Two young scavengers at the dump, filling their sack with valuables. (*Lewis Hine Collection, LC*)

where they were—and what they held. Though the more affluent neighborhoods generated the most waste, it was the least affluent that got the dumps.[10] In Chicago, the bulk of the refuse was carried south and dumped "back of the Yards" on five acres of open fields that had once held rich clay deposits. As the clay was excavated for the nearby brickyards, the enterprising city alderman who owned the pits sold the city the right to fill in the holes with trash. It made little difference to politicians and city officials that thousands of Polish and Slavic families lived adjacent to the fields that were, from the middle 1890s, the chief recipient of the city's wastes. The trash had to be dumped somewhere; why not in this immigrant neighborhood already polluted by the odors of packinghouse and stockyard?[11] According to Upton Sinclair, the odor of the district was so powerful, railway passengers could smell it within an hour of their arrival in Chicago.[12]

The neighborhood children who went scavenging in the dumps "back of the Yards" arrived after school just in time to watch the carts from uptown unload their riches. The children waited outside the gates until the "picker," who had paid fifteen dollars for the privilege, sifted through the piles with his helpers. When the professionals were finished, the children and the neighborhood women who gathered with them were let into the dumps to dig with sticks or bare hands through the mounds looking for something to sell to the junkman: tin cans, milk bottles, wooden boxes, automobile or wagon tires, iron, rags, or something that, cleaned and repaired, might be used at home: old mattresses, worn garments, battered furniture, pots, pans, dishes. The scavengers did their work quickly and quietly, with hope eternal that just under the next mound they'd find the discarded silverware the "picker" had overlooked.[13]

Junking went on wherever there were kids in need of money and dumps with items worth cash to the junkman. Not all dumps were as noxious as the Chicago ones. A 1909 Lewis Hine photograph taken at a Boston dump shows a group of kids having a fine time near the shores of some polluted bay. In the background stands a boy with a pile of wood in his arms, in front of him are ten or twelve others sorting through the rubbish with their bare hands, to the right are two little girls neatly dressed in long, check and plaid dresses, with ribbons in their hair and baskets over their arms. At first glance, it is hard to tell if the children are playing or working. They were, in fact, doing both.[14]

The dumps (especially in cities like Boston, where the garbage was disposed of elsewhere or fed to hogs) were, in Hine's words, "a natural meeting ground" for neighborhood children. What better places to gather and play than wide open fields overlooking bodies of water? Since no adults frequented the dumps except the hoboes, who were seldom any

Boston, October 1909. A group of children playing and working at a Boston dump. Only the adult picker to the far left and the two little girls on the right are excluded from the game. (*Lewis Hine Collection, LC*)

trouble, the children could do as they pleased: run and chase, dig for buried treasure, build forts, "start a warming fire or throw rocks at old bottles without raising the ire of property owners or cops."[15]

While the reformers castigated public authorities—and rightly—for creating and then refusing to clean up their overflowing dumps, the children went right on playing and junking, oblivious to the real and potential health hazards. They were too intent on their work to bother about the danger or the smell or the warnings from the settlement-house workers. They also shunted aside whatever misgivings they might have had about the legality of their expeditions. Junking was, in most of its forms, a combination of trespass and petty theft. The children who forced their way into closed city dumps or railroad yards or vacant lots and construction sites were well aware that they didn't belong there. But they didn't seem to care. Laws that weren't enforced and made no sense could be disobeyed with impunity.

The children had evolved thier own working definitions of junk and private property. And as long as the authorities looked the other way, they could act as if these were the only legitimate ones. Material found unused on public or quasi-public space belonged to whoever had the foresight to collect and make use of it. "Use," not "title," conferred rights of ownership.

As Perry Duis observed in his brilliant dissertation on "The Saloons and the Public City," "Public space in the city . . . tended to depersonalize

93

private property."[16] Items that were found outside in the street or on the railroad tracks or yards did not "belong" to anyone. They were free for the picking.

Though the dumps were usually on city property and the railroad yards and tracks privately owned, the children made no distinction between the two sources of junk. From their perspective, material left behind in the dump or lying unused on tracks was ownerless until claimed. Open-bed railroad cars on poorly laid track threw off a steady supply of coal, wood, and iron. The children, with their wagons, their baskets, and their canvas sacks, collected it daily.

For children with adventure in their hearts and larceny on their minds, the tracks led into the railway yards, where boxcars filled with everything from whisky to wire spools sat unguarded. Theft from the boxcars was as easily rationalized as junking from the tracks. The stuff didn't yet belong to anybody. If it had, it would have been taken away and made use of. Besides, there was so much jammed into the cars, no one could possibly miss a wagonful.

Stan, the future "delinquent" whose story was told and dissected by Chicago sociologist Clifford Shaw, began his life of crime crawling into boxcars and handing out the merchandise to his stepbrother. "Stealing in the neighborhood," he informed Shaw, "was a common practice among the children and approved by the parents. . . . I hardly knew any boys who did not go robbing." Shaw, the expert on crime and juvenile delinquency, agreed with Stanley that acts of petty thievery, like breaking

Fall River, Massachusetts, June 27, 1916. "Pine Street Dump Scavengers" (*Lewis Hine Collection, LC*)

into boxcars, were not morally significant for the boys. "It may be assumed that Stanley's initial experience in delinquency was an aspect of the play activity of his gang and neighborhood. . . . From his point of view, it is probable that his early experiences in stealing had no more moral significance than the non-delinquent practices in which he engaged. . . . There are many areas in the city in which stealing from freight cars is a very prevalent practice."[17]

Though Chicago, with its multiple rail connections, presented junkers with more opportunities than were available elsewhere, children in every city with tracks and yards took advantage of them. Stealing from the railroads was a group activity. The whole neighborhood participated: boys and girls, big brothers and little sisters, all the kids from the block. The little ones squeezed through the pried-open boxcar doors, while the big ones kept watch and carried away the loot to the junkman. Parents did not often help the kids do the junking, but they knew what was going on and made use of whatever their children dragged home. When the police finally caught up with a group of Detroit kids who had, in a month's time, stolen "nine tons of coal, twenty-four baskets of oats, ten barrels of flour, six barrels of sugar, thirty cases of bottled beer, clothing, and more than a hundred dollars worth of perfumery and toilet articles," they found that the stolen goods had been stored in the children's homes, with the exception of the "perfumery and toilet requisites [which had been] used freely by the entire neighborhood."[18] The parents had to

---

Denver, 1910–20: "Where Tommy Costello" got the coal. One of the pictures donated to the Library of Congress by Mrs. Ben Lindsey, wife of the famous Juvenile Court judge, progressive reformer, and writer. This photograph, probably posed, shows three boys scavenging for coal along the tracks. The open-bed cars behind them, bumping along on poorly laid track, threw off enough coal to keep the boys busy all day long. (*Mrs. Ben Lindsey, LC*)

have known—and condoned—their children's action. How else could the kids have hidden so much loot?

In Cleveland, Henry Thurston found that the children who lived near the railroad tracks supplied their homes with coal and wood—with the active connivance of the railroad watchmen. A small group of boys arrested for stealing tobacco from a boxcar defended themselves by claiming "The door was open, no one seemed to be taking care of the tobacco, and we thought they left it for us, as they do the cratings."[19]

The children did not spend their time looking for reasons *not* to carry away loot that *appeared* to have been abandoned. They were too busy making use of the junk to worry over whether it was rightfully theirs to appropriate. Leonard Covello, who became a New York City high school principal and author, grew up in East Harlem "in a neighborhood of rubble and debris and abandoned buildings." The city planned to tear down some tenements and replace them with a park, but the delay between clearing the buildings of tenants and razing them was a long one. The neighborhood children didn't mind in the least. They systematically looted the area of every item they could sell or use. "We stole lead from the primitive plumbing to sell to the junkman. We stole bricks and chipped off the old mortar and sold them again."[20]

For poor kids in rich cities, junk was not an occasional temptation, but an elementary and necessary ingredient in their daily lives. In a better world, the children would not have had to settle for discarded materials. But in the one they inhabited, such items were a never-ending source of enrichment.

Junking provided poor kids with luxuries they could not otherwise have enjoyed. Junk could be turned into cash and then used to buy movie tickets, treats from the candy shop, or special items at the "five and ten." It could be remodeled into toys, games, and sporting goods: pushcarts, pull-wagons, bats, and footballs. It could be swiped from local shops, pushcarts, and open-air markets and consumed on the spot. The older boys built and furnished their dugouts, shanties, forts, and club-houses with junked materials. They built bonfires with scavenged wood and cooked sweet potatoes or fresh ears of corn swiped from peddlers and open markets. Leonard Covello and his gang stole sweet potatoes to "cook in our 'mickey cans' [in our] hide-out under the tenement rubble."[21] Hy Kraft "stole the first slice of watermelon [he] ever ate." It was hot as hell, the pushcart overflowed with juicy slices, and Kraft, too poor to purchase one, could not help himself. "For days I cased the fruit stand on East Broadway and watched every move made by the old man with the beard and funny cap on his head; he wasn't very agile, and he'd leave the stand unguarded every so often to go inside. I can remember rehearsing the raid and then the actual performance, walking in back of

96

an adult, suddenly stepping away, making my quick snatch, the spring around the corner, the dash to the safety of my own block, then hiding in a doorway, making certain that I wasn't followed and enjoying every dripping bit."[22]

Working-class families expected their children to contribute to the family's income any way they could. Those too young to bring home a steady wage could bring home scavenged food and fuel instead. Few families were going to starve or freeze in winter without the children's contribution, but the fact that the children could supply free fruit, vegetables, coal, and wood meant that the family's paychecks could be stretched a bit further.

The amount of material the children brought home was astounding. According to John Madro, a participant in the Chicago-Polonia oral history project, no one in his neighborhood ever "had to buy any fuel, any oil, or any wood." With the help of freight car switchmen and brakemen, the boys collected coal and wood from the tracks. On Saturdays, the men

New York City, early 1890s. "What boys learn on street playgrounds." A photograph by Jacob Riis, purporting to show street kids pilfering fruit from a pushcart. Riis believed that the solution to this particular problem was removing the kids from the streets to supervised playgrounds. (*Jacob Riis Collection, LC*)

and boys on the block cut up the railroad ties and hauled them into their basements.[23] Marie Arendt, another participant in the Chicago-Polonia project, collected unburned, discarded coke from a nearby coke oven and "broken up bread or day old bread and pie" from the bakery down the block.[24] On the Middle West Side of Manhattan, Katherine Anthony, an investigator for the Russell Sage Foundation, found families "almost [living] on waste. The children forage for wood, coal, and ice along the railroad tracks and among the warehouses. . . . It is surprising how large a part of the minimum necessary to support life on the West Side can be picked up from the street by boys and girls whose hunting instincts have been sharpened by necessity."[25]

Children had no trouble at all finding plentiful sources of food and fuel. The Middle West Side kids went scavenging at the "produce depots on Eleventh Avenue for refuse fruit and vegetables."[26] In every city there were similar open-air food markets where the children gathered early in the mornings and late in the afternoons.[27] Philip Davis, who in *Street-land* described the work of Boston's youthful scavengers, found that the children were always one step "ahead of the street cleaner." Their "'red-letter' nights" were Saturday nights and nights preceding holidays, when the food markets, pushcarts, fruit stands, and grocery wagons were only too ready to discharge their refuse. "Specked fruits, tomatoes and cucumbers are either devoured on the spot or taken home. Chicken heads, pigs' feet, and the like, are regarded as spoils of war worth scrambling for every Saturday night."[28]

In Chicago, according to the Juvenile Protective Association, and in Boston, according to the Massachusetts Child Labor Committee, the children were without shame or taste when it came to picking through the discarded, spoiled, overripe, and ruined meat and produce. "These children," reported the JPA, "have been found carrying fruit in every stage of decomposition, and on several occasions dead fowls." The investigators in Boston were just as startled—and disgusted—to find children carrying off in their canvas bags "fruit, vegetables, pieces of meat, fish heads, almost anything which can be eaten or which can be made into soup."[29]

The reformers were a lot more squeamish than the children and their families could afford to be. Food was food. Had the children had the money to shop in the better markets or choose the pick of the pushcarts, they would have. But, as the proverb goes, beggars can't be choosers. A spoiled tomato for free was better than a perfect one too expensive to buy.

While the children scoured the city's dumps, alleyways, and open-air markets for food, fuel, and items to sell to the junkman, the reformers followed at a distance, engrossed in their own collection activities. In

Boston, October 1909. "Carrying home decayed refuse from market." (*Lewis Hine Collection, LC*)

this dawning age of scientific social work, the child welfare experts were determined to back up their assumptions with hard, cold data and descriptions. They surveyed the inmates of juvenile reformatories and discovered that most, if not all, had been junkers at one time or another. The Juvenile Protective Agency of Chicago went a step further and sent questionnaires to juvenile justice experts and officials in various cities. The response from Baltimore, Brooklyn, Colorado Springs, Detroit, Indianapolis, Janesville (Wisconsin), Kansas City, Milwaukee, Minneapolis, New York City, New Orleans, Omaha, Philadelphia, San Francisco, Seattle, and St. Louis confirmed their supposition that junking was not only a "moral hazard," but a significant cause of juvenile delinquency.[30]

The reformers were, in this as in so much else, only half-right. Junking did lead to petty theft. The line between the two was a fine one, often crossed and seldom recognized. What the reformers and the law considered a crime, however, the children considered just another part of the life of the city. If they had learned anything on the streets, it was that one had to seize one's opportunities. The streets were not paved with gold, but they were littered with junk that could be converted into nickels and dimes. If the children didn't do the work and collect the spoils, someone else would.

The children knew the difference between petty theft and grand larceny. Those who were successful in swiping watermelon slices from pushcarts were not about to commit armed robbery. They were petty thieves because they were allowed to be—indeed, even encouraged by the adults around them. Had the railroad guards and the switchmen been less cooperative and the junkyards, streets, and alleyways less stocked with recyclable items, the children might have been able to grow to adulthood with attitudes toward theft as pure as the reformers'. But as long as there was so much "stuff" to rescue, so many junkmen to buy it for cash, and so many families making good use of it, the children would continue to take what they needed and ask no further questions. To have done anything else would have defied common sense and violated the logic of the streets.

Harpo Marx was one of those for whom junking, scavenging, and petty theft were daily experiences. With junkmen and hockshops on every corner, Harpo and his brother Chico made more "mazuma" from scavenging than from any of their other business ventures. There was, nonetheless, another side to the experience. Because, as Harpo knew so well, anything and everything could be ripped off and quickly sold for cash, nothing was safe.

Harpo's childhood memories are replete with stories of loss: from the dishpans he hustled to go sledding in Central Park to his genuine dollar Ingersoll bar mitzvah watch. The dishpans were, within hours of his locating them, "swiped out from under me by bigger kids" who sold them to the junkman for five cents cash. The watch was stolen and pawned by his brother Chico.

"I was pretty damn sore. A present was not the same as something you hustled. I tracked down Chico to a crap game and asked him what about it. He handed me the pawn ticket. I gave the ticket to Minnie [Harpo and Chico's mother] and she reclaimed the watch for me. Then a brilliant idea occurred to me. I would show Chico. I would make my watch Chico-proof, so he couldn't possibly hock it again. I removed its hands.

"Now the watch was mine forever. I wound it faithfully each morning and carried it with me at all times. When I wanted to know what time it was I looked at the Ehret Brewery clock and held my watch to my ear. It ran like a charm, and its ticking was a constant reminder that I had, for once, outsmarted Chico."[31]

100

7

The Little Mothers

We have, to this point, spoken less of girls than of boys—and for good reason. Though girls hawked papers and peddled fruit on the street and went junking in the dumps and alleyways, they were never as numerous as the boys at these work locations. Unfortunately and unfairly, the conditions that made street trading so attractive for the boys made it off-limits for the girls. Young girls were not supposed to be brash, aggressive, and loud. They were not supposed to chase customers they did not know up and down the city's most congested avenues.

Street trading was not only unladylike, it was considered positively dangerous for the young girls of the city. On this, there was as near a consensus as one could get on most subjects in early twentieth-century urban America. From Melvin, a Covington, Kentucky, newsie ("It ain't right for girls to sell papers. . . . They get tough and heaps o' things"[1]), to the middle-class reformers and the parents themselves, it was agreed that girls did not belong on the streets.

The child labor reformers were the most adamant on the subject. Even Elbridge Gerry, President of the New York Society for the Prevention of Cruelty to Children, who supported the boys' right to peddle their papers without state interference, argued vociferously against "the employment of girls selling newspapers." Hawking papers, a wholesome and salutary occupation for boys, was, he proclaimed, "one of the most iniquitous practices" city girls could engage in.[2]

Wilmington, Delaware, May 1910. Two girl newsies and their customer. Girl newsies, though not nearly as numerous as the boys, were not as rare as the reformers would have wished. (*Lewis Hine Collection, NCLC*)

Newspaper publishers and editors, usually uncompromising champions of the children's right to work, surrendered when it came to girls. In what appears to be the draft of a rebuttal to a 1905 Juvenile Protective Association pamphlet, an employee of the Chicago *Daily News*, though disagreeing with everything else the association had to say, agreed that neither the public nor the newspapers were well served by newsgirls. "We [the Chicago *Daily News*] do everything we can to discourage them. I see no good reason why the girl should not be prohibited by law from selling on the streets."[3]

With opposition to their street trading almost unanimous, the child labor reformers had an easy time convincing state legislators to draft special measures to "protect" the girls. In twenty of the thirty states with minimum age requirements for street traders, the ages set for girls were significantly higher than for boys. In six states, boys ten and over could work on the streets, while girls under sixteen were barred. In fourteen other states, the girls had to be from two to nine years older than the boys to trade on the streets.[4]

The laws did not, of course, clear all the girls off the streets. A 1905 Chicago study of one thousand newsies reported that investigators had "seen" twenty newsgirls—though, it added, "a moderate estimate puts them at three times that number." Mary McDowell told a gathering at the 1909 National Child Labor Committee convention that she had, on a recent visit to St. Louis, seen several young girls hawking papers in the vicinity of her hotel and near the railroad station. At the same meeting, a Mrs. E. Gaylord Hunt of Grand Rapids, Michigan, admitted that in her home town there were "a few little newsgirls, perhaps a dozen," loose on the streets.[5]

Though girls could be found trading on the streets of most cities, in only a few could they do so with the protection of the law. The Connecticut legislature, to the consternation of reformers everywhere, expressly forbade the city of Hartford to deny licenses to children "solely on the ground of sex." The lawmakers, reported *Survey* magazine, had found no evidence at all that the newsgirls were "demoralized by the work. . . . The evidence gathered [on the contrary] has shown that 'the Hartford newsgirls are a pretty good sort of girl after all.' "[6]

In Bennington, Vermont, the editor of the *Banner* was also pleased with the work of his newsgirls. As he told Lewis Hine—at the time a field investigator for the National Child Labor Committee—he would have liked to have had more girls on the street, as he thought "they [were] more honest than the boys generally."[7]

These reports from Bennington and Hartford show us that girl street traders were every bit as competent as boys. But competence was not

Hartford, Connecticut, March 1909. A Lewis Hine photograph of newsgirls in one of the cities that permitted girls to trade on the streets. From the way these children are dressed it is clear that they were from homes that were able to provide for their necessities. These children's earnings were probably put towards the family's savings or luxuries like a piano in the parlor or a new icebox for the kitchen. (*Lewis Hine Collection, LC*)

the issue. Propriety and decency were. The only females who had any business being on the streets were "street walkers." Girls under the age of ten might, if properly supervised, hustle flowers or baskets in front of their parents' stands. But those a bit older could not do so without projecting an image of indecency.

The streets bred tough, self-reliant, self-confident young adults. Their lessons were appropriately learned by boys who would grow up to join the world of work and wages. Working-class girls were destined for different futures. Though many would, before marriage or between marriage and motherhood, work for wages in factories, offices, or retail stores, these were considered but temporary detours on the road to motherhood and housekeeping. There was little the girls could learn on the streets that would prepare them to be mothers and wives. On the contrary, it was feared that the streets—with their excitement and adventure—could cause irreparable harm to young girls who, as adults, would have to content themselves with spending the greater portion of every day inside their own homes.

Children who grow up in a society with strictly defined gender roles learn early what will be expected of them. The girls of the early twentieth-century city were no exception. They watched as their brothers were sent out to play while they did their chores. Because the boys were basically useless at home (aside, that is, from fetching the wood and filling the coal bin) and, until they approached ten or eleven, unable to earn much elsewhere, they were free to play in the afternoons. The girls were too useful to be given the same kind of freedom. Six-, seven-, and eight-year-olds were big enough to watch the babies and help their mothers with the lighter household tasks. Ten- and eleven-year-olds could be entrusted with enough responsibilities to fill their afternoons.

Had their mothers had other resources, they might have allowed the girls to stay out at play until they were a bit older. But lacking the money for servants or labor-saving devices, they had to look to their daughters for assistance. It took considerable labor to care for a household and earn money on the side. Household chores required hours of preparation and involved dozens of separate steps. The laundry had to be done by hand from beginning to end: sorted, soaked, rubbed against the washboard, rinsed, boiled, rinsed again, wrung out, starched, hung to dry, ironed with irons heated on the stove, folded, and put away. Cooking involved not only preparing the food and cooking it but hauling coal for the fire, dumping the ashes afterwards, and keeping the cast-iron stove cleaned, blacked, and rust-free. Housecleaning was complicated by the soot, grime, and ashes released by coal-burning stoves and kerosene and gas lamps. Shopping had to be done daily and in several different shops: there were no refrigerators to store food purchased earlier in the week and no supermarkets for one-stop marketing.[8]

Little girls, lacking their mothers' experience, strength, and skills, could not do the cooking, the laundry, or the heavy cleaning by themselves. But they could "help out." Adelia Marsik, who grew up in an Italian immigrant household in Chicago, recalled in her oral history that she began helping with the dishes at five or six years of age. "I started out very early. . . . They would put a chair by the sink and I would kneel there on the chair to do the dishes." Other little girls helped out by sorting and folding the laundry or, like eight-year-old Elizabeth Stern, chopping the "farfel." (According to Stern, farfel was made by "chopping stiff dough into little bits [which were then] cooked with meat as a vegetable.") In families that celebrated the Sabbath, the girls were put to work immediately after school on Friday sweeping the front rooms, dusting the furniture, and preparing the kitchen for the Sabbath meal and celebration. Many young girls did the daily marketing for mothers who had so much to do at home they could not spare the time to shop. They learned how to pick over produce, buy day-old bread (if it were still soft), and bargain with the butcher for a fatter piece of meat and an extra soup bone or two. Investigators in a Polish neighborhood in Chicago found that the children there did "practically all the buying of groceries and staples." From butcher to baker to grocer for canned goods and crackers to the vegetable wagons parked in the street, they traveled each afternoon, their baskets slung over their arms.[9]

The girls' help with the shopping, cooking, and cleaning was important to the proper running of the household, but secondary in comparison with their major responsibility as "little mothers." Elizabeth Stern recalled in her autobiography that she had been put to work rocking the babies and "taking them out for the 'fresh air'" when she was still too young to go to school. Girls old enough to attend school took over caring for the babies when they returned home in the afternoon. Catharine Brody, who grew up in what she called a lower middle-class family in Manhattan, recalled in an article for *The American Mercury* that all the girls on her block minded babies after school. "The babies came in baby carriages. We parked the carriages, generally at the edge of the sidewalk and placed kitchen chairs or footstools together." For Catharine and her

New York City. "Syrian children playing in street." The "little mother," baby in tow, watches a group of smaller boys playing marbles or shooting craps. (*Bain Collection, LC*)

friends, baby-tending was not a chore, but something that little girls did in the afternoon, like embroidering or jumping rope.[10]

In many working-class families, the babies and small children were effectively raised by their older sisters. It was not that the mothers were uninterested or irresponsible. They were, rather, overworked and forced to delegate responsibility to their helpers. Because it was easier to watch the little ones than do the laundry or the cooking or the housecleaning, the girls were given this task. They accepted as a matter of course.

The little mothers were more than baby sitters. They were fully responsible for their charges, often from the time they got home from school until the moment the babies fell asleep. They fed them when they weren't nursing, clothed them, bathed them, diapered them, and put them to bed. The little ones became, in point of fact, *their* babies.

In Chicago, an unpublished report on preadolescent girls in a Polish neighborhood noted that the girls there had "the 'little mother' spirit

New York City. "A little mother." A Jacob Riis photograph and caption. The children were sitting on the stoop because there was no place inside for them to play, sit, or rest. (*Jacob Riis Collection, LC*)

well developed." They not only watched over the smaller children but "took considerable pride in the appearance of the one who [was], at the moment, the baby."[11]

The eleven-year-old girl who told her story in the *Thirteenth Annual Report* of Greenwich House claimed that, during the summer, she minded "Danny, my baby brother, all the time. . . . Sometimes I go to play a little while at night with the other children but I must mind Danny there because he does not like to go to bed until we do. Then he gets so tired he goes right to sleep on my lap and I carry him up. I think my brother is very nice but I get tired minding him sometimes."[12]

The little mothers and "their" babies were as much a part of the life of the city as their "little merchant" brothers. Settlement-house workers referred to the "little mother" problem by name; newspaper reporters described their activities in mocking detail. On the Lower East Side of Manhattan, the Board of Health even organized its own "Little Mothers League" to instruct the girls in the proper care of "their" babies. As Dr. Walter Benzel of the Board explained to the New York *Times*, "much of the time in the summer the babies of the tenements [are] entrusted to the keeping of their older sisters, and it would be almost useless to teach the real mothers unless the 'little Mothers' were also taught."[13]

The girls worked at home and for their mothers. Every increase in their mothers' workload meant an increase in their own. When their mothers took in homework, the girls joined them at the kitchen table hemming skirts, embroidering pincushions, stemming artificial flowers, or sorting nuts. When the mothers took in boarders, the girls helped with the extra laundry, shopping, cleaning, and cooking.

Boarding single men (and an occasional woman or family) was the most common income-producing activity engaged in by married women and their daughters. The American city, so blessed with abundance in other areas, did not have sufficient private housing units for all who needed them. Apartment houses were, as yet, available only for the more prosperous. There were no affordable hotels and few respectable rooming houses.[14]

Boarding out provided immigrants from the old world and migrants from the countryside with the cheapest and most comfortable way to survive in a strange, new urban world. It simultaneously brought the boarding families additional income to close their household budget gaps and save money for land of their own. According to the *Immigration Commission Report* (1908–10), up to one third of urban immigrant families received some part of their income from boarding fees. In areas with a high percentage of recently arrived immigrants, like the Stockyards district of Chicago, the proportion was even higher. A 1910 study of "back of the Yards" Lithuanian and Polish families found that more than half took in an average of three boarders each. In New York City, 48 percent of the Russian-Jewish households took in an average of two boarders each.[15]

Caring for boarders was a working-class and not an exclusively immigrant means of supplementing the family income.[16] Families with children too young to earn regular wages had to choose between mother going out to work or bringing work home. Most decided on the latter course, though not without some thought. Boarders meant less space and less privacy for the entire family. They were also a sign that the man of the house was not able to support his family on his own wages.[17]

Caring for boarders was women's work. It was the mothers' and daughters' task to clear out the front room for the newcomers and find mattresses, beds, or other places for them to sleep. Once the boarder or boarders were settled, it was the women's responsibility to buy, cook to order, and serve their food, make their beds, clean their rooms, and launder their bedclothes, workclothes, and Sunday suits. Though some men did not consider this "work," probably because it was done by women at home, the evidence suggests otherwise.[18]

Taking in boarders was not the only way that mothers and daughters supplemented the family income. Some women brought in money by cooking for single men. Others took in laundry or did sewing. Still more took in industrial homework.

Next to boarders, doing "homework" for small jobbers, middlemen, and contractors was the most common source of income for women who worked at home. It is difficult, perhaps impossible, to estimate the number of households where homework was done—or the number of children working in these households.[19] According to the Immigration Commission, six in one hundred households did some sort of homework, though the percentages varied greatly by city and by ethnic group: from 11.2 percent of all households in Chicago to 1.6 percent for Buffalo, from 25 percent of New York City Italians to 5.3 percent of Chicago Italians.[20] Like caring for boarders, homework was women's work. Unemployed husbands might, in a pinch, join in, but more often they were employed outside the home or, if unemployed, too embarrassed to join their wives at the kitchen table. Their sons, following their lead, stayed as far away as possible. The kitchen and whatever went on in it was not for them.

A photograph taken by Lewis Hine in East Harlem at five in the afternoon on December 19, 1911, shows what was probably a typical scene in a household with plenty of seasonal homework to do. Mary

Mauro, the mother, Angelina, a ten-year-old neighbor, Fiorandi, Maggie, and Victoria, ranging in age from eight to eleven, are sitting at the kitchen table sorting feathers by size. Against the back wall of the tiny, cramped kitchen sit two boys, a little one on his big brother's lap. The boys watch from a distance as mother and girls work intently. A second Hine photo tells the same story. Mother and three children sit at the table sorting nuts. Behind them, taking up the rest of the space in the tiny tenement kitchen, is the father, pipe in hand, sitting in his rocking chair. In a third photo, we see only mother and daughters. Hine tells us that the father had been sorting nuts with the women, but retreated into the bedroom as soon as the visitors arrived, ashamed at being seen or photographed doing "women's work."[21]

The women and girls worked well together. With all they had to do to keep the household in order, mothers had to make expert and efficient use of their helpers. Girls too young to decorate pillboxes or embroider pillowcases could, at least, keep the babies out of the way. Girls a bit

New York City, December 1911. "Mrs. Mary Mauro, 309 East 110th Street, 2nd floor. Family work on feathers, make $2.25 a week. In vacation, two or three times as much. Victoria, 8, Angelina 10 (a neighbor), Fiorandi 10, Maggie 11. All work except two boys against the wall. Father is street cleaner and has steady job." (*Lewis Hine Collection, NCLC*)

older could pull bastings or sort materials. Ten- and eleven-year-olds were old enough to sit down at the kitchen table and do the work of adults.

Because most working-class mothers were "too busy" to leave the house, the job of picking up raw materials and delivering finished goods often fell to the girls. Marie Ganz began her day with a trip to the factory loft to pick up a bundle of unfinished skirts for her mother. "The bundle was always twice as big as I was. Just the bundle and a pair of legs were all the neighbors could see as I passed their windows. 'The bundle with legs' was the way they described it, for the legs seemed to belong to the pack rather than to a human being."[22]

Probably New York City. A young girl probably bringing home "work" for her mother to sew. (*Lewis Hine Collection, NCLC*)

Girls who helped out at home—especially those who assisted their mothers with the homework at the kitchen table—grew up fast, perhaps too fast.

Catharine Brody remembered that the Italian barber's daughters who lived on her block and went to her school never played with the other girls in the afternoon. There was an aura of mystery about these girls, with their long black hair flecked with bits of feathers. What did they do every afternoon? And where did they get the feathers to put in their hair? Only by accident did Catharine discover that the girls spent their afternoons sorting and arranging feathers at the kitchen table.[23]

The eleven-year-old girl who told her story in the Greenwich House Annual Report minded her brother Danny all day during the summer. Her activities during the school year were more varied.

"Every morning before school, I sweep out three rooms and help get breakfast. Then I wash the dishes.

"In the mornings, on the way to school, I leave finished flowers at the shop and stop for more work on my way home.

"After school I do my homework for an hour, then I make flowers. All of us, my sisters, my cousins, my aunts, my mother work on flowers.

New York City, 1912. "Making artificial leaves in tenement attic. . . . The five year old helps. Her sister, aged 10, works until 9 P.M. some nights, although she is nearsighted." (*Lewis Hine Collection, NCLC*)

We put the yellow centers into forget-me-nots. It takes me over an hour to finish one gross and I make three cents for that. If we all work all our spare time after school, we can make as much as two dollars between us."[24]

Not all city girls worked as hard as this child. Girls fortunate enough to have been born into smaller families or families able to survive without having to take in boarders or industrial homework had less to do. Because Kate Simon's father made good money as an "expert shoe worker, a maker of samples," and her mother kept the family small (by having thirteen abortions, as Kate would later discover), Kate's chores were minimal. She was required to wheel the baby a turn or two around the block and help with the cleaning and dishes.[25]

Marietta Interlandi grew up in a working-class Italian family in Chicago with fewer resources at its disposal. Her good fortune came in the shape of an older sister who was enlisted as mother's chief assistant. While Marietta was "always out," skating or playing jacks and ball, her sister "stayed at home with my mother. She helped her out a lot. I was younger, you know. Three years makes a difference."[26]

The little mothers who helped out at home were part-time workers and, like their brothers, were suspended between childhood and adult life. At home and in the classroom, they were expected to follow orders. But out at work—hawking their papers, if they were boys, or shopping for the family's food and minding the baby, if they were girls—they were expected to act like adults. Girls and boys acccepted their ambiguous status without much complaint. It was all part of growing up.

Though most working-class city kids were, by their tenth birthday, doing some sort of work in the afternoons, there were enormous differences between the work assigned to boys and to girls. Like their fathers, the boys earned money outside the homes and were responsible for bringing it home to support their families. Like their fathers as well, they took liberties with their pay checks, holding back a little as a reward for their labor. The girls, on the other hand, like their mothers, earned nothing at their labor. Household chores and baby-tending were entirely unpaid. Caring for boarders brought in income, but it was not considered "work." Industrial homework was, but in this case the income producer was the family of women, not the individuals who comprised it. The girls who joined their mothers at the kitchen table were not earning anything by themselves. They were "helping out."

This situation put the girls at a disadvantage. Aside from the pennies they might earn at junking and the nickel or two they might collect on their birthdays, they were for the most part marooned at home without funds of their own. Every time they wanted to go to the movies or buy a piece of lace to decorate their hand-me-down shirtwaists, they had to go begging to their mothers.

The boys experienced a sort of harmony between their work and the pleasures it bought. The more they worked, the more they could eat, see, and do. The girls' unpaid labor carried with it no such tangible rewards. While the boys' capacity for paid fun and entertainment was bounded only by their earning power, the girls had to petition for every penny. Unlike their brothers, they had to learn to postpone their gratifications and be circumspect in their pursuit of pleasure. They had to find satisfaction instead in the "grown-up" feelings they enjoyed in accomplishing adult tasks, in their neighbors' compliments on their well-behaved babies, and their mothers' congratulations on their outwitting and outbargaining the butcher. When such rewards were not forthcoming, as was often the case, they had to be satisfied, as their mothers "appeared" to be, with the comfort they received from doing their duty without complaint.

The young girls learned early what would be expected of them as adults. They also learned that no matter how difficult or tedious the task, it could be lightened if accomplished in the company of others. Housework in the early twentieth century was fortunately not yet the isolated, anonymous task it would become. The young girls chopped their "farfel" alongside their mothers, watched the baby from the front stoop with their friends, and joined the other girls and women at the kitchen table to hem the new batch of shirtwaists. While, in comparison to their brothers, they remained isolated from the life of the city, they were able to construct their own community of family, friends, and neighbors and draw from it the companionship and comfort they required and deserved.

All That Money
Could Buy

The children who worked downtown crossed the invisible bridge that separated and linked the two parts of the city. Like their customers, the eleven- and twelve-year-old refugees from the slums, the ghettoes, the "Jewtowns" and "Poletowns" and "Little Sicilies" were commuters working in the heart of the city, where money was most plentiful. With eyes and ears wide open, the newsies, peddlers, and shineboys observed first-hand how life was lived by the other half. They watched and listened as the new middle class and the older elites shopped, were entertained, and spent their money. They studied the habits, dress, and style of secretaries and bookkeepers, real estate promoters and railroad magnates, gentlemen and fashionable ladies. They peered through plate-glass windows into lobster palaces and hotel lobbies, window-shopped with department store customers; perused the billboards, marquees, and gaudy, colored posters outside the movie palaces; and read in the newspapers about the life of the city: the fads, fashions, amusements, and personalities. The more they saw, the more difficult it was to return to their home blocks and take up again their childish games. Ring-around-the-rosy, prisoner's base, and building forts in vacant lots quickly lost their attraction.

The children were swept up in the whirlwind of urban life. They, too, wanted to join in the fun and the games and, as they rapidly learned, this was not impossible. The children could not and did not expect to eat oysters in the lobster palaces, shop in the department stores, or see

Denver, 1910–20. Denver newsies smiling for the camera. Every day, these boys left their neighborhoods to travel downtown to sell their papers to the city's businessmen and shoppers. (*Mrs. Ben Lindsey Collection, LC*)

the latest show at the first-class theaters, but they could—for pennies—buy themselves a very good time. There were amusements, entertainments, and fashions to fit every pocketbook, different variations of the same basic model for different classes of urban customers. While fashionable ladies got their shoes and hats custom-made or at the department stores, the girls could—for a fraction of the price—purchase imitations from pushcart peddlers and bargain stores. While society people ate their dinners at the Waldorf-Astoria and Delmonico's and the newly enriched middle classes patronized the lobster palaces, the children could—for a nickel—sit at the counter of a "dairy lunch" and enjoy a big slice of apple pie with ice cream on top. While the upper crust attended the opera and the middle classes the vaudeville palaces and music halls, the children could—for a nickel—see the flickers at the nickelodeon, and—for a dime—watch a cheap vaudeville show from the gallery.

The children had been sent downtown to earn money for their families—and this they intended to do. But the more time they spent away from the block, the more uses they found for the money they earned.

Money bought pleasure *and* a place in the city. The children required

116

both. As the settlement-house workers were the first to understand, reforms in child labor and compulsory schooling laws had, ironically, created a new problem for the children (and for the reformers who looked after their welfare). Boys and girls between the ages of eleven and fifteen were now able to attend school for a few more years. But school, unlike work, let out at three o'clock, leaving the new working-class students with free time in the afternoon—time, the reformers were convinced, that they did not know how to fill constructively.[1]

The reformers, as we saw in Chapter 2, had tried to provide the children with after-school clubs and playgrounds, but had not succeeded. It was difficult to interest the children in regularly scheduled, supervised activities, and even more difficult to raise the funds needed to build the playgrounds, staff the clubs, and supervise the daily activities.

While the reformers watched from the sidelines, frustrated by their inability to solve the leisure-time problem they had helped to create, an army of small businessmen alert to the jingle of coins in the children's pockets proceeded to give them something to do with their free time. Shopkeepers, penny arcade operators, luncheonette and coffee shop proprietors, nickelodeon, vaudeville, and amusement park owners, and the thousands of "Cheap Charlies" who owned corner candy stores opened their doors to let the children in. They provided them—for a price—with amusement, recreation, and a place to gather with the gang. The older children would never again enjoy the kind of compact "playground" they had once had on the block. But, as they soon discovered, they no longer needed it. With money in their pockets, they could buy their way into dozens and dozens of different play areas.

The candy shops were the first and foremost of the small businesses to strike a bargain with the children. Though penny candy shops were not new to city or town, they multiplied in the first years of the century until they were more numerous than even the saloons in the working-class neighborhoods. The children were drawn to the shops like bees to blossoms, lured by the sweets for a penny and, as a Russell Sage Foundation study put it, by "something still more attractive—a place to meet friends, to chat, sometimes to play games—always to talk and skylark a little amid light and warmth, protected alike from the distractions of the tenement home and the inconveniences of the street corner." If the saloon was the workingman's club, the candy shop was the youngster's.[2]

The shop owners, as sensitive and alert to the needs of their customers as the department stores were to theirs, did their best to make the children comfortable. There was a tacit understanding between

117

proprietor and customers: children without money to spend had to stay outside, but those with only a penny were welcome to take all day if they wanted, picking out their treat, savoring every morsel, and hanging around afterward. Some kids stayed inside to play the kiddie slot machines. They deposited their pennies and got, in return, a tiny piece of gum *and* a chance at the jackpot: five, ten, or twenty more tiny pieces of gum. Others played the weekly lottery, with the prize a huge box of candy. In Chicago, the Juvenile Protective Agency claimed that the gambling games in the candy shops had become so popular that children in one school "were pawning their school books in order to get money with which to play."[3] Whether or not this was true (on its face, the claim appears a bit exaggerated), kids were spending their time and their money in the candy stores. And for good reason.

The children experienced in the candy shops a degree of autonomy and independence they could not easily find elsewhere. The freedom of the consumer is, of course, a truncated, degraded freedom. Some would argue—and with justice—that it is no freedom at all. And yet, for the children of the city, it was the best substitute they could find. The marketplace knew no distinctions between children and adults. A nickel was a nickel—no matter who held it. Poring over the selections, choosing what to buy and where and how much, children transcended their minute size and inferior status to assume quasi-adult dimensions. Pennies, nickels, and dimes transformed them from kids to respected customers to be courted and cared for by adult businessmen.

Francie Nolan, the eleven-year-old heroine of Betty Smith's auto-biographical novel, *A Tree Grows in Brooklyn,* was for six days a week just another poor city kid. On the seventh, she became Queen for a Day. Thanks to the nickel in her pocket earned from selling a week's junk to the junkman, the world opened up before her. "Francie had a nickel. Francie had power." She spent most of her Saturday morning shopping with that nickel. She began at the candy shop, then headed for Broadway and "the finest nickel and dime store in all the world. It was big and glittering and had everything in the world in it. . . . Or so it seemed to an eleven-year-old girl. . . .

"Arriving at the store, she walked up and down the aisles handling any object her fancy favored. What a wonderful feeling to pick something up, hold it for a moment, feel its contour, run her hand over its surface and then replace it carefully. Her nickel gave her this privilege. If a floorwalker asked whether she intended buying anything, she could say, yes, buy it and show him a thing or two. Money was a wonderful thing, she decided."[4]

The magic of money rubbed off on the children who carried it. Money was pure potentiality, pure choice. It was as valuable unspent as it was concretized in commodities. The children who had money to spend carried their new freedom—as consumers—into and out of the candy shops and dime stores. It stayed with them wherever they went, enhancing their status and self-esteem on the streets.

Spending money was psychologically important, but it was also—when spent—a powerful means for meeting one's needs. Children with money in their pockets were no longer supplicants dependent on adult largesse. They were free to purchase what they wanted—when they wanted it. Children who earned money on the streets didn't have to wait until dinnertime to fill their bellies. They could, if they chose, satisfy their after-school appetites at Cheap Charlie's or they could eat their way down the block, sampling the wares of the vendors before settling on some combination of peanuts, gumdrops, and chocolate-covered cherries, or, depending on the season, ice cream, watermelon slices, lemonade, hot chestnuts or corn on the cob.

The restaurants and lunch counters, especially those near the newspaper offices where the boys picked up their papers, went after the boys' business with afternoon specials on hamburgers and pie à la mode. In Portland, Oregon, the proprietors competed with one another by advertising in the newsboys' newspaper, *The Hustler*. Woods Quick Lunch ("Say Boys, A hot Hamburger Sandwich 5¢") and Lambs Club

---

Wilmington, Delaware, 1910. "Frank F. Gibson, Western Union, fourteen years old, one year in service, guides soliders to segregated district, smokes, still in school and works from 8:30 P.M. to 12:30 P.M." (*Lewis Hine Collection, LC*)

Dairy Lunch ("We Buy the Best in the Market, Tasty Goods, Cakes, Pastry and Pies are Home Made") were among the paper's regular advertisers.[5]

The young were valued customers in the candy shops and restaurants and in a score of other entertainment establishments. They appeared at precisely the moment when an afternoon lull had set in. The lunch hour was long gone; dinnertime and the homebound commuter rush were still in the future. For those few hours in between and then again after the rush had subsided, the children and their nickels were very welcome.

Because their time was valuable and they had, after all, come downtown to work, the children had to squeeze their paid entertainment into their work schedule. A trip to the ballpark, beach, or amusement park was usually out of the question—unless they wanted to abandon work for the afternoon. Fortunately there were abundant sources of entertainment located on or near the streets where they worked.

The penny arcades and amusement parlors, in part because of their location and in part because they provided their fun in packages of time which fit into the children's schedule, were among their favorite after-school haunts. Most amusement parlors were seedy-looking joints, usually little more than large rooms, open in front, with two or three rows of slot machines "plus a few punching bags, automatic scales, and fortune tellers." The children dropped their pennies into the slot, cranked the handle, and, lo and behold, moving pictures appeared in the peephole. The "movies" lasted only a minute, but that was enough time to experience the excitement of being on a speeding train or observing, unseen, the hootchy-kootchy girls or the mysterious woman "Getting Ready for the Bath."[6] Though the arcades were dark, narrow, and crowded with machines, there was room for three, four, or five boys to gather around the Kinetoscopes waiting for their turns. No adults stood in their way, censored their choices, or told them how to behave.

The only drawback was the expense: a minute's entertainment cost a penny and the pennies mounted up. When, in the early years of the new century, enterprising arcade owners blocked off the rear of their rooms to show movies for a nickel, they were delighted to find customers willing to pay the higher price for a longer show. The new moving pictures were so popular that some owners replaced their Kinetoscopes with projectors, filled their arcades with chairs, and opened the first "Electric Theaters. For Up-To-Date High Class Motion Picture Entertainment. Especially for Ladies and Children."[7]

Though moving pictures had been shown in converted arcades and

120

storefront theaters for several years, credit for the first modern movie theater is usually bestowed upon two Pittsburgh businessmen who in 1905 "converted an empty store into a movie theater" and then with a flair for show business "gave their store-theater a luxurious appearance which distinguished it from other store theatres and arcades and impressed the spectators. They added the innovation of piano accompaniment, which increased the grand air of the show. Then, to advertise their theater's cheapness and at the same time maintain its dignity, they named it the 'Nickelodeon.'"

The first "nickelodeon" made so much money—so rapidly—that within a year there were a hundred more—in Pittsburgh alone. By 1908, there were between eight and ten thousand in the nation. In New York City investigators counted more than six hundred entertaining between seventy-five and a hundred thousand children daily. Nickelodeons had, as Jane Addams wrote from Chicago, "sprung up suddenly, somehow, no one knows why," in every working-class and immigrant district in the city.[8]

The early theaters and nickelodeons catered to an almost exclusively working-class audience. As Milton Berle remembered in his autobiography. "The movies were something for the lower classes and immigrants. Nice people didn't go to the 'flickers.'"[9] Barton Currie, writing for *Harper's Weekly* in 1907, ridiculed the better classes who, never having been to one, assumed the theaters were no more than dark dens for pickpockets and their victims. Whom, he asked, were the thieves going to rob? The audiences in the neighborhood theaters were composed entirely of people with empty pockets: "workingmen, . . . tired drudging mothers of bawling infants [and] the little children of the streets, newsboys, bootblacks, and smudgy urchins."[10]

It was this latter category that made up a sizable portion of the early audience. The children fueled the expansion of the nickelodeons, converting what could have been fallow afternoon, early evening, and Saturday matinee periods into virtual bonanzas. According to Roy Rosenzweig, "Virtually all observers of early movie theater audiences noted the presence of large numbers of children and young people. 'The nickelodeon,' wrote one in 1908, 'is almost the creation of the child. . . .' 'Children are the best patrons of the nickelodeon,' added a trade press correspondent that same year. . . . Children, a range of different studies agreed, composed about one-quarter to one-half of the new movie audience."[11]

Author and critic Edward Wagenknecht, who saw his first pictures in Chicago in 1905 or 1906, attended the Family Electric Theater "on the southeast corner of Ogden and California Avenues, just across the

Wilmington, Delaware, May 1910. "Where some of the newsboys' earnings go." One of a series of photographs with this caption. Here Hine shows a boy on his way into the nickelodeon. (*Lewis Hine Collection, LC*)

street from Douglas Park. There was no box office. The proprietor, a man named Brown, stationed himself at the end of a long dingy corridor, and you passed in, handed him your nickel, and took your seat. . . . The rule at the Family Electric Theater was three reels of film [each no more than ten minutes long] and an 'illustrated song' for a nickel. The illustrated song would be one of the popular ballads of the period—'Clover Blossoms' or 'In the Good Old Summertime' or maybe 'Come Away with Me, Lucille'—sung by the girl Sophie who played the piano (her cousin Helen was in my room at school) to the accompaniment of colored slides on the screen."

Wagenknecht remembers being utterly "fascinated" by the movement on the screen. He didn't really care what was up there, as long as it moved. [12] The children never knew what they were going to see—but enjoyed whatever it was. To attract repeat customers—especially children—the nickelodeons changed their programs daily, twice on weekends. To supply the thousands of nickelodeons, each changing its program daily, movie producers/directors turned out thousands of one-reel films, borrowing ideas where they could. Because the "Great Train Robbery" was the first blockbuster story film, hundreds of imitations were produced, with shoot-outs, stick-ups, criminals, lawmen, and lots of chasing. Some producers, aware that their audience was almost entirely made up of working people and children, borrowed their themes from subjects closer to the daily life of their viewers. In "The Eviction," "The Ex-Convict," "A Desperate Encounter," "She Won't Pay Her Rent," "The Eleventh House," and hundreds of others, they projected onto the big screen their own melodramatic representation of life in the big city. [13]

In this era before screen writers and screen plays, the easiest way to get a script was to steal a story. The movies stole shamelessly from current events, Shakespeare, opera, novels, short stories, history, even the Bible. There was no telling what you might find on the screen in front of you: *King Lear, Parsifal, The Scarlet Letter, A Tale of Two Cities, The Boston Tea Party, The Life of Moses.* There were also slapstick comedies, risqué light dramas, fantasy films, cowboy films, and more cowboy films. [14]

In the first two decades of the century, there were more movie "theaters" than there would ever be again, so many that it was the rare city kid who had to walk more than a block or two to get to one. The nickelodeons, housed in converted storefronts, were soon supplemented by neighborhood theaters built specially to show films and, after 1914, by lavish movie palaces decorated and furnished to attract new middle-class audiences.

Children who worked downtown had their choice of theaters. They could attend the "nickel dumps" in their neighborhoods or, for an extra nickel, watch the flickers at the new "palaces." Most preferred the dumps. Why spend a dime when you could see the same show for a nickel? The nickelodeons were also more hospitable to their young customers. While the palaces did whatever they could to keep the street kids from tarnishing their image and dirtying their new carpets, the nickel dumps welcomed them with open arms. Edward Wagenknecht remembers that the proprietor of the Family Electric Theater in Chicago handed his customers "five cent packages of chewing gum" as they entered the theater. In many neighborhoods, children were admitted two for a nickel on Saturdays. In his autobiography, Sam Levenson, the comedian, recalls the scene outside the theaters as "dozens of two-cent kids would congregate . . . chanting the movie matinee call: 'I've got two. Who's got three?' "[15]

The Bijous, Pictoriums, Theatoriums, Jewels, Electrics, and Dream-lands became the children's "general social center and club house." "Young people," Jane Addams reported from Chicago, "attend the five cent theaters in groups, with something of the 'gang' instinct, boasting of the films and stunts in 'our theater.'" When the lights went down, they were free—as they were free nowhere else indoors—to behave like children: to shout, scream, howl, laugh aloud, and jump up and down in their seats. "They were called silent pictures," Sam Levenson remem-bers. "Maybe the pictures were silent, but the audience certainly wasn't. When 'talkies' came in, it was two years before we noticed the change."[16]

The children's behavior, though disturbing to middle-class critics, was consistent with a long tradition of working-class conduct at cultural events. As Roy Rosenzweig reminds us in his study of working-class leisure activities in Worcester, Massachussetts, "Modes of conviviality, active sociability, and liveliness remained the norms for the working class." Adults and children socialized, ate, drank, cheered, growled, and stamped their feet through all sorts of theatrical performances. The audience was part of the show, part of the fun. The nickelodeon and theater owners, many of them from the neighborhood, did not seem to mind. When the fun got a bit too frantic, they tried to channel the energy in other directions. If the projector broke down—as it often did—slides would be quickly projected onto the screen and the piano player enlisted to play the song the slides illustrated. With luck, the children would stop throwing food and insults long enough to join in the singing, until the lights were dimmed again and the screen lit up with cowboys or criminals, pirates or policemen. Phil Silvers, future film actor, Broadway star, and "Sergeant Bilko," began his entertainment career quieting the crowd at his local theater by singing aloud whenever the reels were changed.[17]

The younger kids on the block had to rely on their parents' largesse for tickets to the Saturday matinees. If they were very lucky, they might also get to accompany their mothers to a Sunday show. The children who earned their own money had no such restrictions placed on them. They could go to the flickers whenever they pleased. The nickel price and the short length of the show—twenty or thirty minutes in the era

Jersey City, New Jersey, November 1912. "Going to the movies: 2:30." (*Lewis Hine Collection, NCLC*)

before features—made the movies as accessible as they were entertaining. The street traders could easily take a half hour off from their work on slow days or stop in for a show on their way home for dinner. In Birmingham, Alabama, Esther Rider discovered that most of the boys who hawked papers finished their work day at the cheap theaters. In Chicago, William Hard, a journalist, claimed to have found a group of children who sold papers every afternoon for the sole purpose of raising money for movie tickets. They worked until they had their nickels for admission, quit to see the the show, and then returned to "work again until they [had] another nickel to be spent for the same purpose at another 'theatorium.' "[18]

While the children saw nothing wrong with spending their hard-earned nickels at the movies, the adult reformers and settlement-house

125

workers were worried about the physical, mental, and moral toll of so much time spent in darkened rooms watching moving images, some of them of subjects best kept secret from growing children. There were dozens and dozens of investigations of the effects of the movies on the children who watched them. Common to every one of them was the investigators' amazement at the number of children who went to the movies and the number of times they went each week. In Madison, Wisconsin, a 1915 Board of Commerce study of recreation found that the average child spent five to six hundred percent more time at the movies than on religious activities. A 1911 Russell Sage Foundation study in New York City revealed that 62 percent of the school children interviewed "declared that they were accustomed to go to moving-picture shows once a week or oftener. . . . A truly astonishing proportion, 16% of the total, avow that they go daily." Of the 507 newsies Ina Tyler interviewed in St. Louis, 87 percent "frequented moving picture shows and cheap theaters." One boy claimed that he had attended "a show of some kind every night for four months."[19]

The movies had become such an attraction that one social worker reported that the Irish mothers on Manhattan's West Side had started giving their young boys money for the "nickel dumps," afraid that if they didn't, the boys would steal it. Jane Addams claimed that a major source of juvenile crime was the children's quest for the price of admission to what she called the "house of dreams." "Out of my twenty years' experience at Hull House I can recall all sorts of pilferings, petty larcenies, and even burglaries, due to that never ceasing effort on the part of boys to procure theater tickets."[20]

The settlement-house workers, reformers, and educators were worried by what they saw around them. Eleven- to fifteen-year-olds were too influenced, too affected, too attracted, even addicted, to the pleasures of paid entertainment. The theaters were, as Jane Addams called them, "houses of dreams." Adolescents were prone to dreaming, even without the stimulus of the big screen. What the movies did, the reformers feared, was exaggerate this tendency to dangerous levels. At an age where the boys and girls should have been anchored more firmly to the real world, they were indulging in daily flights of fantasy in darkened movie theaters and nickelodeons. The images before them not only distracted them from the crucial task of preparing themselves for adult life, they impeded their socialization by inflaming their desires. Children who spent too much of their childhood dreaming were going to find it difficult to adjust to the discipline and responsibilities of adult life.

The children were impervious to such criticisms. They paid their nickel and enjoyed the show, whatever it was, wherever it took them.

Contrary to the adults' fears, the young did not confuse what they saw on the big screen with life on the outside. The movies were *not* real life. That was why they were so enjoyable. In the real world, bounded for the children by home, school, and the street, dreams did not come true, villains were not always punished, virtue seldom rewarded. The children entered the movie theater as they opened their storybooks: expecting to find there an alternate world, with different values, settings, people, and a guaranteed happy ending. When they left the theater—or put down their stories—they reentered the world they had temporarily vacated. What harm could there be in taking these brief vacations from work and the city? The same street, the same city, the same life would be there when they came out into the light.[21]

The children who enjoyed the world presented on the big screen would also have thrilled to the melodramas, the music hall shows, and the legitimate English- and foreign-language theaters. Unfortunately live drama cost more than they could afford. The cheaper theaters had almost all been put out of business by the competition from the movies.[22] The only forms of inexpensive live entertainment that remained by the second decade of the century were the cheap vaudeville halls with galleries where, for a dime, the children could sit for hours watching the acts march past: dancers, singers, instrumentalists, magicians, tumblers, comedians, and animals. Like the nickelodeons, the vaudeville galleries offered the children space of their own to do as they pleased. Far above the stage and the better-paying audience, so far above they were almost in a different world, the children sat surrounded by their friends, singing with the singers, giggling at the suggestive jokes, hooting the boring acts off the stage, and staring in amazement as the magicians defied gravity and common sense.[23]

Vaudeville and the flickers, the lunch counters and the penny candy shops, the arcades and downtown amusement parlors: these were not treats or luxuries reserved for special occasions. They were, in combination, an integral part of the children's daily life. Poor, underage, and often immigrant, the children were triply handicapped in their quest to join the life of the city. They were outsiders looking in, guest workers allowed downtown to hawk their wares. Only with money in their pockets were they welcomed to stay and become a part of the city they worked in.

The children of the city were not ascetics or martyrs or heads of

St. Louis, May 1910. "Where the boys spend their money." Lewis Hine took a number of photographs under this caption. This particular one shows a boy in front of a vaudeville theater. The gallery seats cost only ten cents, and there were matinees every day for the boys to attend. (*Lewis Hine Collection, LC*)

household who had to save all their money to support their families. They were children who worked hard and wanted to enjoy the fruits of their labor. They did not look to their parents for handouts or allowances. They did not believe that those who did not work were entitled to play. They had as little use and as much contempt for idle aristocrats as their parents. They asked only that they be allowed to spend some of what they earned.

Their parents refused the request.

9

The Battle
for Spending Money

Adults—engaged in a daily struggle to put food on the table, pay the gas bill, and save a bit for a ship's ticket for relatives in the old country, a down payment on a house, or a new icebox—did not look favorably on their twelve-year-olds' demands to be allowed to spend their money as they pleased.

In most working-class families, the children were expected, even required, to hand in their earnings to their mother, who would return to them what she believed they required for carfare, lunch, and entertainment. Mothers were not to be questioned when it came to spending money. They alone knew what the family took in every week and what it had to pay out. They alone had the discipline and foresight to carefully husband the family's resources. They alone could estimate—to the penny—what could be put aside for savings and special treats.[1]

Parents were not averse to spending money on their children. In good times and bad, they had no choice but to buy them shoes, stockings, and decent clothing for school. There was usually a nickel on Saturdays for the matinee and perhaps a penny or two for a treat at Cheap Charlie's. When everyone was working steadily and the dreaded "slack" periods were a distant memory, there might even be something left over for a new pencil box, a family outing to Coney Island or Luna Park, perhaps violin or piano lessons.

What the parents would not do was allow the children to spend money on their own. Money did not belong in their hands. On this there was near universal agreement among adults. Settlement-house workers and working-class parents closed ranks against the children, convinced that they were, by definition, too young, too irresponsible, too susceptible to the temptations of the city to be left alone with their nickels and dimes. As Fannie Fogelson, a "janitress" on East Sixty-second Street, told an investigator from the New York Child Labor Committee, "the possession of money would spoil the best child. . . . No money that a child may bring into the home can repay the home for the spoiling of the child—child earnings is the dearest money in the world."[2]

Adults feared the "filthy lucre" for the same reasons that the children cherished it. Children with their own money to spend could do as they pleased away from home, could consume or hide the evidence, and no one, least of all their parents, would be any the wiser. According to Joseph Bosco's mother, a widow struggling to carry on her deceased husband's junk business, money made children into "little grown-ups and took the childhood out of them—if they had money they were acting grown-up and only doing the bad things of grown-ups."[3] The boys could smoke cigarettes, spend every afternoon in the nickelodeons, and stuff themselves with hamburger specials; the girls could purchase fancy ribbons, laces, and the silk stockings their mothers refused to let them wear. Money erased the distinctions between childhood and adulthood and, in so doing, tore apart the hierarchical basis upon which the family rested.

Children with money got "spoiled." And spoiled children could not be saved. Those that developed a taste for spending money—and the pleasures it purchased—would, their parents feared, never again be able to do without it. The only way to protect their innocence and keep their eyes, ears, and taste buds closed to the temptations of the street was to keep money out of their hands.

It was easy to protect the younger girls, most of whom did their work at home for no pay. Because they earned no money, they had no money to spend. Their brothers presented a different case. They were, from the age of twelve or so, out on the streets selling papers, blacking boots, and peddling candy and gum. They made their own sales and collected their own tips. When they arrived home in the evening, they were supposed to empty their pockets, which they did. But how were their mothers going to be sure that the change dumped into their laps was the sum total of what had been earned? It was so simple for the boys to deduct a nickel or two and spend it on the way home: for a hamburger in a cheap restaurant, a handful of gum drops at the candy store, a ticket to the nickelodeon, or the latest installment of Oliver Optic's adventures.

Children who were obedient in every other regard did what they

131

had to to preserve some part of their earnings for themselves. They lied, they cheated, they hid away their nickels and dimes, they doctored their pay envelopes. The possession of spending money was too important an item in their daily lives to be voluntarily surrendered.

Their parents were seldom fooled. When the New York Child Labor Committee in 1918 sent investigators into the homes of newsboys to ask about the boys' spending habits, up to 30 percent of the parents confessed, reluctantly, to fears that their boys were cheating them. (Many more probably suspected as much but were not going to admit it to an investigator they did not know and could not trust.)[4] Dominick Abbruzzese's parents had no trouble at all figuring out that he had been devouring his earnings in the form of cake and candy when he became suddenly "unable to eat his supper."[5] Other parents came to the same conclusion when their children lost their appetites, came home later than usual, or stared uncomfortably at the floor as they emptied their pockets.

The parents knew what was happening. But they didn't know how to prevent it. Those who suspected their children of cheating had few options. If their charges were denied, parents could either forget the matter or accuse the boys of being liars and cheats. And then what? If they locked the boys in their rooms, they, the parents, forfeited any possibility of getting any money from them. If they punished them further, the boys just might run away.

The fact that the children contributed something to the household's income gave them leverage within the family. Parents who used their children's earnings to help out at home knew that they put this money at risk every time they questioned them. In the Brusco household, where the father, "a shovel worker," brought home money only when the weather was good, Frank's contribution of fifty cents a night made up an important part of the family's income. Every afternoon, Frank traveled to his corner at Madison and Fifty-ninth Street, where he sold papers until 8 P.M. When he returned home at 9 or 10 P.M., or later, he handed his money to his mother and refused to answer any questions about where he had been or what he had been doing. Frank's family knew that the boy was holding out on them, that he spent money on the movies and trash to eat, but they had no influence on him. He "gives the 50 cts and thinks that is enough and no questions should be asked."[6]

In the La Polla household, the same conditions held. Anna La Polla told the investigator from the New York Child Labor Committee that she knew her son Dominick made more than the dollar a week he brought home, but, with three younger children at home, the baby Delia only six months old, and her husband, a porter, bringing home twelve dollars a week, she was not about to risk a confrontation.[7]

Though in theory all children were supposed to turn in their earnings, and in practice most objected, only the boys were able to win significant concessions. Some mothers, like Anna La Polla, looked the other way as their sons cheated them; others negotiated settlements that allowed the boys to keep a certain percentage of their earnings for themselves. The boys, explained one mother, had to be pacified because they could "run away if you don't do the right thing by them." The girls, who could not run away, had no bargaining power and no choice but to follow the dictates of the household. Even those who had taken full-time jobs outside the home at age fourteen and now earned more than their fathers had to "coax, cry, or quarrel with their mothers whenever they wished independent spending money."[8] And yet they, too, needed an independent source of spending money.

The older girls (fourteen and over) who lived at home and worked downtown or in the neighborhood had no choice, or believed they had no choice, but to spend money on proper clothes and accessories. They walked to work on public streets and rode in streetcars or subways. In the evening, they went to the movies or for a stroll with their girlfriends. Wherever they went, whatever they did, they could not escape the gaze of the anonymous other. Urban space was public space, demanding of those who used it set standards of behavior, deportment, and dress. Eight-year-olds who played all day on the block could dress like peasants for all anyone noticed or cared. Their older sisters had to pay attention to what they wore.[9]

This is not to imply that only girls were fashion-conscious. Lucky Luciano (as he would later be known to the public) and his friends regarded fancy, expensive clothes as a visible sign of success, one of the few available to adolescents. Charles Angoff recalls in his autobiography that in his Boston neighborhood the boys fought with their fathers over shoes: the boys wanted low ones, their fathers insisted on buying them high ones. On the Lower East Side, where Harry Roskolenko lived, the boys were as particular about their caps. Only ones with large visors were acceptable because, as everyone knew, the larger the visor, the tougher the kid underneath.[10] Still, though the boys made distinctions between the stylish and the unstylish, to be in fashion was for them an option, not a necessity. Only for their older sisters were the right clothes mandatory.

Working girls could not help comparing their dress and deportment with that of the city's fashionable women. All they had to do was look around them, read the daily department store advertisements in the papers, and view the pictures of society people in the Sunday supplements and magazines. It was not possible to close one's eyes to the fashionable or to make believe that such standards need not intrude in one's own personal space. A Polish-language newspaper in Chicago did its best to explain to parents that their fashion-conscious daughters were not acting aberrantly, but were very much in tune with the American city they now inhabited. "It is evident that most of our young Polish girls of teen age are . . . afflicted with [the American] passion for fine clothes. The old saying, 'Clothes do not make a person,' does not appeal to our women. We must regretfully admit that our girls are being influenced by and are quickly adopting the habits and customs of the American girls."[11]

Of all the articles and accessories that were required of the well-dressed girl, none was more important than the hat. Girls who could afford only one item of fashionable dress had no trouble deciding what that item would be. Hats not only stood out above the crowd, but also were—and had always been—the bearers of important social messages. In the Old Country, as the mothers never ceased to remind their daughters, "women below the middle class" did not wear hats, but went bareheaded or wore simple kerchiefs. In the new world of the American city, as the daughters reported back to their mothers, hats remained

Twenty-third Street and Sixth Avenue, New York City, June 12, 1896. An Alice Austin photograph of a newsgirl selling at the entrance to the "El." Her hat and veil had undoubtedly been purchased from the proceeds of her street trading. (*Alice Austin Collection, Staten Island Historical Society*)

socially significant. They signified that the girls who wore them knew enough, cared enough, and were able to spend enough to stay in fashion. Girls who saved for an ostrich plume or bird of paradise feather hat were committing no social crime; on the contrary, they were affirming their allegiance to their new land.

In Chicago's stockyard district, Louise Montgomery found that the American working-class daughters of foreign-born parents all placed "an exaggerated importance upon the possession of a fashionable hat." Girls who practiced thrift and economy in every other area would not compromise when it came to buying the right hat for themselves. Eight hundred miles away, Ruth True described the same situation among the daughters of American-born Irish and German parents. One working girl reportedly spent a whole week's wages "on a willow plume. 'We starved fer that hat,' her mother said, 'just plain starved fer it, so we did.' "[12]

It was easy to poke fun at the girls for their devotion to fashion and the fashionable. The Polish-language newspapers in Chicago ridiculed the girls for their shoes as big as sleds and the incongruity between the "silks and satins" they dressed in and the "shack[s] bending to the ground" they called home.[13] Yet the girls, while devoting a large percentage of their spending money to their clothing, were not acting unreasonably. Fashionable clothing was not an affectation or frivolity. Girls had to dress properly not because the right outfit would lead to better jobs or transport them from dreary, congested flats to suburban cottages: they had to dress properly because out on the streets they would be judged by their appearance and nothing else. In the eyes of others, they were what they wore.[14]

The cities were socially stratified—with an escape clause. Working girls could, if they properly distinguished themselves, avoid the opprobrium visited upon the poor, the immigrant, and the outsider. The proper outfit covered a multitude of social sins. On Manhattan's West Side, the manager of a large pattern factory, as cognizant as the girls of the hat's social significance, urged his young workers "to wear their hats to and from work so as to avoid being taken for factory girls."[15] As Mary Simkhovitch, director of Greenwich House (a New York City social settlement) and author of The City Worker's World in America, wrote in 1917, the girl whose hat and shoes were in fashion carried "with her as she goes to church, to the theater or to work, no outward mark that betrays the meanness of her tiny room, nor the slenderness of her daily fare. She will be judged by her appearance, and that to her means her clothes."[16]

Like their street trading brothers, the girls who worked full-time had to lie and cheat to get the money they needed—and then lie again

St. Louis, 1910. Three young working girls, probably no more than fourteen years old and just out of school, wearing hats probably paid for with their own earnings. (*Lewis Hine Collection, NCLC*)

to buy what they wanted without divulging the true price to their mothers. It was easier on everyone involved to lie than to argue, whine, and plead for extra spending money. A working girl on Manhattan's West Side explained to Ruth True, an investigator for the Russell Sage Foundation, how most of the girls she worked with got the money they needed. "Oh sure, there's a lot of girls that 'knock down.' You take this week in our place,—we all made good overtime. I know I got two forty-nine. Well, I guess there wasn't a single girl but me that didn't change her [pay] envelope, on our floor. Whatever you make is written outside in pencil, you know. That's easy to fix—you have only to rub it out, put on whatever it usually is, and pocket the change."[17]

The children did not enjoy cheating their parents. They took no pleasure in lying, especially when they suspected that their parents recognized the lie. And yet they could find no other way to get the funds they needed. It cost money to have fun, money to belong, money to join in the life of the city. The children were not spendthrifts, thrill seekers, or bums. They took only what they had to have and surrendered the rest to their parents. The loyalty and sacrifice of teenage girls to their families was legendary. Even the newsies, who were considered much less reliable and responsible, turned over the bulk of their earnings to their parents. Harry Bremer, in his detailed study of New York City newboys, found that though most cheated their parents, almost all held back less than they handed in. Similar studies in Cincinnati (1919), Milwaukee (1911), and selected Connecticut cities (1921) confirmed these findings.[18]

The parents would not have been comforted by this bit of information. They demanded—and were convinced that it was their right to demand—all, not some of their children's earnings. There was no solution to this conflict, no compromise that would have left both sides content. The parents saw work as the core activity in life, with entertainment an infrequent break from routine. Adults were not in principle opposed to spending money for a good time, but they lacked the funds—and the financial security—to do it on a regular or casual basis. Even when times were good, there was tomorrow to worry about. Slack times, short weeks, pay cuts, and layoffs were facts of life. So were sickness in the family and workplace accidents.

Had the children had the responsibility of providing food, shelter, and clothing for large families, they might have agreed with their parents that money was too valuable to be spent on fun and games in the afternoon. But the circumstances of their daily lives militated against such conclusions. Here they were, only children, but children with money in their pockets in a city full of wonders. If the movies had cost a dollar or been located deep within the bowels of the fancy hotels, if pie à la mode at a lunch counter had cost more than a nickel, or a gallery seat for the vaudeville show more than a dime, the attraction would not have been as great. But the fact that pennies could buy a good time made that good time irresistible and those pennies a necessary part of life.

10

The Children
and the Child-Savers

The eleven- to fifteen-year-olds who worked and played on the streets of the city lived, as Samuel Ornitz put it, "several kinds of lives, traveling from planet to planet."[1] There were no magical moments of transition from childhood to adult life; one assumed adult responsibilities and shed childish roles over an extended period of years. Young teenagers had no choice but to live in two worlds at once: as children at home and in the classroom, as quasi-adult workers and consumers outside on the city streets. They and their parents regarded their alternating status as an unattractive but inescapable fact of urban life. Only the child labor reformers and their supporters refused to accept it as immutable. It was their belief, buttressed by theoretical concoctions based on G. Stanley Hall's work, that children under sixteen were not prepared to assume adult work roles and responsibilities, even part-time after school. Children forced into the workplace before they were constitutionally able would, it was argued, grow up morally, intellectually, and physically stunted.[2]

The argument was not without merit when applied to the reformers' primary targets: the textile mills, coal mines, canneries, and berry fields that employed children full-time. In each of these workplaces, youngsters were forced to sit, stand, stoop, or lie on their bellies, hour after hour, day after day. They emerged in the end with twisted bodies, damaged eyesight, and senses numbed by inactivity and lack of stimulation. They had, as the reformers argued, been deprived not only of their childhoods but of any reasonable chance of leading normal adult lives.

When the reformers turned their attention from the mill, mine, and cannery children to the street traders, their arguments lost their force and much of their validity. The street traders were not physically confined or constrained, nor were they deprived of sensory stimulation for the better part of the day. They were, on the contrary, freer to move on the streets than in the classrooms and no less stimulated. The street, as a workplace, was not without its dangers, especially vehicular, but these paled beside those that faced the children who carried molten glass in tongs from the furnace, shucked oysters with sharp knives in ice water that numbed the fingers, or picked through coal fragments sharp enough to slice fingers in light too dim to see.

The child labor reformers and their allies feared for the street traders not because they were exposed to physical danger or deprived of sensory

Paso Christian, Mississippi, February 1911. "All of these children shuck oysters and tend babies at the Pass Packing Company. I saw them all at work long before daybreak. Photos taken at room in the absence of the superintendent who refused me permission because of Child Labor agitation." The knives held up by the boys to the left were sharp enough to slice fingers to the bone. (*Lewis Hine Collection, NCLC*)

stimulation or physically confined during the daylight hours. They set out to save them from a different order of evils: from too much, not too little freedom, stimulation, and excitement.

To the untrained eye, the crowded downtown streets might not appear particularly dangerous. But for the reformers, the sources of danger to unformed morals and awakening libidos were ubiquitous. Primary among them were the signs, symbols, and displays of sexuality. As *Current Opinion* magazine reported in the summer of 1913, echoing the unspoken fears of many child-savers, "It has struck 'Sex O'Clock in America:' A wave of sex hysteria and sex discussion seems to have invaded this country." The invasion had first struck in the downtown sections of the city, where young middle-class women were for the first time seeking amusement after dark in public places "where neither the activities of the entertainers nor the behavior of the customers could be considered entirely respectable or predictable by nineteenth century standards." They dined in lobster palaces with unmarried men, attended the vaudeville show, danced the turkey trot in public, watched and applauded scantily clad chorus girls in girlie shows, smoked, drank, used "powder, rouge, lipstick, eyelash and eyebrow stain," and appeared to be practicing birth control to such an extent that President Roosevelt felt obliged to warn the nation of the dangers of "race suicide."[3]

Sex had reared its head in the tenement and working-class districts as well, and there was no way to hide the sight from the children. Reformers had always been worried about the effect on maturing children of growing up in overcrowded tenement flats with unrelated boarders sharing sleeping quarters and privies. This danger from inside the dwelling was now magnified a hundredfold by the explosion of sexuality on the street and in public. There were lewd posters outside the movie theaters and suggestive images on the screens. Even in cities where the movies were censored, dangers lurked inside. The Chicago Vice Commission, composed of reformers from organized religion, law, medicine, education, and the business community, warned the public about the darkened theaters where "boys and men slyly embrace the girls and offer cheap indignities." According to the commission, danger stalked the children not only in the movie theaters and cheap burlesque halls, but in the back rooms of confectionery and ice-cream parlors, in the amusement parks, dance halls, and lake steamers where corrupt young males waited to pounce on unsuspecting virgins, and even in the schools, where young girls had been spotted studying and "passing to one another" pornographic literature, pictures, and poems "describing in a most suggestive and obscene manner the experience of lovers."[4]

There was no way to shield the children from the sights they should not see. Prostitutes lived and worked in their neighborhoods, where rents were cheapest and neighbors least able to call for police or politicians to get rid of them. "They occupied vacant stores," wrote Mike Gold of his Lower East Side block. "They crowded into flats and apartments in all the tenements. The pious Jews hated the traffic. But they were pauper strangers here; they could do nothing. . . .

"They tried to shut their eyes. We children did not shut our eyes. We saw and knew."[5]

Prostitutes were a part of the life of the streets. The children played with them, teased them, and ran errands for them. There were no secrets—and very little shame—between the groups. They shared the same public space and had little choice but to get to know one another. The Chicago Vice Commission reported having discovered "a man [being] solicited by a prostitute standing on the porch of her home . . . while a number of young boys were playing in the street in front of this house." The commission was shocked; the children took it all in stride.[6]

Young teenagers were, the reformers feared, at risk on the streets of the city. Newly awakened to the passions and pressures of sexuality, they had to be protected from the city and from themselves. The boys especially seemed not to understand the gravity of the situation. They regarded neither the bums who gathered in the newspaper alleys nor the older men with money who solicited them after hours as true threats to their virtue. They did not often succumb to the adults' entreaties, but neither, to the reformers' distress, did they always flee in horror. The reformers were no doubt correct about the dangers, but they refused to understand that the boys were, most of the time, capable of taking care of themselves. Seldom did they venture into dark alleys by themselves— one did not sell very many papers in such places. There were some street gamins who sold themselves, but they too knew what they were doing: poverty as much as desire led them to accept the older men's offers.

The boys who sold themselves or gave themselves to men were few and far between. The danger, as the reformers presented it, was potential rather than actual. Far more real was the "threat" to the boys' "virtue" posed by easy women and prostitutes. The boys who sold papers late into the evenings or delivered messages to whorehouses could not help but come into contact with ladies of the night. Stories of messenger boys who had contracted venereal diseases from prostitutes were commonplace in the street trader tracts.[7]

The girls were, from the reformers' perspective, even more vulnerable. No matter how much the boys tomcatted about, they were not going to get pregnant. This was, of course, a major reason for the parents' differential treatment of their boys and girls. Though they might have disagreed with the reformers about the dangers posed to teenage boys,

Norfolk, Virginia, June 1911. "Raymond Bykes, Western Union No. 23, Norfolk, Va. Said he was fourteen years old. Works until after 1 A.M. every night. He is precocious and not a little 'tough.' Has been here at this office for only three months, but he already knows the Red Light district thoroughly and goes there constantly. He told me he often sleeps down at the Bay Line boat decks all night. Several times, I saw his mother hanging around the office, but she seemed more concerned about getting his pay envelope than anything else." (*Lewis Hine Collection, NCLC*)

they seemed to accept the warnings about their daughters. As one Irish mother confided to Ruth True in 1914, " 'You've got t'keep your eye on a girl. Now it's different with a boy. He can take care of himself. But you never can tell, if don't keep a watch, when a girl's going to come back an' bring disgrace on you.' "[8]

The streets were unhealthy and unwholesome for girls—with saloons on every corner, brothels within walking distance, and men and boys lurking nearby with their winks, their flattery, their coy invitations and rude remarks.[9] These first decades of the twentieth century brought a virtual avalanche of novels, first-person narratives, pamphlets, newspaper articles, and official Vice Commission reports on the perils that awaited young girls on city streets from young blades acting on their own, pimps who made a living corrupting innocent young girls, and the notorious white slavers. Much of it, especially the white-slavery reports and tracts, was exaggerated or just plain fictitious. But the public read the novels, and the newspapers reported on the Vice Commission findings—because, true or not, they articulated an anxiety that would not go away. Parents of young girls did not sleep easily at night, not because they feared turbaned white slavers would abduct their daughters, but because they knew how easy it was to get pregnant and what the consequences were for girls who were not married (or could not marry the prospective father).[10]

Every block had its "fallen girls." Every settlement-house worker had horror stories to tell about pregnant girls who had been thrown out of their homes or locked in basements by parents who wanted nothing more to do with the "soiled" creatures. For unmarried mothers and girls "in trouble" or suspected of sexual misconduct, there were few places to hide and fewer to turn for help. Not even the juvenile courts, the most "progressive" of legal institutions, showed mercy or understanding. While "delinquent" boys were routinely placed on probation, girls accused and convicted of sexual misconduct or precocity were sent away to reformatories or country workhouses. In *The Lost Sisterhood*, a history of prostitution in America, Ruth Rosen recounts the story of fifteen-year-old Deborah Horwitz, who "was brought into court for staying out with boys and 'flaunting' her sexual activities. Her probation officer, after ransacking her belongings, found a racy letter that the girl had written to a sailor, along with photos showing her with the top button of her blouse undone and her hat off. . . . Deborah, for her part, defiantly insisted that she had never coaxed or invited anyone's sexual attention. Nevertheless she was committed to the state reformatory for girls."[11]

Few girls landed in such difficulties, but such were the risks that had to be considered. The parents and reformers who spent time worrying about the girls' morals did so not because they were especially prudish or mistrustful but because they thought they knew the city and its dangers better than the girls did.

The adults should not have worried as much as they did. City kids were not nearly as naïve or as easily corrupted as they believed. Within their own circle of friends, they probed the mysteries and learned of the dangers—and the delights—that awaited them. Sex, though a forbidden topic of discussion with adults, was a constant one among the children. "There was a great curiosity about sex among the adolescent children of Williamsburg," wrote Betty Smith in *A Tree Grows in Brooklyn*. "There was a lot of talk about it. Among the younger children there was some exhibitionism (You show me and I'll show you). A few hypocrites devised such evasive games as 'playing house' or 'doctor.' A few uninhibited ones did what they called 'play dirty.'" In the Bronx, Kate Simon, who discovered at age ten that she was "lost" when it came to the important topics of discussion—"things, breasts, love"—quickly sought out the "older girls who knew everything." By age twelve, she too believed she knew everything.[12]

Neither boys nor girls sought information or advice from their parents. Sex was something you discussed with your friends but didn't mention to adults. Children kept quiet because they did not want to confess that they thought about such things *and* because they knew no adult would answer their questions.

The more one reads in the autobiographies of the children who grew up in this era and in the reports of the Vice Commissions, the settlement-house workers, the child labor reformers, and Juvenile Court officials, the more apparent it becomes that it was the adults, not the children, who were most obsessed with juvenile sexuality. While some girls "played dirty," and some boys visited whorehouses, few ventured into areas they could not extricate themselves from. The reformers and parents were too worried by the potential dangers of city life to notice how well the children handled their environment.

There were two possible solutions to the problem the reformers diagnosed: they could cleanse the city of its moral pollutants or quarantine the susceptible. Since the first option was impossible because it neces-sitated infringing on the right of businessmen to make their living, the reformers were compelled to take the second. They campaigned to remove the children from the street because they were convinced that the less time they spent there, the less vulnerable they would be to its dangers. The street and its extensions—the movie theaters, vaudeville halls, amusement parks, penny arcades, and candy shops—were the only places where the children were free of adult supervision and control, the only places where they were allowed, even encouraged, to act more grown-up than was good for them. By isolating them from the environ-ments that fostered precocity, the reformers would succeed in returning them to the status of full-time children, protected morning, noon, and evening from the temptations, the excitement, the sounds and sights of urban life.

The task was overwhelming, but the reform community was not without its allies and its resources. Together, the child labor activists, settlement-house workers, juvenile justice authorities, and the legions of professionals and well-meaning amateurs who supported their campaign accomplished a great deal. With the unacknowledged assistance of the economic shifts that had rendered the children less vital a component of the labor force, the reformers succeeded in passing omnibus compulsory schooling and child labor laws in most states outside the south. As the reformers, however, were quick to discover, it was one thing to get laws passed and quite another to get them enforced. Legislation, by itself, accomplished nothing. Only when the parents—and the police—agreed with the aims and ends of the legislation could it be enforced. Such was the case with the statutes that prohibited girls under a certain age from working on the streets. When it came to the large number of statutes that regulated and limited the work of the boys, however, the laws might as well have never been written.

From the reformers' perspective, the chief culprits were the police. They not only were sworn to uphold the laws but should have under-stood—far better than the parents—the necessity for enforcing them. Policemen were ready to hassle child gamblers, junkers, trespassers, but they did not go out of their way to enforce the laws that restricted those without proper licenses from peddling or hawking papers on city streets. The problem with the policemen—again, from the reformers' perspec-tive—was that they thought too much like the children's parents. Youngsters trying to earn money on the streets were not, they believed, doing anything terribly wrong. Why then should the police have to waste their time and energy arresting and testifying against them in Children's Court?[13]

Because the police could not be counted on to enforce the street trader ordinances, the reformers tried to secure enforcement powers for civilians—and succeeded. In cities across the country, agents of child welfare organizations, truant officers, factory inspectors, and in some states "any person" who wished to make and prosecute a complaint were empowered to arrest children violating child labor laws.[14]

In New York City, the Gerry Society—the children's nickname for the Society for the Prevention of Cruelty to Children (taken from the society's President, Elbridge Gerry)—was able to put its own private policemen onto the streets in great enough numbers to keep the children on their toes. According to Lillian Wald of the Henry Street Settlement, the society's special officers became such a bugaboo that the children invented their own "Gerryman" game: the child chosen as "it" had to chase the other kids on the block.[15]

While the Gerry Society regarded all city kids as within its purview, it devoted special attention to those who worked on the stage. Like the Juvenile Protective Association in Chicago, the society did all it could to "protect" child actors and performers working in amateur shows, on vaudeville stages, and in legitimate theaters. Though, to the audience,

New York City, July 1910. "Against the Law in New York City—But 'Who Cares'?" Hine's caption comments on the fact that the policeman instead of arresting this girl for breaking the law smilingly poses for a photograph with her. (*Lewis Hine Collection, NCLC*)

the child performers might appear secure and protected, the reformers were convinced that they were endangered by their work: compelled to stay up too late, to linger before and after their performances in darkened theaters, and to spend too much time in the company of actors and actresses, not the most wholesome of adult companions.[16]

According to Milton Berle, the Gerry Society's campaign in New York City was so successful that most kiddie acts were forced to flee the Broadway theaters for the neighborhood vaudeville halls, where the Gerrymen were less likely to find them. Even in the sticks, however, the children had to take special precautions. When Milton performed at the Mt. Morris Theater at 116th Street and Fifth Avenue, he sang his songs from a box overlooking the stage so that he would not be arrested by the Gerrymen for performing *on* the stage.

As Berle remembered in his autobiography, Eddie Foy had enough clout to perform with his "seven little Foys" whenever he wanted. Buster Keaton "could work because he looked older. (When he was old enough to work without fear of the Society, he took an ad in *Variety*: 'Today I am a Theatrical Man—Goodbye, Mr. Gerry!')" Milton, unfortunately, looked ten when he was ten. With his Buster Brown haircut and kid's tuxedo—white shirt with dark buttons, jacket, knickers, and long socks—

146

he was a target wherever he appeared. On one memorable evening, he was greeted by a policeman as he left the stage. "Mama was there too, and, just like so many of the heroines she had loved in silent movies, she pushed herself with an arm-outspread gesture between the cop and me. 'What? What is it, officer? Don't you dare touch that boy. . . .'

" 'Well, we've had a complaint from the Gerry Society that minors were working on this stage. I'm going to have to take the kid down to the station.'

"Mama was always a fast thinker. 'What station house? Which one?'

"The cop told her. Mama smiled. 'I don't think you'll like it when you bring my son in. Isn't the sergeant on duty there named McCloskey?'

Mrs. Berle went on to explain that she was a fellow officer of the law, a store detective, and on the best of terms with all the big shots in the precinct. " 'I sure don't think Sergeant McCloskey's going to like it when a fellow law-enforcement officer's child is arrested and put away like a common criminal.' "

"The poor guy was sweating. 'Well, I didn't know. . . . Look, I think we can forget this whole thing, but why don't you take your son and get out of here fast, okay?' "

Mama and Milton won that battle, but not the war. They eventually had to relocate in Philadelphia, where the society was not strong enough to "protect us [child actors] right into the poor house."[17]

The stage children were a special breed. They were part of an adult world and worked as individual acts rather than as a group. They were, as a result, easy pickings for law enforcement agents. The children who hustled on the streets were more fortunate. They worked their own turf, in groups, and were too numerous to be effectively policed. Periodically, when the pressure from the reform groups grew too great to be deflected, the mayor would contact the police commissioner, who would call out his men in a street trader raid. Unlike the brothel owners, who were also subject to this brand of law enforcement, the children paid no one off and were not warned in advance of the raids.

On May 20th, 1913, the New York *Times*, in a front-page story, reported that "Seventeen little boys and two small girls were arrested at the New York end of the Williamsburg Bridge last night." The children ranged in age from twelve to fifteen and had been nabbed for selling chewing gum and candy. (Children under sixteen were too young to get licenses to sell anything but newspapers.) Though the newspaper article said only that "a complaint" to the mayor's office had led to the raid, we can trace its genesis through documents in the Lillian Wald Papers at Columbia University.[18]

Miss Wald, a well-known member of the city's reform community and one of the founding members of the New York Child Labor

147

Committee, had on May 15th written a long letter complaining to the Gerry Society about the child peddlers at the entrance to the Williamsburg Bridge. "A little girl, twelve years old, Gussie Cohen of 109 Essex Street sells gum and candy at the head of the stairs leading to track No. 6 every afternoon except when her place is taken by her little brother, who is considerably smaller. Their mother sells papers at the entrance outside. Two or three boys who do not appear to be more than ten years old have been noticed selling gum at other entrances to the Bridge."

The Gerry Society, on receipt of the letter, must have contacted the mayor's office, which pressured the police commissioner to set up the raid that led to the arrest of the "seventeen little boys and two small girls." On June 11th, a Mr. Walsh of the society wrote back to Miss Wald informing her that the children selling gum had "been taken into custody. . . . In the case of the Cohen children, the case was brought before Children's Court where the mother was warned by Justice Mayo who on May 24th released the children to her custody on suspension of sentence."

We do not know if Gussie and her brother returned to the bridge to sell gum. We do know, however, that within six weeks of the first raid, enough children had resumed their trade to bring the police back a second time.

As might have been expected, the second raid was as unsuccessful as the first. Miss Wald, on July 26th, again contacted Mr. Walsh. "For a few days after the arrests made by your Society on July 10, there were very few, if any, children to be seen, but I am sorry to say that there are now as many of them as ever, both girls and boys. On Thursday afternoon of this week, at about five o'clock, I counted fifteen children peddling gum, and I have seen these or other children each afternoon. A boy of ten, named Tushberg, sells gum at the head of the stairs leading to the Brooklyn Elevated trains. . . . Three sisters named Rosen, the youngest apparently not more than nine, sell gum at various entrances to the Bridge. They are sharp little things, and run away if they are asked any questions. . . . I regret to say that some of the child peddlers now recognize me as what they call 'a detective lady' and keep out of sight at the time when I usually appear. It may be necessary for me to go to the Bridge at unexpected times hereafter in order to keep track of the situation."[19]

Miss Wald could have moved her parlor onto the bridge; she was not going to clear it of child peddlers. The children were too smart to be intimidated. They knew, perhaps even better than she, that business at the bridge would return to normal the day after each raid. The police were not interested in arresting child peddlers on a daily basis. The Gerry Society might have been, but lacked the resources to do the job.

The children were also protected by their informal organization. As Miss Wald had discovered, the young street traders had their own early-warning system. Should trouble appear in the form of police, truant officers, "detective ladies," or other suspicious adults, the word was quickly, quietly, and efficiently passed up the street, round the corner, and down the next one. The "word" and the children moved too fast for the adults.

The reformers ran themselves—and at times the police—ragged in their attempts to get the children off the streets. In a 1905 issue of *Charities* magazine, James Paulding described a series of raids on New York City newsies. The New York Child Labor Committee, which had campaigned for and won legislative approval of a newsboy licensing law in 1903, had since then been battling with the police commissioner to get the law enforced. After much stalling, Commissioner McAdoo agreed in the spring of 1905 to detail a special squad to arrest crooked newsies. According to Paulding, the four-man squad, though taking care to disguise themselves in plain clothes, had not succeeded in making many arrests. "The boys are very quick to 'spot' a 'copper', even when he is in plain clothes, and a rumor of the presence of these particular men was quickly noised abroad."[20]

Nothing united the kids or spurred them into action like the sight of a truant officer or policeman rounding the corner. As Harpo Marx put it, "one way, the only way, that all of us kids stuck together regardless of nationality [or gang] was in our cop-warning system. Much as I loathed and feared the Mickie gang or the Bohunk gang, I'd never hesitate to give them the highsign if I spotted a copper headed their way. They'd do the same for me and the other 93rd Streeters."

The children's cooperation on the streets extended beyond such early-warning systems. In those cities with licensing requirements for street traders* the children did their best—and it was usually enough—to foil the intent of the laws.

The licensing or badge system was, in theory, an efficient and effective way to regulate street trading. Children who wanted to sell papers (and, in some cities, other items as well) had to secure licenses or badges and wear them when they worked. Those too young or too far behind in their schooling or too weak, sickly, or small would be denied licenses and, thus, barred from the streets.

Had the children cooperated, the laws might have accomplished their end. Children without licenses would have been easily spotted by

---

* Boston has in 1892 passed the first city ordinance requiring newsies to apply for and wear badges when selling on the streets. By 1915, eleven states and several municipalities had similar legislation.[21]

law enforcement officials and removed from the streets. Unfortunately for the reformers, the children saw no reason to cooperate. They were not lawless creatures. Their own laws of the street, though unwritten, remained sacrosanct. Only those laws that made no sense or were intended, as they saw it, to harass or limit their mobility, autonomy, and profits had to be broken—and broken they were.

The children did not subvert the law by organized protest or resistance. They simply played with it and with the officials who tried to make it work. Children eligible for badges applied for them even though they had no intention of using them. Those who had other jobs or were so big no one would ever accuse them of being underage, sold their badges to kids too young or far behind in their schooling to get their own. Some bigger kids secured licenses, sold them to little kids, then— claiming they had lost their badges—got new ones for their own use. Children forged their parents' signatures, used aliases, and gave wrong addresses to keep the authorities from visiting their homes. In Newark, officials were baffled by the way the children flung open their coats to

St. Louis, 1910. (*Lewis Hine Collection, NCLC*)

reveal the badges underneath until they realized that the newsies were mimicking what policemen did in the movies when asked for identification. In New York City, the boys wore their badges close to the body under layers and layers of clothing. When asked to produce them, they protested at first and then began stripping down to their long underwear, embarrassing the officials and giving their friends without badges plenty of time to disappear around the corner.[22]

In city after city, the officials responsible for the enforcement of the street trader laws were outmaneuvered and outwitted. According to published and unpublished reports from Newark, Birmingham, Milwaukee, Cleveland, and Cincinnati, the children either disregarded the law or played with it.[23]

In New York State, where the Child Labor Committee undertook two extensive investigations of enforcement, they were dismayed but not surprised to find that in most cities the officials had given up entirely. In Syracuse, the school authorities reported in 1909 that they no longer issued badges because "it was a waste of time and material." In Albany, the truant officers were overwhelmed with so much other work that "it is impossible for them to give any time to newsboys." In Utica, the officials had tried their best to enforce the law but had been made fools of by the children. "When the law became effective we announced that all boys must have badges, and immediately there was a rush, and something like four hundred were issued." Unfortunately, few of the four hundred boys who applied had any intention of using their badges to sell papers. Most bought them to resell to kids too young to obtain theirs legally.[24]

In 1918, when the committee dispatched Ethel Hanks to evaluate the enforcement of the child labor laws in the state's smaller cities, she found that only Auburn among the nine cities she visited was enforcing the laws "with a fair degree of success." In Binghamton, the superintendent of schools had stopped issuing badges three years before because "it was impossible to secure full cooperation from the police in keeping small boys off the streets." In Elmira, Niagara Falls, Poughkeepsie, and Jamestown, the law was enforced only "partially." Some boys sold with badges, some without. The police didn't seem to care one way or another. In Tonawanda and North Tonawanda no one wore badges. In Kingston, no badges had been issued because the superintendent of schools did not know—or so he claimed—that the law applied to his city.[25]

Supervisor Purcell of New York City's Second Attendance District and his assistant, Attendance Officer Wheatley, were not far from the mark when they complained that enforcing the laws had become nearly impossible because of a "free masonry among the boys."[26]

Ironically, it was in those cities where the reformers were most active and effective that the laws were most useless. In Boston, often cited by other reformers for its model street trader ordinance, the newsies neither applied for nor wore badges, the truant officers were too few in number to enforce the law themselves, and the School Committee which had been given responsibility for enforcement had no money to hire new truant officers and no way of enforcing the law without them.[27] In desperation the School Committee hired Philip Davis, the future author of *Street-land,* as Supervisor of Licensed Minors and entrusted him with full responsibility for enforcing the street ordinances.

Davis recognized at once the golden opportunity created by the breakdown of the system. Concluding from recent experience that the only way to establish enforceable laws was to enlist the boys in writing and enforcing them, he set out to interest the newsies and the School Committee in an experimental, self-government, self-enforcement plan.† With the support of the School Committee—and of the boys themselves—elections were held in the local public schools to choose delegates to a "constitutional convention." On June 17, 1908, Bunker Hill Day, some three thousand newsies gathered in the Boston Theater to ratify their new constitution and officially establish the Boston Newsboys' Republic, the now official governing body for all city newsies, eleven to fourteen years of age.[28]

The Boston newsies took their republic seriously, as Davis had hoped they would. Now that they had the power to make the laws and enforce them in their own courts, they would try to bring them into harmony with the demands of their trade.

To the delight of the adults, the boys' first official acts were raising the minimum ages (for bootblacks from ten to twelve and newsies from ten to eleven) and lowering the curfew (from 10 P.M. to 8 P.M. for all street traders). The boys were not motivated in either of these decisions by the belief that children did not belong on the streets. They were simply trying to bring some order into their trade. Restricting the younger kids removed the competition of little ones who relied on cuteness and innocent looks to steal customers from establishe newsies. Cutting back the curfew reduced working hours without decreasing sales or profits. If adult customers knew that the curfew was going to be enforced and that they would not be able to find newsies or bootblacks on the streets after eight, they would get their papers and shines earlier in the evening, leaving the boys free to go home—or to the movies. When, a year and a half later, the boys realized that their eight o'clock curfew was too early on those special nights "like the night of the million dollar South End

---

† As Davis himself later admitted, his idea was not original, but modeled on the George Junior Republic in upstate New York and the Newsboys' Association in Toledo, Ohio.

fire" when people stayed out late, they petitioned the School Committee for permission to extend the curfew for these occasions. The committee, impressed by their arguments, accepted their proposal.[29]

The cornerstone of the republic was the newsboys' court. With its boy judges (none older than fourteen), its mock-judicial style, and the wisdom embodied in its judgments, the court made quite an impression. In an article for *Outlook* magazine, Lyman Beecher Stowe reported enthusiastically on his visit to the court. "On the bench sat two boy judges, one a Polish Jew, who was acting as presiding Judge, and the other a Negro." The first case involved a twelve-year-old who had been caught jumping on and off streetcars. The judge reprimanded him, warning him that hopping cars was "not only dangerous . . . but there's no money in it, because they was covered at the terminal by the big fellers an' there isn't hardly anybody gets in between there an' this crossing. So you run the risk of gettin' hurt and losin' your license for nothin'."[30] (Translation: Most streetcar riders boarded downtown at the station where they bought their evening papers. The independent newsie, jumping on and off the cars, would consequently find few customers to sell to.)

Judgments such as this were accepted by the boys because they

Boston. Downtown newsies jumped on and off streetcars like this one, selling their papers in the aisle, then moving on to other cars full of potential customers. (*Lewis Hine Collection, NCLC*)

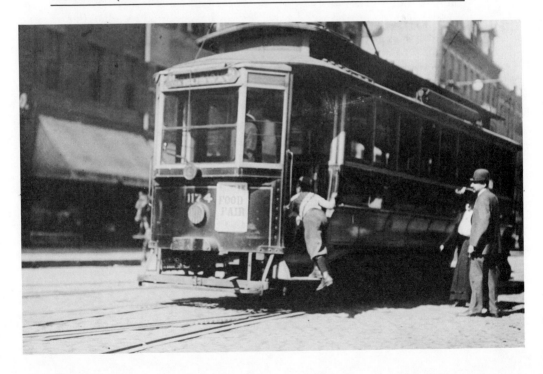

were so eminently reasonable. The judge was not moralizing or treating the accused as an irresponsible minor. He was not even saying that "hopping cars" was wrong because it was dangerous. He was merely pointing out that the potential profit involved in hopping this particular streetcar was not worth the risk of bodily injury.

The next case was that of a boy charged with illegally lending his badge. "The mother of the boy who had lent the badge appeared and explained that they did not need the money which the boy made, and that she and his father would much rather he would not sell papers. She urged the Court to revoke his license.

"The young Judges then questioned the boy. If the family did not need the money, why did he want to sell papers? He wanted to earn some pocket money. Didn't his parents give him any spending money? They never had. At this point the Court asked the mother whether she was able and willing to give the boy some spending money. She said she was, and she finally agreed to give the boy 20¢ a week, provided he would give up selling papers. The boy agreed, and the Court sealed the bargain by canceling the license."[31]

Here too, the court, fully cognizant of the child's point of view, reached a solution to the problem acceptable to both parties. Not all cases were settled as easily as these and not all judgments rendered with as much common sense and as little moralizing. Still, the court provided its adult observers with a changed perspective on the boys' capacities for self-government. The boys behaved with a maturity and dignity befitting their situation. They displayed respect for one another and for the law which, in this courtroom at least, they were committed to upholding.

Not least among the wonders of the court were its judges, all of whom were newsies elected by their peers. An article in *Survey* magazine for December 2, 1911, entitled "Horatio Alger, Then and Now," described the 1911 election for new judges. The election assembly was called to order by sixteen-year-old Judge Harry Hornstein, "one of the original newsboys court judges," who exhorted the newsies to see "the best boys win out, no matter what their color or religion or school is." The five candidates presented their positions, the votes were taken and counted, and Michael Berman, Abe Resnick, and Henry Brown were duly elected. Brown was, the article reported, "a colored boy from Dorchester."[32]

When Lyman Beecher Stowe visited the newsboys' court, he carefully observed this black judge (or perhaps another) deferring to his Polish Jewish colleague. While the latter was active in every stage of the proceedings, the black judge sat quietly on the bench saying little, if anything. At the conclusion of the session, Stowe approached the white judge to ask why the "colored judge appear[ed] to take so little part.

. . . 'Oh [the boy answered wistfully] he does his share all right, only he kinder lies low because, you see, some people don't like niggers.' " Stowe, impressed and moved by the courage and tolerance of the boys who, despite the racism rampant in their community, had seen fit to elect a black judge, took this as one more sign of the boys' capacity for self-government. He concluded his article with the plea that other cities follow the Boston example.[33]

Stowe was going to be disappointed. Though, according to Philip Davis, cities "from Portland, Maine to Portland, Oregon" inquired about the Boston system, only Birmingham (Alabama) and Milwaukee "adopted [it] in whole or in part."

It was in Milwaukee that the system got its truest test. The Milwaukee Newsboys' Republic, established in 1912, was modeled on the Boston one. The boys elected their own congressmen, policemen, and judges; they wrote their own laws and held their own newsboys' court. According to the published reports, the Milwaukee experiment proved as successful as the Boston original. Taxpayer money was saved as cases were shifted from the Juvenile Court to the newsboys' court, and the street trader laws, which had been "practically useless" because unenforceable, were rescued from oblivion.[34]

Though the boys no doubt accepted and supported the republic because it gave them the power to regulate their own trade, the adult reformers who celebrated the experiment in Milwaukee were more impressed by the "splendid opportunity" it furnished "for the training of future citizens." According to *Outlook*, the republic "bids fair to make for law and order among the boys who have always constituted one of the worst problems of the social workers. . . . It cannot fail to be a splendid instrument for the making of future citizens of the United States. When one considers the cosmopolitan character of Milwaukee's population, this little democracy, with its American Chief Justice, its German President, and its Russian-Jew Vice-President, becomes an important agent for the assimilation of our second and third generations of foreigners."[35]

Common sense and practical success did not lead to longevity or expansion for these experiments in self-government. Philip Davis and Perry Powell, his counterpart in Milwaukee, might have trusted the children to regulate their own trade with justice, efficiency, and wisdom. But these were exceptional men. Elsewhere (and in Boston after Davis's retirement), it was the accepted wisdom that the street traders were too young, too foreign, and too common to be given any responsibility at all. The self-government plans foundered because they gave the children precisely what most adults, including the reformers, were convinced they should not have: a degree of autonomy on the streets. The newsboys' republics might have succeeded in putting back into operation long-disregarded ordinances and statutes, but they had accomplished this at a price most reformers were not willing to pay. When given the choice, most preferred allowing the laws to remain unenforced to giving the children the responsibility for managing their own affairs.

The Boston Newsboys' Republic survived only as long as Philip Davis remained Superintendent of Licensed Minors. His successor, on taking office, disestablished the republic and replaced the court's newsie judges with an appointed adult. As might have been expected, the boys refused to accept the new superintendent's authority. Instead of cooperating to enforce the laws, as they had done under their republic, they pulled together to evade his futile attempts to police the streets by himself. According to one investigator, Davis's successor was quickly and easily outwitted by the children he was supposed to be supervising. "The boys know him too well and give warning up and down the line as soon as he comes in sight." Madeleine Appel, in her own informal canvas of

Boston, January 23, 1917, 4 P.M. "Group of newsies selling in front of South Station. Four of them said they were eleven years old. Saw no badges in evidence." (*Lewis Hine Collection, NCLC*)

the busier Boston districts, found that less than one half of the boys were properly licensed. The majority hawked their papers in open violation of the laws.[36]

In the long run, it was those adults who believed in the sanctity of the laws who suffered the most from the failure of the experiments to take root. Without the children's cooperation, the street trader laws were unenforceable—and the children knew it. Try as they might, the reformers could not solve the problem. They rewrote the laws, shifting responsibility for enforcement from police to school officials and back again. It made little difference. The children had learned from experience that as long as they cooperated to regulate their own trade and evade laws they considered unreasonable there was little the officials could do. The children were too many, and the strength of their informal ties too strong, for the adults to succeed in regulating their activities on the street.

Working Together

T he reformers could not help worrying about the street traders. How, they wondered, could eleven- to fifteen-year-olds care for themselves away from home, school, and the block? What the adults failed to understand was that the children who left school and home to work downtown were not abandoned like orphans to the storm. They entered the life of an active, organized community with its own structures of authority, law, and order. The streets were not jungles and the children were not savages.

The children, as we have seen, took care of one another at play on the block. They continued the practice on the downtown streets of the city where they worked every afternoon. Big kids watched after smaller ones, experienced hustlers taught newcomers the rules of the game, streetwise veterans took the rookies under their protection. As an editorial writer in the trade journal *Editor and Publisher* observed of the newsies, "To the credit of the bigger lads be it said, the younger boys, if they behave decently and honorably are actually pushed in and helped by the elder."[1]

Instead of bullying or beating up the little ones, the older hustlers entered into cooperative business relationships with them. The newsies had their own apprenticeship system. Children starting out on the streets could, if they chose—and many did—work as "strikers" for older boys. In return for a commission of up to 50 percent, the big boys provided the strikers with papers to hawk, a place to sell, and protection when necessary. While the big boys expanded their coverage and their profits, the younger ones were spared the hassle of dealing with circulation managers, paying cash in advance for their papers, and having to worry about those they could not sell.[2]

The older children helped out the younger ones as a matter of course *and* because it was good for business. It was the accepted wisdom on the streets that customers would rather buy from a cute young kid than an adolescent who needed a shave. The little ones were also better salesmen. While the older boys were too mature and dignified to run up and down the streets shouting their wares, "the youngster," according to Maurice Hexter in Cincinnati, "takes keen delight in making his voice resound because he just 'loves to holler' and looks upon salesmanship as a game."[3]

Though self-interest was no doubt behind much of the elder boys' cooperation with the rookies, there were many instances where the big ones had nothing to gain from helping out but helped out nonetheless. Harry Bremer, an investigator for the National Child Labor Committee, discovered on a Saturday night visit to Jersey City that the younger children who sold the *Sunday World* on Saturday evenings got their papers from the older newsies, who routinely went "over to the World Building in New York . . . to bring back a supply for all." The same informal arrangement held among the Elizabeth, New Jersey, newsies. "The older boys go in to New York City about four o'clock Sunday morning and bring papers out" for themselves and the younger boys to sell.[4]

There was nothing in the least extraordinary about such cooperative relationships. Children of different ages were quite accustomed to working and playing together on the streets. Today, when children are more likely to accept the propriety of strict age grading carried over from the classroom, fifth-graders play only with fifth-graders, fourth-graders with fourth-graders. At the turn of the century, such age segregation made little sense. Though most of the boys, as David Macleod has observed, probably preferred playing with children no more than three years younger than they were,[5] children regularly worked and played on the streets with their siblings and with their siblings' friends and classmates. The arrangement benefited everyone. Older street traders got the use of younger brothers and sisters as unpaid assistants, the little ones got to stay out on the streets with their older brothers and sisters, and parents rested easier knowing that the older children were watching over the younger.

A good many of the tiniest street traders—who appeared to be alone—were in fact working with older siblings. A concerned citizen who lived on Madison Avenue in New York City contacted the Charity Organization Society in 1906 to report a boy no more than six years old who she claimed was selling papers in all sorts of weather on the street corner. The society, a reform group which investigated such cases, sent out a special "visitor," who promptly reported back that the child in question was neither abandoned nor orphaned nor the victim of parental exploitation. He was simply helping out his big brothers, who owned the corner newsstand.[6] In Chicago, another concerned citizen, this one a lawyer, made a similar request to the Illinois Humane Society. Touched by the plight of a "girl about eight years old who has only one leg [and] sells papers at 18th Street and Wabash," the lawyer informed the society that he had "on evenings bought all of her papers and at other times [given] to her 20¢, 30¢, and 50¢." He asked the Humane Society to find out if the girl were indeed a worthy recipient of charity. The investigator sent out on the case never did find the little girl; but he did track down her mother, who admitted readily that the girl sold papers on the street, but always in the company of her brother. Surely, the mother asked the investigator, there could be nothing wrong with a little girl helping out her big brother. As the investigator departed, the mother asked that he please see that the gentleman who had been leaving the large tips was thanked for his kindness.[7]

Not all family groupings were as innocent as these. The good samaritans who worried about the little ones alone on the streets never seemed to notice their big brothers—for a very good reason. The big boys stayed out of sight so that the little ones would appear to be by themselves. Living tableaux were artfully constructed to elicit sympathy, sales, and tips from well-meaning customers. Tiny, innocent-looking children properly presented were worth their weight in pennies. The well-tutored "waif," standing alone on a corner meekly holding out some item for sale, was hard to resist. Only the trained observer would look for the older sibling across the street.

William Hard, a Chicago journalist, followed 'Jelly,' an Italian newsboy, one Saturday night on the way to the elevated railway station to meet his ten-year-old sister. "She had dressed herself for the part. From her ragged and scanty wardrobe she had chosen her most ragged and her scantiest clothes. Accompanied by his sister, 'Jelly' then went to a flowershop and bought a bundle of carnations at closing prices. With these carnations he took his sister to the entrance of the Grand Opera House. There she sold the whole bundle to the people coming from the performance. Her appearance was picturesque and pitiful. . . . As soon as the flowers were sold and the people had gone away, 'Jelly' took his sister back to the elevated station. There he counted the money she had made and put it in his pocket. He then handed her out a nickel for carfare and, in addition, a supplementary nickel for herself."[8]

The children of the street cooperated with one another for purposes other than deceiving potential adult customers. They worked together to regulate their trade and protect their profits from the employers, suppliers, circulation managers, and publishers, who were interested in soaking the last ounce of profit from their labor. The eleven- to fifteen-year-olds who worked every afternoon on the downtown streets of the city did not have to read Locke or Rousseau to understand that, without some form of "social contract," life on the streets would be pure hell. Each downtown district had only a finite number of busy intersections, streetcar stops, train stations, and good "corners." Had all the children battled daily for the few key spots, none would have had time or energy left to sell their wares.

The children maintained order on the streets by respecting one another's property rights. They did not recognize the rights of railroads to the "stuff" on the tracks or the rights of landlords to the copper wire left behind in empty houses, but children who had built up a trade on a corner deserved to have their property protected.

Adult observers were astounded by the children's loyalty to one another and their unwritten laws. Jacob Riis questioned one thirteen-year-old newsie as to why he didn't try to take away the "corner" from the older boy who owned it. "He has no more right to the corner than you have," Riis egged the boy on. "Why don't you fight him for it?"

" 'He's my boss,' was the dogged reply.

" 'But suppose some stronger fellow drove him away?'

"The answer was prompt:

" 'I'd get other boys and get it back for him.'. . .

" 'Did you ever hear of anyone taking a boy's corner—just taking it?'

" 'I hearld of it, but I never knowed it. It is *his* corner.' "[9]

In Milwaukee, Alexander Fleisher engaged another newsie in the same dialogue; he, too, was intrigued by the boys' commitment to their laws. Right, not might, seemed to rule on the streets. Fleisher asked one of the bigger boys why he didn't take over the "Palm Garden," one of the better spots for selling papers. The boy answered that he would not even consider moving into territory "owned" by others. "If the policeman did not interfere, the other boys on the street would, and in the end it would be impossible for him to sell papers at all."

By collectively legitimizing the property rights of established street traders, the children brought order to the streets and provided for a smooth transition from generation to generation. When traders got ready to leave the streets for other work, they could hand over title to their corners—and their customers—to younger brothers or sell it to the highest bidders. There was a going rate for each piece of real estate, established by the children who bid on it. Once the new owner paid the price, the location became his. Any child who wanted to work there had to pay him a commission.[10]

The children enforced their laws in their own ways. The police were not going to do it for them. The standard punishment for trespassing was being chased away and, if caught, beaten up. Dominic Pavano, who had been chased off a corner at Park Row near City Hall, explained to a New York Child Labor Committee investigator that "a big boy, stranger to him, accosted him, asked him how much he made, and then took the money from him by force and ran away, telling him he would be killed the next time he came there." Harry Browne had also been "chased off" a corner that did not belong to him. Harry complained to the investigators that "it was very hard for a 'white boy' to make anything at paper selling [because] the Jews and Italians hung together to hold the most profitable places and corners." Harry would either not admit or had not yet figured out that his problem had less to do with race than with the territorial imperatives of street trading. He had been chased away not because he was "a white boy," but because he had been horning in on someone else's trade and territory.[11]

Most newsies did not get into trouble as Dominic and Harry had. They stayed away from "owned" corners or made a deal with the owner. The unwritten laws of the street were so well known and obeyed that there was little need for violence. Mervyn LeRoy, the Hollywood producer, recalled in his autobiography that in San Francisco, just after the 1906 earthquake, "newsboys had to battle it out for choice corners."[12] But his experience was exceptional. Other autobiographical accounts and the dozens of published and unpublished newsboy studies report little in the way of violence. The children were too busy trying to earn money to waste time fighting one another. They were, in fact, so well organized and law-abiding that one New York City truant officer complained that the small boys who should have been looking to the police for "protection as to trade and territory" were looking to the older newsies instead.[13]

Most newspaper circulation managers relied on the boys to regulate their own street trades. They not only refrained from interfering, but did what they could to enforce the boys' unwritten laws by refusing to sell papers to newsies who did not properly "own" the territory they sold from. As the Seattle *Post-Intelligencer* informed its readers in October 1917, "Newsboys hold squatter title to corners and buy and sell them from each other. The newspapers have no financial interest in the corners, but, with the police, recognize established 'titles' in the interest of order."[14]

Unwritten laws governed the boys' behavior in the newspaper offices and distribution centers as well as in the streets. The sooner the boys got their papers in the afternoon, the sooner they could start selling them; no newsie wanted to be stuck in line while outside in the streets customers began looking for their afternoon editions. In most cities, the boys established and followed a simple seniority system. The older newsies got their papers as soon as these arrived from the press rooms. When they had been served, the rest of the boys lined up to get theirs.[15]

The circulation managers and their assistants worked with the boys to smooth out kinks in the distribution system. In Portland, Oregon, where there had been "continual fighting and hard feeling over the Saturday night places" on the line, the "circulator," a former newsie,

---

St. Louis, May 1910. A photograph of "Burns Basement Branch." The boys have lined up to get their afternoon papers from the assistant circulation manager. The older boys are at the front of the line, the younger ones just behind. (*Lewis Hine Collection, LC*)

proposed a solution. The "regular midnight boys" who sold every night would get their papers first, followed by the "boys who only sell Saturday nights." The new procedure, it was hoped, would "eliminate some of the hard feeling and wrangling." The boys, knowing that the better regulated the distribution process, the sooner they would all get their papers, agreed to give the proposal a trial run. If it worked they would support it; if not, they would return to the old system. The decision, in any event, would be theirs.[16]

Newsies, unfortunately, did not always get along so famously with the adults they did business with. The boys helped to organize their own distribution systems when they could. There were, however, times and places where this was not possible. In cities where the boys were too spread out for centrally located distribution offices to serve them all, the circulation managers hired truckers to deliver the papers at their corners. Though this system saved the hustlers a great deal of time, it made it more difficult for them to join together to protect their interests. In Cincinnati, for example, the boys, isolated from one another geographically, found themselves at the mercy of the supply men who, according to Maurice Hexter, regularly extorted bribes to insure delivery "at the earliest possible moment, when the demand for the edition is strongest. One little chap told [Hexter] that he usually gave his supply man a silk shirt for Christmas"—probably in addition to weekly bribes.[17]

When the publishers and circulation managers were too thickheaded to understand the children's worth or their potential organized strength, the boys had to—and did—take special measures to bring them back to their senses. In Boston, where the newspapers in 1901 unilaterally changed the distribution procedures, the newsies appealed directly to the publishers for a return to the status quo. When, as should have been expected, the publishers refused to listen to their grievances, the boys organized themselves into a union, applied for and were granted an AFL charter, and sent off an official delegation to bargain with the manager of one of the city's leading dailies. When they were again rebuffed and even humiliated by the manager, who refused to negotiate and "took occasion to make sport of [their union, the boys] declared a boycott. . . . The result was a surprise not only to the manager of the paper but to the newsboys themselves. The circulation of the paper fell off rapidly and advertisers complained. The manager invited the Union to a conference." In the end, the boys won everything they demanded—and more.[18]

The street traders carried with them from their home blocks the inchoate sense of unity that had suffused their play communities. Just as in their play communities they had experienced what Huizinga referred to as the feeling of being " 'apart-together' in an exceptional situation,"[19] so downtown were they united by their shared isolation from the adult world that surrounded them. They were separated from the other inhabitants of the downtown shopping, entertainment, and business streets by age, class, and need. They were different—and they could not but perceive that difference every time they shouted their wares, collected their tips, or made their way back home to their working-class neighborhoods.

In the long run, the unity born of that difference made their experience at work more enjoyable and more profitable. The children trusted one another rather than the adult suppliers, circulation managers, and deliverymen. Their trust and cooperation made it easier for them to establish and enforce their own territorial laws. And those laws, in turn, smoothed the conflicts and eliminated the contests that might have arisen between them.

The child labor reformers who observed and reported on the boys at work were surprised by the degree to which they cooperated with one another. In their relationship with their adult suppliers and customers, the little hustlers were little demons. But in their relationship to one another, they were friendly and supportive. Street trading was not a

Philadelphia, 1910. This Lewis Hine photograph shows us three newsies who work together every afternoon and on Saturday nights till midnight. The middle boy, Morris Goldberg, is Jewish; his companions, "the Mellitto Boys," are Italian. (*Lewis Hine Collection, NCLC*)

solitary but a group activity. Multiple connections—work, play, classroom, and neighborhood ties—held the children together in friendship, not rivalry.

The child experts attributed such attitudes and behavior to the children's lower evolutionary state. Children, as G. Stanley Hall argued (persuasively enough to convince observers of children as astute as Jane Addams), were in their development recapitulating the evolution of the human species. Adolescents at play and at work embodied the savage personality in their eschewal of individualistic competition for the comforts of membership in and solidarity with the group.[20] The experts—and there were dozens of them who accepted Hall's formula—were unable to see beyond their own theoretical framework. The children's community of the streets was no atavism, but a response to their social situation. The children worked together because they had more fun that way and earned almost as much money.[21] They cooperated because solidarity with other children meant protection for all against the adults they did business with.

Unions and Strikes

J oseph Pulitzer, nearly blind, so sensitive to sound he exploded when the silverware was rattled, and suffering from "asthma, weak lungs, a protesting stomach, insomnia, exhaustion, and fits of depression,"[1] managed his newspapers in absentia for the last twenty years of his life. Nearly every day he received memos from the New York *World* office providing him with the information he required: financial reports, circulation figures, summaries of lead stories and features, lists of headlines in the *World* and its rivals, office gossip, and evaluations of key personnel. In July of 1899, a new subject appeared in the memos. Don Seitz, managing editor and chief correspondent, noted that the paper had "had some trouble to-day through the strike on the part of the newsboys." A July 21 memo headed "On the Newsboys Strike" reported further that the strike would "probably be sporadic for some days" but assured Pulitzer that "we have the situation well in hand." Twenty-four hours later, the tone of the memos had changed: "The newsboys strike has grown into a menacing affair. . . . It is proving a serious problem. Practically all the boys in New York and adjacent towns have quit selling." By the twenty-fourth, panic had set in. "The advertisers have abandoned the papers and the sale has been cut down fully ⅖. . . . It is really a very extraordinary demonstration."[2]

Indeed it was. The New York City newsies had formed their own union and gone out on strike against not only Pulitzer but also William Randolph Hearst, publisher of the rival New York *Journal*. Before their strike was over, the boys would succeed in seriously cutting back circulation of the two afternoon papers and forcing the two most powerful publishers in the nation to alter their distribution practices.

The story of the 1899 strike has never been told. In his mammoth history of journalism, Frank Luther Mott refers to it in a sentence.[3] No one else, to my knowledge, has ever given it that much notice. Children bringing down big-city newspapers by unionizing and striking is too improbable a scenario for anyone, even historians, to take very seriously.

The children of the city, as we have seen, took their money-making seriously. When their earnings were threatened, they did what they had to in order to protect them. They cemented their informal communities of the street into quasi-formal unions, held mass meetings, elected officers, declared strikes, paraded through the streets shouting their demands, "soaked scabs," and held together as long as they possibly could. Along the way, they tried to have a good time. The children's strikes were serious matters, but they were also occasions for community celebration, for marching en masse up the avenue, for playing dirty tricks, for making and wearing signs, and for ganging up against troublesome adults, especially the boss's still loyal employees and the police who tried to protect them.

The New York City newsies were, in 1899, in the enviable position of being irreplaceable. Their successors, as we shall see, would not be so well situated. As it became apparent through the early decades of the new century that there was money to be made selling papers, more and more adults would move into the business, setting up news distribution companies or opening and operating independent newsstands. At the turn of the century, however, the children were still, by far, the major distribution source for the afternoon dailies. Publishers and circulation managers could threaten, intimidate, and try to bully them back to work when they struck, but they could not replace them.

The event that was to lead to the newsies' strike of 1899 was the wholesale price increase that Hearst's *Journal* and Pulitzer's *World* had instituted in 1898 at the height of the Spanish-American War circulation boom. The publishers, especially Hearst and Pulitzer, had been spending far more money competing with one another in extra editions, splashy front pages, and eyewitness reports than they could hope to recoup on advertising and sales.[4] By raising prices to newsies from five cents to six cents for ten papers, they expected to reduce their losses to manageable levels.

The boys, as long as they were making money hawking extra editions

City Hall Park, New York City, late 1890s. Hawking the *World* on the steps of City Hall. These children had probably walked a number of blocks from their homes to City Hall to sell their papers. Without papers to sell, they would have been out of place; with them, they became as much a part of the landscape as the adult businessman to their right. (*Alice Austin Collection, Staten Island Historical Society*)

with horror-story front pages, did not protest the price increase. By the summer of 1899, however, as the news grew tamer and the headlines shrank, they began to feel the pinch of the penny increase.

It is difficult to say where or precisely how the strike began. The first reported actions took place in Long Island City, where the newsies discovered that the *Journal* deliveryman had been cheating them. On July 18, they took their revenge by tipping over his wagon, running off with his papers, and chasing him out of town. Flushed with success and in a fighting mood, the boys "decided to make a stand against the *World* and *[Journal]* for 50¢ per hundred." (This had been the price before the increase.) They demanded a price rollback and gave notice to their supply men that they were no longer going to buy the Hearst or Pulitzer papers. According to Don Seitz, who reported on all this in his letter to Pulitzer in Bar Harbor, the news of the Long Island City action traveled quickly into Manhattan, where "a young fellow named Morris Cohen, who sells about three hundred *Worlds* a day in City Hall Park got hold of the boys and got them to strike."[5]

Seitz notwithstanding, it is unlikely that Cohen by himself precipitated the strike in Manhattan. (His name was never to appear in any of the newspaper reports of the strike.) The boys who sold papers downtown, in the City Hall and Wall Street districts, gathered every afternoon outside the newspaper offices on Park Row, nicknamed Newspaper Row, and in City Hall Park. Most were students who worked part-time, but there were a significant number—many more than there would be in later years—who had left school entirely to hustle for a year or so until they were old enough to find steadier, more lucrative employment. The full-time hustlers sold the morning papers and the early editions of the afternoon ones. They were joined after three o'clock by the schoolboys, who arrived in plenty of time for the afternoon rush. During the spring and summer of 1899, the boys' afternoon discussions must have been punctuated by denunciations of Pulitzer and Hearst and strategic discussions on how to fight back. When word arrived about the Long Island City action, the downtown newsies, perhaps called together by Cohen, put away their red-hots, closed down their crap games, and assembled in City Hall Park. That afternoon, July 19, they organized their union and announced that they would strike the next day unless Pulitzer and

City Hall Park, New York City, late 1890s. Two bootblacks in City Hall Park, where in 1899 the newsboys would organize their union and their strike. (*Alice Austin Collection, Staten Island Historical Society*)

Hearst rolled back their prices. Officers were elected, a "committee on discipline" chosen, strategy debated, and delegates sent out to spread the word to the newsies at Fifty-ninth Street and in Harlem, Brooklyn, Long Island City, and Jersey.[6]

The newsies acted swiftly not because they were children, but because the moment was fortuitous. The Brooklyn streetcar operators were already on strike, and though they would ultimately be defeated they were, for the latter part of July, tying up the police so tight there were few left on the downtown Manhattan streets. As Boots McAleenan, aged eleven, explained to a reporter from the *Sun*, "We're doin' it now because de cops is all busy, an' we can do any scab newsboy dat shows his face widout police interference. We're here fer our rights an' we will die defendin' 'em. At de rates dey give us now we can't make on'y four cents on ten pape's, an' dat ain't enough to pay fer swipes."[7]*

On the first afternoons of the strike, the downtown boys gathered in front of the newspaper offices on Park Row to physically prevent the delivery wagons from leaving with papers for uptown and the suburbs. As the *Sun* reported on July 22, "Fully a hundred boys were gathered in Park Row at the hour when the first editions of the 'yellows' usually come out, and as soon as the wagons started there was a great howl and a shower of missiles which made the drivers' jobs uncomfortable. The police came on the run and the boys scattered hastily, for an order [from the Committee on Discipline which was running the strike] had gone out, it is said, that the police are not to be injured. All the boys were armed with clubs and most of them wore in their headgear placards denouncing the scab extras and calling on the public to boycott them."[8]

Though they did their best, the downtown boys were soon "scattered by the advance of the constabulary." The trucks—with their newspapers— rolled out to the distribution points uptown and out of town. The drivers who delivered to Columbus Circle were the first to discover what the newsies had in store for them. A crowd of four to five hundred boys had gathered at Fifty-ninth Street to await their arrival. "They had decorated the newsstands and lampposts with banners inscribed, 'Please Don't Buy the *World* or *Journal*,' 'Help the Newsboys,' 'Our Cause is Just', 'We Will Fight for Our Rights,' and other pregnant sentiments. As soon as the wagons came up the boys pressed forward and began to hoot and

---

* The progress of the strike was reported in the New York *Times, Daily Tribune, Sun, Herald, Mirror, People* (the Socialist Labor Party weekly), and the Brooklyn *Daily Eagle,* none of which had raised their prices and none of which were struck. As might have been expected, these papers, especially the *Sun*, had a field day, cheering the boys on in what they described as a mock-epic struggle of dirty-faced Davids against the twin Goliaths.

howl. . . . Though pushed back [by the policemen], they did not scatter. They formed a circle, and as fast as any man got his bundle of papers and tried to get away with them they swept down upon him with yells of 'Kill the scab!' mauled him until he dropped his papers and ran, then tore the sheets into small bits and trampled them in the mud."[9]

At other distribution points, the same scenario was played out. In Brooklyn the boys "appointed committees to meet the delivery wagons and every driver who dared defy the newsboys was bombarded with a choice collection of stones, with which the pockets of the rebellious youngsters bulged."[10] The Jersey City boys met the wagons at the ferry and tore up the papers as they were thrown down.[11] The Yonkers group sent delegations to the incoming trains to capture the papers as they arrived.[12]

The boys were in constant communication. The strike committee, elected by the downtown boys, sent representatives to the outlying regions; the outer suburbs elected delegates to travel downtown to Park Row. The *Sun*, glorying in this successful strike against its two major competitors, reported in full the visit of Spot Conlon, District Master Workboy of the Brooklyn Union, who, attired in pink suspenders, walked across the Brooklyn Bridge with "greetings an' promises of support. . . . 'We have tied up de scab sheets so tight dat y' can't buy one fer a dollar in de street. Hold out, my gallant kids, an' to-morrer I meself, at de head of t'ree tousand noble hearts from Brooklyn will be over here t' help youse win yer noble scrap fer freedom an' fair play.' "[13]

The *Journal* and *World* did not, at first, take the strike very seriously. Their opponents were after all only children, too small, inexperienced, and irresponsible to win a contest with adults. It was not until the advertisers began requesting "allowance on their bills on account of the strike" that the publishers realized the gravity of the situation. The newsboys were not only on the way to shutting down street circulation; they had won a public relations battle for the sympathy of the public. "The people," Seitz reported to Pulitzer on July 24, "seem to be against us; they are encouraging the boys and tipping them and where they are not doing this, they are refraining from buying the papers for fear of having them snatched from their hands."[14]

The strike closed down distribution of the papers in Manhattan and, within days, spread uptown to Fifty-ninth Street and Harlem and across the rivers to Long Island City, Brooklyn, Jersey City, and Newark, where according to Seitz "the paper was completely obliterated."[15] In Mount Vernon, Staten Island, Yonkers, Troy, and Rochester, New York; Plainfield, Trenton, Elizabeth, Paterson, and Asbury Park, New Jersey; New

Haven, Connecticut; Fall River, Massachusetts; and Providence, Rhode Island, local newsies joined the strike.[16]

Though it is not possible to do an ethnic census of the strikers, the names reported in the papers provide evidence that boys of all backgrounds participated in all aspects of the strike. Among those arrested were Abe Greenhouse, Ike Miller, Joe Mulligan, Frank Giasso, Donato Carolucci, 'Grin' Boyle, Albert Smith, Edward Rowland, Mikki Fishler, and William Reese and John Falk (the latter two identified by the *Sun* as "Negroes"). The elected strike committee included Barney Peters, Jim Galty, Crutchy Morris, Abe Newman, and Dave Simons.[17]

The boys, all of them, were in dead earnest about their strike. The fact that the publishers refused to take them seriously just spurred them on. Every day, they met the delivery wagons at the distribution points, pelted them with stones and rotten fruit, captured as many bundles as they could, and then paraded up and down the streets with banners, leaflets, songs, and cheers, proud of their accomplishment but on the constant lookout for any scab papers that might have gotten through.

The children used their wits—and numbers—to advantage. The *Sun* reported an incident from the third day of the strike, when a small boy appeared in front of the *Journal* office with a stack of papers and a policeman by his side. The strikers, poised outside to make sure no one got away from the office with papers to sell, were at a loss as to what to do. "Barefaced defiance by a mere 'kid' would demoralize the rank and file if left unpunished. Yet there was the policeman with a night stick and there was the lesson of three of their number already sent to juvenile asylum for assaulting scabs. . . .

"Up spoke Young Myers, sometimes called Young Mush, on account of his fondness for taking his girl to Corlears Hook Park Sunday evenings.

" 'That cop's too fat to run fast an' I'll get him after me if you'll tend to the scab when he gets away,' he said.

"The leaders promised to attend to the scab if Young Myers would remove the policeman. Walking innocently up to the *Journal* boy, Myers grabbed a handful of his papers and ran as fast as his legs would carry him. The *Journal* boy yelled for help and away went the policeman after Young Mush. The *Journal* boy watched the pursuit with interest. A second later he had other things to think about. Fifteen strikers surrounded him and the blows came in thick and fast. The *Journals* that he had were taken away and torn into ribbons."

A second policeman rescued the boy, who retreated to Frankfort Street; there he was met by the strikers, who "invited him to join them, which he did in a hurry. A half hour later he was leading an attack on a boy who was trying to smuggle some *Worlds* and *Journals* over to Brooklyn."[18]

The "bluecoated servants of capital," as the *Sun* referred to the policemen, did their best but were overwhelmed by the persistence and sheer numbers of the strikers. They managed to arrest a boy here and there but were powerless against the huge crowds that gathered at the distribution centers and marched down the main streets on the lookout for scab papers.

The newspapers, now frightened by the recognition that the strike was for real, called in their favors from politicians and police captains. As Seitz reported to Pulitzer on July 24, "I have been up to headquarters, arranging to break up certain strike points, with the help of the police, to-morrow." The *Journal*, which had been running editorials condemning the police for their actions in other strikes, quickly reversed itself: offending editorials were "suppressed," including a full-page diatribe against the police as "friends of monopoly." With its editorial policy now favorable to the department, the *Journal*'s editor made his way "to see Mayor Van Wyck in the matter of better police protection." According to Seitz, the "Mayor had expressed his friendly purpose towards us; very friendly purpose I judge from what Los [*Journal*'s editor] said."[19]

The publishers needed police protection for the army of scabs, thugs, and assorted toughs they had hired to get the papers on the streets. When their supply of available adults was exhausted, they sent their agents to the Bowery lodging houses with the offer of two dollars a day plus commission for any man who would sell *Worlds* or *Journals*. The boys followed the agents into the flophouses to explain their case. According to a story in the *Sun* on July 23, the bums agreed to support the boys: "I'm a Bowery bum . . . and one of about a hundred that's signed to take out *Worlds* and *Journals* to-morrow. But say, we ain't a-going to do it. It's all a bluff. We told them scouts that we'd do it when they offered $2 a day, but everyone of us has decided to stick by the newsboys and we won't sell no papers."[20]

Those few who appeared at the newspaper offices the next day did so only because they had found a way to make their two dollars without breaking the strike. As they left the offices with their bundles, they dumped their papers in the streets; then, after a short while, returned to the publishers, demanding their money. " 'Say, dis is easy,' said one of them: it's a reg'lar cinch. But don't give it away. I wouldn't be doin' it but I needs de money.' "[21]

The only trouble the boys had was with the women who owned their own stands. Though Annie and "Mrs. Cry Baby, the only name by which they [had] ever known the eccentric German newspaper woman

174

who is a familiar figure at the [Brooklyn] bridge entrance" were with them, other "newswomen around the bridge entrance," while pretending to support the boys had "been caught selling the boycotted papers, hauling them out from under their shawls when they [were] called for by customers. This base deceit . . . angered the boys very much, but they [were] at a loss to find a remedy."

" 'A feller don't soak a lady,' said Kid Blink, 'and yer can't get at them women's scab pape's without soakin' them.' " The best they could do was to threaten the women and try to coax their customers away from them.[22]

The boys were well aware of the value of public support. To publicize their cause they took up a collection, and, with the eleven dollars they secured, printed up thousands of circulars to stuff in the nonstruck papers and hand out in the streets and at the bridges, train stations, and ferries. They organized parades and street demonstrations, and, whenever the opportunity presented itself, made their case to the reporters from the nonstruck dailies.

For the boys, and for the public who read about their strike, the highlight of the two weeks was the mass meeting held at New Irving Hall on Broome Street. Some five thousand boys from all over the city showed up to shout their support. The two thousand who were able to squeeze into the hall were greeted by Frank Woods, the voice of the Polo Grounds and a former newsie. A few local politicians saluted the strikers, songs were sung, strikers cheered, and scabs booed.

The newsboy speakers played to the larger public through the medium of the reporters from the nonstruck papers. Early in the evening the chairman, conscious of the effect favorable reports might have on building public support, asked the reporters present to please refrain from quoting "the speakers as saying 'dese' and 'dose' and 'youse.' "

Bob the Indian, one of the first speakers, promised the boys that they were going to win their struggle, but pleaded with them to keep the violence down. "Now I'm to tell yer that yer not to soak the drivers any more. . . . No you're not to soak 'em. We're a goin' to try to square this thing without violence; so keep cool. I think we'll win in a walk— on the level I do."

Kid Blink, a strike organizer, urged the boys to stick like "glue" and a moment later like "plaster." "Ain't that ten cents worth as much to us as it is to Hearst and Pulitzer who are millionaires? Well, I guess it is. If they can't spare it, how can we? . . . I'm trying to figure how ten cents on a hundred papers can mean more to a millionaire than it does to newsboys, an' I can't see it."

The boys sat or, rather, stood and cheered through speech after speech. Crazy Aborn told how the circulation managers had tried to bribe him; Newspaper Annie shouted her encouragement; Dave Simons, president of the union, presented the assembly with a set of resolutions to vote on; Warhorse Brennan, the oldest newsie, and Jack from Park Row saluted the boys. Racetrack Higgins reported that the Brooklyn boys had hired a band to lead them over the bridge to Irving Hall but were prevented from "parading" by the police commissioner, who denied them a permit. The last scheduled speaker of the evening was "Hungry Joe Kernan, the newsboy mascot [who] sang a pathetic song about a one-legged newsboy." With a few brief remarks by a few more newsies, the meeting came to a halt, the boys reinvigorated and ready to carry their strike to its conclusion.[23]

The boys held together for the rest of that week and the next. Though there were rumors of scandal and a hasty trial and removal from office of two of the strike leaders, the boys continued to keep the *World* and *Journal* off the streets. Seitz, summarizing the effects of the strike for Pulitzer, admitted that "the loss in circulation . . . has been colossal." The press run had been reduced from over three hundred sixty thousand to one hundred twenty-five thousand, while returns more than doubled from the customary 15 or 16 percent to an average of 35 percent. "It is really remarkable the success these boys have had; our policy of putting men out [adult scabs] was not helpful, yet it was the only thing that could be done. We had to have representation and the absolute disappearance of the paper was appalling."[24]

The publishers conceded defeat in the second week of the strike by offering the boys an advantageous compromise. The price would remain where it was, but the *World* and *Journal* would henceforth take back *all* unsold papers at 100 percent refund. The boys agreed to the offer and on the second of August returned to the streets.[25] (Frank Luther Mott claims that the "strike . . . was eventually successful" in forcing the papers to rescind their price increase. I have not found any evidence to support his claim.[26])

The newsboys' union did not survive long enough to take credit for the victory. Toward the end, all that remained were the leaders and their statements to the press. The union had done yeoman work in getting the strike started, arranging the mass meeting, and spreading the word to the boys and the public. Once the boycott took hold, however, its days were numbered. The strike was so decentralized that the citywide organization had little to do. Each group of newsies policed its own district: the Harlem boys patrolled theirs, the Jersey City boys theirs. Though each group considered itself part of the larger whole, none felt obligated to accept decisions arrived at outside the local district.

Had the publishers formally negotiated with the union, the organization might have been strengthened or at least given something to do. But the publishers, perhaps wisely from their perspective, ignored the union. When they decided to compromise with the boys they simply spread the word—through the circulation and branch office managers— that they were going to accept 100 percent returns. The boys, without formal vote or decision, accepted the agreement and queued up to buy their papers.

The New York City union, like most of the other children's unions, was an ephemeral organization with a limited life span. The children paid no dues, had no salaried officers, and probably did not expect their union to outlive the particular struggle it had been called into being to address.

The children's unions owed their existence—and whatever strength they possessed—to the informal networks that preceded them. The boys knew and trusted one another from the neighborhood and the streets. No extensive organizing campaigns were necessary to convince boys to join a union with their friends. Ironically, the informal community structure that made establishing unions so easy had the opposite effect on sustaining them. Because the boys were already tied together in multiple social relationships, they did not need permanent unions to regulate their trade or create a community of mutual interest.

The New York newsie strike of 1899 left no organization behind it,† but it did not recede into the past without leaving its mark up and down the East Coast and as far west as Cincinnati. Children everywhere learned about the New York City strike from their local papers. In Lexington, Kentucky, the newsies followed the New York boys' example and called a strike against the city's major afternoon paper. In Rochester and Syracuse, Philadelphia and Pittsburgh, Boston and Cincinnati, the messengers went out on strike. As the papers reported, with less and less levity as it spread, a "strike epidemic" had broken out.[27]

The children, it appeared, felt some sort of generational pull to go out on strike in support of one another. From Providence, Rhode Island, to South Jersey, children who sold the *Journal* and *World* went out in support of the New York boys. In Cincinnati, the newsies went out in support of the messengers.[28] And in New York City, still the hub of activity, the messengers and bootblacks joined the newsies in what nearly became a children's general strike.[29]

Although, unlike the newsies, most of the messengers and shineboys

† The only newsboys' union to survive the strike that had precipitated its organization was the Boston Newsboys' Union.

177

had left school and worked full-time, they too belonged to the children's community of the streets. Like the part-time street traders, they lived at home and were expected to turn in their wages to their parents. Like them, also, they held back part of their earnings to spend on their own good times.

Of all the children's strikes, the shineboys' provided the nonstruck newspapers with the best copy. Here was the perfect strike: no individual or business was going to suffer, and the mostly Italian boys—with their exaggerated accents—were even more colorful in print than the newsies with their "deses" and "dems." The shineboys, for all the good cheer with which their action was reported, did not leave their stands to amuse the rest of the city. They had real grievances and no other way to force their employers to act on them.

The boys who shined on the Staten Island and East River ferries were employed by a Vincent Catoggio, who owned all the "concessions" on the ferries and made between twelve and fourteen thousand dollars a year from them. While the boys slaved away, Catoggio, they claimed, lived like a prince with diamond rings on all ten fingers. To make matters worse, the boss had recently instituted a new and, for the boys, degrading system. To make sure that no boy pocketed the proceeds from a shine, Catoggio required them to ring a bell each time they got a customer.

"Of coursa, we go on a strika," Looking-glass Wadalup (named for the quality of his shines) was reported as having said only days after the newsies had led the way with their strike. "Da bossa he maka all da mona, and he wanta maka da men rings upa da shina same like da monka ringa de bell in de circ. Nexta ting we know he wanta putta colla and chaina ona da men sama lika jocko."

The boys threatened to throw their stands into the sea should their demands not be met. Catoggio offered them a 20 percent wage increase to six dollars a week. They took it, though as "Tony Rocco, who shines shoes on one of the Staten Island boats," confided to a reporter, the boys were still looking for seven dollars. "We maka our union stronga first. Then we strika for the seven doll."[30]

Like the bootblacks, the messengers were galvanized into action by the newsies' example. As the *Sun* reported, "The boys haven't any more cause of complaint now than they have always had, but simply yielded to the strike epidemic." The boys, it was true, were not striking to overturn recently established practices, but they were not playacting, as the *Sun* implied. Their major grievance was the "tax" they were charged for their uniforms and, in the case of the American District boys, for clean white linen collars. "Mind yer," one of the boys told a reporter, "they take 50¢ a week out for uniforms and before yer wear one out yer've paid for it a half dozen times over. But d'yer own it then? Not on yer life. They takes it away, gives yer one that some large boy has grown out of, and keep right on taking yer 50¢ a week."[31]

The boys wanted nothing more than what was due them as American workers and citizens: the right to buy and wash their own uniforms and collars. The American District and Western Union boys also objected to their companies' policy of shifting their work hours and not telling them until the night before when they were going to work. They demanded as well full pay for every telegram they carried out of the office, not simply for those which were delivered.[32]

The messengers' strike was called for July 24, just four days after the newsies went out. Though the boys from the different companies had different demands—and different schedules—they tried to coordinate their actions. If they were successful, they could close down the city or, at the very least, slow down Wall Street. The Postal Telegraph Company boys were the first to go out. "They made things lively downtown . . . and seriously impaired the company's service" until the police arrived to chase them away. That afternoon the Western Union boys joined the strike, but trooped back to work when the district manager agreed to their demands. The American District boys waited until the next day, payday, to walk out.[33]

As might have been expected from the difficulty the boys had coordinating their actions, their strike was going nowhere. The boys had been in such a hurry to get started, they had not bothered to form a union—even a weak one, as the newsies had. Their lack of organization did not help their cause. Neither did help come from the older boys, out of school, out of work, and only too ready to take the places of the striking messengers. As the *Tribune* reported on July 27, three days after the boys had walked out, the strike "like a badly charged rocket has about fizzled out, after a few weak sputters."[34]

It is difficult to imagine a different outcome. The companies and the business community had too much at stake to allow the boys to close down shop for even an afternoon. The city could survive without shined shoes or afternoon papers, but not—in this era, at least—without its telegrams. In Cincinnati, when the boys struck, the companies and their clients hired cabs to deliver the strikebreakers and their messages. Elsewhere, the strikes were quickly broken by a combination of intimidation, cabs, scabs, and police guards.[35]

The messenger boy strikes of 1899 achieved little. The boys' grievances remained simmering until 1910, when a new generation took

New York City, 1896. The photograph on top shows three independent bootblacks looking for shines on a busy city street. Above is one of the new "stands" that was putting the independents out of business. Few customers would pay a nickel to a boy with a shoeshine box when for the same price they could sit on a throne on one of the stands. (*Alice Austin Collection, Staten Island Historical Society*)

up where the old one had left off—unfortunately with much the same results. Thought the boys in 1910 had a solidly organized union behind them and assistance from union organizers and other sympathetic adults, they were no match for their employers. In New York, in 1910, and in Detroit, where the boys struck for higher rates in 1914, the telegraph companies beat them down with the telephone and with "Bowery bums" hired by the day. The bums were paid at rates much higher than the boys. Once the strikes were broken, the boys were offered their old jobs—at the old rate of pay.[36]

In unionizing and striking to protect their rights and their profits, the children were behaving precisely as they believed American workers should when treated unjustly. Unions and strikes were part of the urban environment. It was the rare working-class boy or girl who did not have a father, brother, sister, or relative who was a union member or sympathizer. The papers the children hawked were full of stories—and not unsympathetic ones—about strikes for better wages and working conditions. The New York City boys who struck in 1899 had that very week hawked papers with banner headlines describing the strike of the Brooklyn streetcar operators. The Boston boys who struck in May of 1901 had spent a good part of the preceding month shouting headlines about the brewers', plumbers', linesmen's, and machinists' strikes.

The newsies were themselves independent merchants, but that did not prevent them from patterning their organizations after labor unions, calling them "unions," and applying directly to local and national federations for certification and support. The Boston boys who joined the AFL in 1901 were so serious about their union affiliation that they raised money to send newsie Thomas Mulkern to the 1906 Annual Convention, where he introduced a resolution calling on the adult unionists to "make a special endeavor during the coming year to organize the newsboys throughout the country." In Detroit, the boys in 1914 appealed directly to the Detroit Federation of Labor for assistance when the *News* unilaterally broke its unwritten agreement with them. In Chicago, where in 1912 the Hearst papers locked out the pressmen in a complicated, long-simmering dispute, the newsies not only refused to handle any struck dailies but tried their best to prevent Hearst's imported scabs from selling them. The strike was a bloody one, with more than one newsboy's head smashed before it was over.

Fortunately for the newsies, such actions were rare. So, too, were the occasions on which the boys felt compelled to unionize and strike to protect their interests. As long as business was good, the publishers were content to abide by their unwritten agreements with the newsies. For a decade and a half after the 1901 Boston strike, business was good—so good on the retailing end that adults were encouraged to move into the distribution business. By the beginning of World War I, a significant number of adults, some of them independent newsstand owners and operators, others employees of large distributing companies, had joined the children on the streets.

As had occurred during the Spanish-American War, circulation increased during the World War I years; but costs, propelled upward by a newsprint shortage and wartime revenue measures, rose even faster. Publishers struggling to maintain their profit margin or simply survive had to raise their advertising rates or their prices.[37] Since competition with other papers and with the magazines prevented them from boosting the advertising rates, they attempted to balance the books by charging the public more for their papers. The newsies and the independent dealers assumed that they would retain the same percentage of the selling price under the new price structures. They were mistaken.

The Pittsburgh papers were among the first to boost their prices. In December of 1916, the newsies were informed that under the new price structure they would take home a much smaller percentage of the sales price than they had been getting. Outraged by the publishers' unilateral decision to break what they considered a long-standing though unwritten agreement, the boys refused to sell any papers at the new prices. According to *Editor and Publisher*, "a virtual boycott was placed . . . on the sale of newspapers in the city." Regrettably, the boycott did not hold long enough to force the publishers to the bargaining table. Recognizing that the boys were not going to voluntarily return to work, the publishers set out to force them back—or replace them entirely. They erected newsstands at key locations throughout the city and staffed them with loyal adults. The boys, unable to keep papers off the stands or customers from the papers, were forced to concede defeat and call off their strike.[38]

In Seattle, Minneapolis, and New York City, the newsies reacted as the Pittsburgh boys had to the publishers' attempts to unilaterally change the unwritten agreements that governed their street trades. They were no doubt encouraged, as their predecessors had been, by the example of adult union members, who were in these same years resorting more frequently to strikes to redress their grievances. The second wave of newsboy strikes occurred during a period, 1916–18, in which more than a million adults struck each year—"more," according to David Montgomery, "than had ever struck in any year before 1915."[39]

The Seattle and Minneapolis newsies had better luck than their Pittsburgh counterparts, in large part because the publishers in those cities were less prepared for battle. The Seattle newsies had, for the past

182

seventeen years, abided by an agreement reached between their former union and the publishers. In 1917, when the Seattle *Post-Intelligencer*, citing increased paper costs, broke the agreement by raising its prices and changing its pricing structure, the boys quickly organized—or, more properly, resurrected their old union—and went out on strike. Both the AFL-affiliated Central Labor Federation and the rival IWW chapter offered assistance. The *Post-Intelligencer*, out on a limb as the only paper to have raised its prices and be struck, caved in at once.[40]

In Minneapolis, the newsies also went on strike the moment the publishers raised their prices. They were, from all accounts, enormously successful. On the third of July, the day after the strike, the New York *Times* reported: "Virtually no newspapers were sold or delivered in Minneapolis today, several hundred vendors and carriers having gone on strike." The publishers, not about to surrender to a bunch of children, tried to get their papers into the streets with scab vendors. The newsies attacked, "several severe riots" ensued, and, according to *Editor and Publisher*, the governor intervened, notifying "the Mayor and Chief of Police that unless the disturbances were stopped immediately, he would suspend them from office." The pressure from the top forced the publishers to the bargaining table.[41]

The Minneapolis boys had been so militant—and so successful—in pressing their demands that they frightened into existence a new coalition of concerned citizens and reform groups. The "concerned citizens" blamed the "recent boycott" not on the publishers, but on "the effects of street life upon growing boys." The boys were obviously learning the wrong things on the streets: to organize, protest, strike, and survive. The only solution was to remove them from the streets—and quickly—before another generation was similarly corrupted. "We believe it would be for the ultimate welfare of the newsboys themselves to eliminate their business entirely."[42]

The New York City publishers were among the last of the big-city publishers to raise their afternoon prices. (Could they have remembered what had happened the last time they'd tampered with the newsies' profit margin?) On January 16, 1918, without advance notice, they made their move. Every New York and Brooklyn afternoon paper which had sold for a penny raised its price to two cents. The vendors were informed that 0.6 cents, or 30 percent of the new selling price, would go to them; the remainder was for the publishers. The newsies objected immediately and strenuously to the new pricing formula and demanded a return to the old one (under which they had received 40 percent of the selling price).[43]

The strike began in Brooklyn but quickly spread to Manhattan and from there to the Bronx. There were battles at the Brooklyn Bridge,

Times Square, uptown at 125th Street and Eighth Avenue, and every-where else scabs tried to peddle the struck papers.

For the first week of the strike, the boys were rather successful in keeping the papers away from the scab newsies. According to the *Tribune,* "In the greater city the only papers to circulate freely were 'The Call,' . . . and 'The Brooklyn Times,' . . . These two papers were peddled everywhere by iron-lunged 'newsies,' who besought all to 'help the newsies win the big strike.' "[44]

The newsies kept the scabs off the streets, but they could not keep papers out of customers' hands. The newspaper distribution business had changed in the twenty years since the boys had last gone on strike. Though still a fixture on the streets, the children were no longer the essential link between publisher and customer they had been in 1899. In New York City, the boys had been helped out by a series of legal restrictions on the construction of newsstands. By the second decade of the century, however, such restrictions had been effectively nullified by the graft that greased the palms of the city officials who approved the licenses. Permanent enclosed stands—owned and operated by indepen-dent dealers or employees of large distributing companies—had been erected on street corners, in subway stations, ferry houses, train terminals, office buildings, and hotel lobbies.[45]

When the strike began, the adults who owned their own stands went out with the boys. The company-owned stands not only stayed open, but "did land office business" selling to customers who ordinarily got their papers from the boys or the independents.[46] The publishers, reported their journal, *Editor and Publisher,* were "ready to fight to a finish." Within days of the strike, they chartered a new company to build and operate even more newsstands and arrange delivery to private homes and apartment buildings.

With the police guarding the stands that remained open, the publishers building new ones, and the public unwilling to do without its papers, the newsies and small dealers were outgunned and outmaneu-vered. On February 7, they called off their strike, accepting a compromise proposed earlier in the week. The boys agreed to accept the new pricing structure in return for a guarantee that they would be able to return their unsold papers for full refund.[47]

The compromise held for six months, until the War Industries Board, citing the ongoing white paper shortage, outlawed "refunds," charging that the practice of allowing the boys to return unsold copies encouraged them to buy more than they could sell.[48] The boys were back where they had started—with one crucial difference. They knew now that they were not able to win a strike against the publishers.

Unable to strike, but unwilling to let the matter pass without a struggle, the newsies decided to selectively boycott the Hearst papers. Hearst, never their favorite, was, they believed, ripe for a tumble. He was a bully, a millionaire, and, as the publisher of the only major New York City paper urging a negotiated end to the war, suspiciously sympathetic to the Germans. He was also, they claimed, the publisher most responsible for raising prices in January.

The boys and the independent adult dealers who joined them expected that some of the publishers would support them, or at least look the other way. To their surprise and dismay, only the *Tribune*, which had been waging its own war against Hearst, took their side. Every other publisher backed Hearst by directing its circulation managers to deny papers to vendors who joined the boycott.

For the first few days of their boycott, the boys managed to outwit the publishers arrayed against them. Some of the boys bought a few copies of a Hearst paper "for no other purpose than to make themselves eligible to buy other evening papers." Others "did in" the scab newsies and raised such a commotion that customers were frightened away or encouraged to honor the boycott.

The boys held out as long as they could, which, in this case, was not long at all. The publishers took no chances. At their insistence, city officials moved quickly to revoke the licenses of all newsstand operators and newsies who refused to sell the Hearst publications. Under a newly invented interpretation of their licensing authority, the officials charged that vendors who did not offer *all* publications for sale were not serving the public and were, thus, no longer entitled to their licenses. The boys and their adult allies hired lawyers, enlisted local politicians, and even got Al Smith, the Democratic candidate for governor, to intervene on their behalf, to no avail. The boycott ground on, less and less effectively, through August and into the fall. Only the *Tribune*, still violently anti-Hearst, kept it in the news by reporting daily on the activities of Andrew Stanton, president of the Newsboys Union, as he journeyed through the city, enlisting empty declarations of support from adult unions with nothing else to offer. The carpenters, boilermakers, painters, engineers, housesmiths and bridgemen, cement and concrete workers, bluestone cutters, flaggers, bridge and curb setters, metal lathers, sheet metal workers, blacksmiths, steamfitters, and United Hebrew Trades all expressed their support for the boys and their union. Unfortunately, victory in the union halls did not compensate for defeat in the streets. And the boys had been defeated.[49]

They had done their best but lost the battle and the war. Even had their strike been 100 percent effective, it would not have brought Hearst to the bargaining table. He and the other publishers did not need the newsies, as they had in the past. There were other outlets for their papers. The eleven- to fifteen-year-olds were helpful but no longer necessary in the distribution process.

The loss of the strike weapon was symbolic of the street traders' loss of power and status. While few had ever engaged in strikes, they knew that such actions had occurred in the past or elsewhere and could, if necessary, be employed where they worked. The possibility of unionizing and striking, even if never called on, protected their interests and their self-image. Children whimpered for their rights; adults struck or threatened to strike to protect theirs. Without the strike weapon, the street traders had no mechanism for forcing the adults they worked with to treat them as business associates rather than children. They were losing their special place on the streets and their special status as little merchants.

13

End of an Era

The events of 1918–19 signal the close of an era in the history of urban childhood. Children would continue to work in the city but never again would they occupy the place the street traders had. Future child laborers would not be granted the same degree of autonomy and freedom at work on the streets. The adults they worked with would treat them as children, nothing more, nothing less.

The reign of the street traders was a brief one, no more than a moment in the history of childhood and the history of the city. By the 1920s the children of the city had been pushed to the side by the automobile, which cut off their play and work space, by tougher and better-enforced child labor laws, and by adults who moved into the trades they had once monopolized.

The substitution of adults for children was a gradual one. From the 1890s on, year by year, the downtown business, entertainment, and shopping districts brought more and more people into the city. Improved interurban and suburban transportation systems made the commute simpler than ever, better street lighting encouraged people to stay out later, and department stores, restaurants, theaters, and movie palaces gave them more to do. Sidewalks on the busier streets became as congested as the inner rooms of tenement house flats. As pedestrian traffic increased, so did business for street traders. The more business, the more profits, the more adults.

The first of the street trades to be taken over was the shoeshine business. Greek and Italian immigrant adults joined the children who blacked boots in the central business districts. With little money and less fanfare, they erected shoeshine stands on the streets, in saloons and railroad terminals, and on the ferries to greet the burgeoning armies of white-collar workers in need of shiny shoes. Within only a few years, the adult bootblack barons had succeeded in cornering the market on downtown shines. According to a 1903 confidential report to the New York Child Labor Committee, "The business of blacking boots has become so concentrated and systematized that it can now be described only as an industry."[1]

In New York City, Italian immigrants controlled the new "industry." Elsewhere, according to the 1908 Immigration Commission, the major force was a group of Greek immigrants who had built parlors in cities across the nation and imported young boys to work in them. The imported Greek shineboys had little in common with the other street traders. They worked from six in the morning until nine or ten at night, slept in overcrowded, underventilated rooms rented by their padrones, and survived—day after day—on bread and olives or cheese. For this they received, in addition to their room and board (and an initial sum paid to their parents) an average of $120 to $180 a year. Any tips collected went directly to the padrone.[2]

The child labor reformers, incensed—and rightly—by the situation, did what they could to stop the importation or, at the very least, free the boys from what amounted to indentured servitude. They were stymied at every turn by the boys' reluctance to testify against their padrones. By American standards, the boys were paid miserably and treated worse. By Greek standards, their food, clothing, and shelter were adequate; their pay, outstanding. Some of the imported boys, like Nicholas Gerros of Cincinnati, even got the chance to go to night school. Had they been given the opportunity to renounce their contracts and return to Greece, few would have accepted. No matter how bad conditions were, they lived better than they had in the Greek slums they'd left behind.[3]

Throughout the country, bootblack parlors and stands—with or without imported boys from the Old World—were forcing independent child bootblacks out of the business. As Philip Davis reported from Boston in 1915, "The old-fashioned bootblack who knocks about the streets with his shine-box over his shoulder in quest of trade is gradually being eliminated."[4] In New York City, as we have already seen, the boys who shined on the ferries worked for wages. Child labor investigators in Tennessee and North Carolina found that most black boys who shined shoes after school and during weekends and holidays worked for adults who owned and operated the downtown parlors. The few who continued to work on their own were reduced to clustering outside saloons and railroad terminals, literally begging for shines. In Wilmington, North Carolina, one investigator reported finding "little colored boys . . . gathering in front of the station entrance with their bootblack boxes and crying, 'Throw us some money, boss, and watch us scramble for it.' "[5]

Boys who worked on their own were not going to lure customers from the parlors—and they knew it. Most stayed away from the downtown sections of the city, except on holiday eves, Saturday nights, and Friday

A southern city, 1901. A bootblack identified only as being from a southern city. (*Detroit Photographic Company, LC*)

afternoons in the Jewish districts, when everyone on the streets appeared to be in the market for a shine. Many independent bootblacks worked only in locations scorned by adults. Where there were no parlors in sight, they had a fair chance of getting enough shines to make it worth their while. In New York City, shineboys could be found offering cut-rate two-cent shines to the bums in the Bowery. In Chicago, the boys clustered with their wooden boxes at Madison and Halsted—"Hobo land." Anthony Sorrentino, who shined shoes on the weekends, worked the wholesale fruit and vegetable markets on Saturday afternoons. On Sundays he covered "the cheap hotels and lodging houses, cat houses, and taverns on West Madison Sreet."[6]

The children, if we can believe the testimony of two of them,

New York City, 1910. "While the boss exchanges gossip with a neighbor, this bootblack keeps his mind on the job." This Lewis Hine photograph shows one of the new "stands" that put the independent shineboys out of business or forced them to become employees of the stand owners. (*Lewis Hine Collection, NCLC*)

contributed to their own decline and fall. As Harpo Marx notes in his autobiography, shining shoes was hard work. It also required some investment of capital. Joe E. Brown, the future comedian, unable to invest the proper amount, had to run away from his first customer. He was ashamed to admit that he owned only a can of black polish and could not shine tan shoes. George Burns was as deficient, though not nearly as sensitive, a bootblack. With the profits earned by selling newspapers, he recalls, "I bought a can of polish for a nickel and got myself a little wooden box that I hung on a strap over my shoulder. I'd walk along the street selling shines for either two or three cents. For three cents I'd use a little polish, for two cents I'd just spit and rub. All I had was black polish, so if a customer had brown shoes, I'd sell him a newspaper."[7]

The demise of the errand boys and messengers is told in much less detail. They fell victim to the telephone, the most efficient and, after the introduction of message-unit pricing, the cheapest way for businesses, small and large, to communicate with their customers.

In most city neighborhoods, the candy stores, grocers, and druggists were the first to get phones. The whole neighborhood wrote down the phone numbers and used them as their own. When calls came in, kids were roused and sent out to bring back the person wanted on the phone. As the number of phones—business and residential—increased in the first decades of the new century, the need for children to bring people to phones or carry messages from business to business or business to home decreased. Many errand boys and part-time messengers were automated right off the streets.[8]

Of all the city's street traders, the newsies held their place on the streets the longest, until they too fell prey to adult competition. The children could not outbid adults for the better street locations; they could not raise the money to get licenses or build permanent enclosed stands; they could not sell morning or early afternoon papers while school was still in session; they could not even guarantee their customers dry papers when it was raining or snowing.

The independent child hustlers were squeezed out of business from two directions: by the adult dealers at their weather-proofed, all-day newsstands and by the new breed of professional circulation managers called into existence to extend circulation and bring order to the one area in the business that had lagged behind the others in efficiency and organization.

By the second decade of the new century, the era of extras by the score and widely fluctuating circulations had passed into history. Advertisers demanded regularity in the circulation of evening as well as morning papers. They were unwilling to take chances—as the newsies had to—on sudden tragedies boosting circulation. They wanted guarantees that the editions in which they advertised would reach a certain minimum number of customers—day after day after day.

The easiest way to build stable circulations was to bind customers to buy by the week or month instead of on the spur of the moment. Home delivery to subscribers guaranteed circulation managers—and advertisers—a secure circulation base. As C.M. Schofeld of the Worcester (Massachusetts) *Gazette* informed his fellow circulation managers at their annual convention in 1917, "Advertisers Invariably Prefer Home Delivered Newspapers to Street Sales: A publisher wants home delivered circulation for several reasons. A street sale paper is uncertain, as it depends on the weather, the number of people on the street, and the boys on the street corners." Home delivery, on the contrary, was as regular as clockwork. Customers paid for their papers by subscription and had them delivered daily to their front stoops, regardless of the weather, the day of the year, or the size of the headlines.[9]

The circulation managers went to work to change the balance between street sales and subscriptions. They offered coupons, contests, and special inducements to subscribers. They divided the metropolitan areas into districts and the districts into delivery routes. Motorized trucks replaced horsedrawn wagons and pushcarts. Improved distribution systems, more efficient mailing rooms, and better wire-tying machines enabled them to get the late editions to the outlying districts before the city boys were even home from school.[10]

The expansion of home delivery cut into street sales. Morning papers had always been delivered to the homes, but evening papers had been exclusively the preserve of the newsies and the adult dealers. Now, as afternoon paper sales began to shift from the streets to home delivery, the hustlers found themselves with fewer and fewer customers—and this at a time when they were already suffering from the competition of adult newsstand owners.

Though children would continue to hawk papers on city streets through the 1920s and 1930s, and on into the middle decades of the century, the balance between street hustlers and residential carriers would shift dramatically. The working-class city kids who had once been the bulwark of the afternoon sales force were reduced to a distinct minority by circulation managers who sought out a "better class" of boys to deliver subscribers' papers to the front porch.

Any child with the money to buy papers could hawk them on the streets. Carriers had to meet specific requirements—and agree to abide by a set code of laws—before they were given routes. In St. Paul, Minnesota, the carriers for a major daily were required "to pay for their papers one month in advance and in addition deposit, upon taking charge of their routes, a sum of money equivalent to two weeks' paper bill." In Lincoln, Illinois, the *Courier-Herald* hired only boys "who have telephones in their homes and own bicycles." Such requirements limited and sanitized the carrier force. In Seattle, Anna Reed noted that the "carriers," unlike the street hustlers, were seldom foreign-born" and almost never of southern European birth." In Yonkers, Margaret Beard found that while over one third of the carriers were "American," with another 25 percent Irish, English, or Scotch, only 5 percent of the street hustlers were American and only 5 percent more Welsh or Scottish. The differences were as significant in their fathers' occupations: the carriers' fathers were more than twice as likely as the street sellers' to be store owners, factory bosses, white-collar workers, or professionals."[11]

The work of the carriers had little in common with that of the street traders. Though the newspaper publishers made much of the training they gave their boys, the carriers learned less on their routes than the street traders did on their corners. As employees—employees who were children and treated as such—they were required to follow adult orders from the moment they got their routes until they outgrew them. They were told what to wear, how to ride their bicycles, what to say to their customers, when to pick up their papers, how to fold them, and where to put them. At the Indianapolis *News*, which William Scott, author of *Scientific Circulation Management*, described as the paper with the best circulation department in the nation, there were no less than twenty-one different categories of rules governing the boys' behavior. As Scott put it, "The outstanding fact about the . . . rules is the absolute control, amounting to a 'benevolent despotism' exercised by *The News* over its distributing force."[12]

Though eclipsed in numbers and importance by adults and home-delivery carriers, the street hustlers did not disappear from the city's streets. City boys, fifteen, sixteen, and older, continued to hawk their papers on the streets, though never—after 1920—in the same numbers or with the same profitability or degree of freedom as earlier in the century. As Harry Shulman of the New York Child Labor Committee observed in 1931, the importance of the boys to the newspapers lay not in "the actual number of copies they [sold], which is an inconsequential drop in the circulation bucket, but [in] the value which accrues from having these newspapers thrust before the public eye with a fever of energy which only youngsters are willing to display. The child news-seller is omnipresent; in restaurants, at theatres, movies, prizefights, on the street, in subway and elevated trains. . . . He is good indirect advertising and for that reason his use is apparently not discouraged by tabloid newspaper publishers."[13]

Here stands the final epitaph to the newsies and their fellow street traders. The children who had once rocked the Hearst and Pulitzer empires were now prized by the publishers for their value as "good indirect advertising." How the mighty had fallen.

Epilogue

T he early twentieth-century city was a city of strangers. Most of its inhabitants had been born or raised elsewhere. Only the children were native to the city—with no memory, no longing, no historic commitment to another land, another way of life.

The children of the city grew up with the city and with the century. They were present when the nation won its "splendid little war" with Spain and built its empire. They observed the first automobiles chugging through the streets. They played in the freshly dug tunnels and then rode the subways. They window-shopped in the department stores and joined the crowds in the downtown entertainment districts now glowing with electric lights. They were there when the movies were born and watched as that small cottage industry became big business, its studios transported from New Jersey to Hollywood, its theaters transformed from storefront nickelodeons to lavish movie palaces.

The streets that they grew up on were self-contained environments, separate from those of home and parents. Children who stayed at school and work until dinnertime grew up regarding home as the place they left in the morning and returned to at night: it was not nor could it be the center of their existence. Work, money, and the fun that money bought were located on the streets of the city.

The boys who found their fun outside the home would as adults continue to seek their amusements elsewhere. The girls who had spent their early years working inside as little mothers would, in a similar

fashion, continue to spend more time at home. There was nothing new
in this. For generations previously, workingmen had left home and family
for the saloon while the women had found their companionship closer to
home. What was new to the twentieth-century city was the quality,
quantity, and pull of the amusements that drew both boys and girls into
the streets. Though they would not have occasion, in childhood or adult
life, to share equally in the life of the city, both boys and girls would
grow up believing there was nothing wrong or selfish or irresponsible or
immoral about using one's earnings to have fun or seeking that fun outside
the bosom of the family. Families that generations before might have
worked, played, worshiped, and celebrated together did less of this in
the new century. Aside from a small but vocal army of mid-century
moralizers prattling about the joys and virtues of "togetherness," no one
seemed to mind. Leisure time was too important to be wasted or sacrificed
to the abstract virtues of family solidarity.

The children grew up understanding far better than their parents
the place of entertainment in twentieth-century urban life. A good time—
at the movies, at the amusement park, or shopping in the dime or
department store and wearing your new finery—was more than the
reward for work: it was the reason one worked. As Daniel Bell pointed
out in his 1956 essay on "Work and Its Discontents," twentieth-century
Americans were driven to work not by physical hunger or the residual
demands of the Protestant ethic but by a "new hunger," the "desire for
goods" and entertainment.[1] The children had experienced this hunger—
and the pleasure one derived in sating it—at the turn of the century.
Their nickels had kept the nickelodeons in the black. The dollars they
paid as adults would create and sustain a variety of new, multimillion-
dollar entertainment industries.

It was not simply their spending money but their attitude toward
entertainment that would actuate the final stage in the transformation of
American culture from the production orientation and work ethic of a
Benjamin Franklin to the consumption ethos of *Playboy* magazine. Early
American culture heroes had worked hard and saved their money for a
rainy day. Their twentieth-century counterparts worked hard but then
played harder, spending what they had, then borrowing a bit more and
spending that too.

The children had learned in childhood that there was always
something else to see or buy, that the entertainment marketplace had
more to offer than they could ever consume. There was a feverish quality
about their search for fun. The pleasures of paid entertainment were
ephemeral and addictive; yesterday's good time could not satisfy today's
need for more. The new entertainment industries fed the hunger, but

196

in such a way that it was constantly renewed. Few could ride all the rides at the amusement parks. There were new shows daily at the nickelodeons—two on Saturdays. There were more Oliver Optic adventures and Horatio Alger novels than a kid could read in a year.

The children who had been pulled—or had jumped—onto the entertainment merry-go-round remained there as adults. The discontents of modern labor and living made entertainment a necessity; the commodification and mass production of leisure-time activities made its pursuit a serious undertaking. Like the children they had been, the adults were whirled round and round from the marketplace where they bought their fun to the workplace where they earned enough for more. They kept their balance without getting dizzy or evidencing any great desire to jump off.

From their vantage point on the streets, the children observed the life of the city and joined in its work. Daily they left their working-class neighborhoods for the downtown business, shopping, and entertainment districts. Doing so, they could not but notice—and try to make sense of—the disparities between their parents' poverty and the wealth they saw paraded on the downtown streets.

In the movie theaters, on the newspaper pages, in school, and on the streets, the children observed that material success appeared to come to those who spoke without accents, who dressed properly, who knew their way around the city. Jerre Mangione understood as a child that though his Sicilian relatives looked down upon the Americans, their language, their morals, and their table manners, they admired and respected them at the same time. "After all, to be an 'Americano' [or a Sicilian who behaved like an 'Americano'] was a sign that you were getting on in the world. The bosses were Americans. The police were Americans. In fact, nearly anyone who had plenty of money or a good steady job was either an American or was living like one."[2]

The children and their parents misconstrued the effect as the cause. Children were expected to succeed where their parents had failed because they were more American, spoke better English, and had been raised on the city's streets and schooled in its classrooms. Those who were not handicapped by Old World accents and habits, those who had grown up in the city would, it was hoped and believed, find success here.

The older generation, especially the recent immigrants, harbored an optimism born of suffering and the hope that that suffering would be redeemed in the next generation. Harry Golden wrote of the Lower East Side Jews that they "did anything for the children. They wanted the

197

children to enter the American middle class. My son will be a doctor, they'd say, or a lawyer, maybe a teacher. I never heard anyone express lesser hopes for his child."[3] It is traditional to attribute such hopes to the Russian Jewish immigrants, but others felt precisely the same way about their children's futures. Leonard Covello's father, born and raised in Sicily, also expected his son to achieve the material success he, the father, had not attained. " 'Nardo,' my father repeated again and again. 'In me you see a dog's life. Go to school. Even if it kills you. With the pen and with books you have the chance to live like a man and not like a beast of burden.' "[4]

The children of the city absorbed their parents' dreams for the future. No matter what that future would bring, it would not entirely erase the expectations formed in childhood. Using Freud to correct Marxists who, he claimed, had forgotten their own childhoods, Jean-Paul Sartre has reminded us that we were not conceived as adult wage earners.[5] We live our lives moving forward to catch the possibilities we set out before us as children. We fashion and project our own personal opportunity structures from the experience of the world we lived in as children. The lessons the children learned on the street were not interred with their childhoods, but were cast forward to frame their perceptions of the society they would join as adults.

The street bred a gritty self-reliance in its children. It was their frontier. In meeting its dangers and clearing a play and then a work space for themselves, they developed confidence in their strength of purpose and their powers to make their own way. The city held few mysteries for those who grew up with it. They would not—as adults— be shocked by its violence, bewildered by its diversity, overwhelmed by its congestion, or confused by its traffic patterns. Their early responsibilities would prepare them for future adult ones. "Little mothers" who had bargained with butchers and cared for infants would not be frightened by the tasks they would confront as wives and housekeepers. Little hustlers who had negotiated with hard-nosed circulation managers and suppliers would not enter the workplace as innocents ripe for exploitation.

The children of the city would grow up to exert an influence on American culture far out of proportion to their numbers, their wealth, or their political and social power. Though there were among them children who would become United States senators (Jacob Javits), Supreme Court justices (William O. Douglas), heavyweight champions of the world (Jack Dempsey), corporate executives (David Sarnoff), philosophers (Morris Raphael Cohen), bestselling novelists (Meyer Levin), educators, critics, and journalists, in none of these fields would the former street children displace older, established elites. Only in the entertainment industries which grew up with the children would they achieve an influence that was both profound and predominant.

This book is filled with the names of vaudeville stars, comedians, and Broadway and Hollywood directors, producers, writers, and actors. As we argued earlier, the children who achieved fortune and fame in show business were in many respects representative of their generation.[6] Though their individual talents and ambitions and their ultimate success would mark them off from their contemporaries, they grew up in the same tenements, played on the same streets, attended the same schools, had the same sorts of fights with their parents, and hawked papers, shined shoes, and peddled gum just like the others. We can, in examining their adult lives and work, locate—in microcosm—the influence of the streets on their generation. We can also trace that generation's contribution to the shaping of twentieth-century American culture. The entertainers were the vehicle through which the street children exerted their particular influence on American culture. Embedded in their songs, their comedy routines, and their movies were the lessons they had learned years before on the streets of the city.

Though the movies, as Gilbert Seldes has written, came from America, they were made here by immigrants and their children.[7] The nickelodeon owners who moved to Hollywood to establish and then manage the first studios (Harry Cohn, William Fox, Samuel Goldwyn, Sam Katz, Louis B. Mayer, Spyros B. Skouras, Marcus Loew, and the Warner brothers) were children of the late nineteenth- and early twentieth-century cities who had played, worked, and grown up on the streets. In the decades between the wars, it was they who exerted the greatest influence on the shape of the image and the sound of the dialogue that reached the screen. Though the studio heads did not supervise every project from conception to script and screen, the men who worked under them were always alert to their probable reactions. The projects that were bought, shaped into scripts, produced, and distributed were those that appealed—or that the producers, directors, and screenwriters believed might appeal—to the moguls' tastes.[8]

The moguls were businessmen, who sought above all to maximize their profits by shaping their product to the market (and the market to their product). But they were also former street children who believed in the messages they projected on the screen. Edward G. Robinson, who on his arrival in Hollywood was amazed and a bit frightened by the personal attention and power the moguls focused on their films, saw at once that no matter what their habits, moralities, or life styles, the studio heads "imposed their childhood moralities on the screen."[9] They considered the studios their personal property. Anything that might offend them was barred from production, but projects they approved of were supported from beginning to end. The Andy Hardy films received star treatment from Metro-Goldwyn-Mayer because Louis B. was captivated by the project. With his interest, support, and sometimes interference (he once had a scene rewritten because he was convinced that Andy was not praying the way he should), the series ran to fourteen films. Had Mickey Rooney not grown up and gone off to war, fourteen more might have been produced.[10]

It was in the 1930s that the movies attained "the zenith of their popularity and influence," with the introduction of sound temporarily postponing the impact of the Depression on box office receipts.[11] Though the Warner Brothers' *The Jazz Singer*, starring Al Jolson, was the first film to talk (or rather sing), it was the gangster films that made the most of the new technology. In the early 1930s the studios turned out one after another, with Warner Brothers leading the way.[12] The first of the 1930s' gangster films—and among the most successful commercially— was *Little Caesar*, bought by Jack Warner, a street kid from Youngstown, Ohio, produced by Hal Wallis, a street kid from Chicago, directed by Mervyn LeRoy, a former San Francisco newsie, and starred in by Edward G. Robinson from the Lower East Side. Each of these men had a special relationship to the film. In their autobiographies, Warner, Wallis, and LeRoy[13] each claim to have initiated the project, and Robinson explains how he tried to convince producer Hal Wallis that the part of "Rico" was made for him. He, Robinson, and "Rico" (he could have added, Wallis, Warner, and LeRoy, as well) were ambitious men who fought to be "different, above, higher." They came from the "humblest, the most dispossessed" of backgrounds. They feared that their ambitions to rise in the world would eventually lead to self-destruction.[14]

The gangster films are films about the city. The gangster, as Robert Warshow has written, is "a man of the city, with the city's language and knowledge, with its queer and dishonest skills and its terrible daring. . . ."[15] The films present the street as a determinative influence in the lives of the adults who grew up on it. We are reminded again and again—sometimes, as in *The Public Enemy*, in the film's opening scenes— that the gangster is a former child of the streets. So too, we learn, is his counterpart, the "good" or reformed brother or friend: Rico's sidekick

Joe Massera (Douglas Fairbanks, Jr.) in *Little Caesar*, Baby-Face Martin's old playmate Dave Connell (Joel McCrea) in *Dead End*, Tom Powers' (James Cagney's) war hero brother in *The Public Enemy*. Gangsters and good guys have grown up with the same tough-skinned determination, strength of will, and ambition. They are urban frontiersmen who know what they want and possess the self-reliance, courage, and confidence to get it. What in the end distinguishes good guys from gangsters is luck (Dave, in the play from which the film *Dead End* was adapted, suggests that Baby-Face Martin was ruined not by the streets alone but by being sent to reform school for some minor prank[16]) and the gangsters' inability to set limits to their ambition. There are, for the gangsters, no indecent, immoral, or evil means to their ends. They will do whatever they must to reach the top.

The gangsters represent in exaggerated, almost mythologized form the children of the city. For one reason or another, neither home nor family, neither school nor church have tempered the streets' influence on them. They are loyal to family, friends, and the gang, but beyond that are committed to nothing but their own personal success. The street is their strength and their undoing. It has given them the skills, the drive, the cunning they require, but also the unbounded ambition that must lead to their ultimate self-destruction.

The gangster films enjoyed a brief ascendancy in Hollywood, but their gritty realism and unhappy endings were not as well suited to the Depression years as the charm, gaiety, and good times of the screwball comedies which succeeded them as the most popular film genre. There were many reasons why, as historian Robert Sklar has written, "Hollywood's contribution to American culture [in the 1930s] was essentially one of affirmation."[17] The studio heads and their managers, producers, and directors did not want to reawaken the crusades against film that had kept them on the defensive through much of the industry's early years. They also understood as well as anyone that, in an era of economic depression and political anxiety, audiences wanted to be amused and reassured, not challenged by what they saw and heard on the screen.

Hollywood had no difficulty providing the audience with what it wanted. The former street children who reigned in the studios had grown up with a belief in America and its institutions. They were only too pleased to project this faith onto the screen. The screwball comedies that they produced in such abundance in the late 1930s presented a wonderfully optimistic vision of the social world. Rich and poor were separated by circumstance and misunderstanding, no more, no less. In the blockbuster of screwballs, *It Happened One Night,* written by Robert Riskin, a former New York street kid, and directed by Frank Capra, a former Los Angeles newsie, a poor working stiff and a rich girl meet, fall in love, and, in a succession of "screwball" acts prove to one another that they are more alike in personality than separated by class. What counts in the screwballs is spunk, confidence, and inner strength, not money or breeding. In *Easy Living,* a "Wall Streeter" takes delight in marrying his son to a "plain Jane working girl."[18] In *It Happened One Night,* Claudette Colbert's grumpy millionaire father helps Clark Gable win his daughter's hand in marriage because he admires his character.

Frank Capra's films were not as blissfully oblivious to social problems as most of the comedies and musicals of the 1930s, but they shared with them the "common assumption that America is the last, best hope of mankind, the country where the fate of the common man is of the utmost importance."[19] Even in his so-called "populist" films, where Capra describes a social and economic order despoiled by bankers, corrupt politicians, businessmen, and the misguided "masses," the disorder is only temporary, never permanent. In the end, it is Mr. Deeds, John Doe, and Mr. Smith who set things right again. They, the common men, triumph—and with them, America and capitalism.

While the Marx Brothers films are perhaps the most wildly satiric and subversive of the 1930s' Hollywood productions, they resemble the others in their happy endings. The world, so artfully taken apart in the course of the film, is always put back together again in the end—with lovers united, sanitariums, circuses, and tenors rescued, and villains unmasked and humiliated. Class differences are not always bridged by love, but neither do they loom large in the fates of their characters. The world of the rich and powerful exists to provide the brothers with a source of amusement and funds. Like the street children arriving downtown to sell their wares, the brothers appear as aliens visiting a social world they do not belong in: hotels, opera houses, country estates, ocean liners, and big stores. The comedy develops from the confrontation between the brothers and the established society they are thrown into. Harpo plays himself throughout: the cheerful cherub who converts his environment into a playground. But Chico and Groucho are presented, in different ways, as hustlers who must make their living from the rich. Chico is a street kid, hustling, peddling, hyping, wheeling and dealing. Groucho takes another approach. Like the street performers and newsies looking for a tip, he plays to his patron, Margaret Dumont, at once flattering, cajoling, and entertaining her. He is a rogue, a hustler, and will do nothing to hide it. This is his particular way of making a living, he declares through his actions and words, and it is no more or less corrupt than anyone else's. There is so much money around, why not take what you can, when you can?

From *A Night at the Opera:*

"**Dumont.** Mr. Driftwood: three months ago you promised to put me into society. In all that time, you've done nothing but draw a very handsome salary.

Groucho. You think that's nothing, huh? How many men do you suppose are drawing a handsome salary nowadays? Why, you can count them on the fingers of one hand. . . ."[20]

From *The Coconuts:*

"**Dumont.** What in the world is the matter with you?

Groucho. Oh, I . . . I'm not myself tonight. I don't know who I am. One false move and I'm yours. I love you. I love you anyhow.

Dumont. I don't think you'd love me if I were poor.

Groucho. I might, but I'd keep my mouth shut."[21]

The Marx Brothers recall the streets not simply in the content but in the style of their comedy. Like many other entertainers who grew up on the streets and served an apprenticeship in vaudeville, they translate to the screen the energy and drive that propelled them forward on the street and the stage. There was, as Gilbert Seldes observed in the 1920s of Fanny Brice and Al Jolson, both former street children, an almost " 'daemonic' heat and abandon" in their performances,[22] the same manic energy that fueled the Marx Brothers movies and stage and screen performances by Danny Kaye, Eddie Cantor, George Jessel, Milton Berle (especially in his "Texaco Star Theater" television shows), and Phil Silvers (as Sergeant Bilko on television), all of whom grew up on the streets.

The former street traders performed as adults without a trace of self-consciousness or a hint of embarrassment—and they never slowed down. What Irving Howe has identified as "the almost hysterical frenzy with which many of them worked" was, as he put it, a direct spin-off from their immigrant experience and their Jewish backgrounds.[23] It was also a lesson learned in their youth. The street traders' and performers' energy and exuberance betrayed an anxiety that anything less than total effort would not suffice. Their customers demanded everything they had. Child newsies, peddlers, and performers had to make themselves heard, seen, and noticed; they had to create their customers and their audience out of anonymous passers-by. There was plenty of money out there on the streets, but it had to be corralled and coerced out of adult pockets. One had to shout, gesticulate, and perform day after day. And even then, nothing was guaranteed.

From stage and screen, and later on radio and television, the former street children broadcast to the nation the lessons they had learned on the streets and their faith in themselves and in America. While a few, like Samuel Ornitz, made headlines by defying inquisitors from the House Committee on Un-American Activities, most went out of their way to parade their love of the nation, middle-class pieties, and capitalism. James Cagney, under some suspicion in the 1930s for his activism in the Screen Actors Guild and his left-liberal politics, volunteered (through his agent brother) to star in a movie version of George M. Cohan's life not only because the role of the "damndest patriotic man in the country"[24] would rescue his reputation, but because he considered himself as much a "Yankee Doodle Dandy" as Cohan. George Jessel dressed in his Uncle Sam suit, Eddie Cantor selling war bonds, Burns and Allen transporting their vaudeville routines into a suburban setting (with their WASP neighbors, the Mortons), Milton Berle as television's Uncle Miltie, Irving Berlin writing and singing "God Bless America"—all were unmistakably former street kids, but they were also 100 percent American and, as they never ceased to remind themselves and their audiences, very proud of it.

The street children of the city, those who attained fame and fortune in show business and those who did not, grew up with a faith in themselves and a faith in America. They had won the battle of the streets—as children—and come home with change in their pockets, enough to help support their families and buy themselves a good time. They carried into adult life the vision of a social world where one's earnings were usually sufficient to satisfy one's needs for subsistence and amusement.

Those who had been born with the century and had taken their first full-time jobs in the 1920s were hard hit by the Great Depression (with the exception, of course, of some of the Hollywood stars), but not hard enough to destroy the faith that had been built on the streets of the city. There was too much wealth in the nation. And they were too shrewd, too smart, and too disciplined by their apprenticeship on the streets to be shut out for long. Nicholas Gerros, a Greek immigrant who had shined shoes as a boy and opened up a small clothing store in the late twenties, recalled of the Depression that it "influenced [but] didn't bother me too much because I was young [i.e., new] in the business and I also was young."[25] Jerre Mangione, another former street child, spent the Depression years in New York City employed in a dozen capacities as writer, critic, and editor. Through the ups and downs, he remained, as he put it, "more responsive than ever to the Horatio Alger syndrome implanted by my public-school teachers. . . . The promises proffered in the demonic Manhattan landscape, though often based on quicksand premises, held me enthralled."[26]

If the Depression tested but did not upset the street traders' faith, the boom that began on the home front during World War II and extended with periodic brief recessions through the 1960s served to reconfirm it. Those who held jobs—and very few of the former white male street traders did not—found that their paychecks were large enough to cover the necessary expenses of home and family and buy goods and services their parents had never dreamed of. Democrats or Republicans, liberals or conservatives, they accepted the social world as it was or could become with minor adjustments. They might complain about prices, taxes, and wages. They might even protest government policies and strike against employers. But they never doubted that they lived in the best of all social worlds. Their patriotism, often bordering on chauvinism as they grew older, came naturally. Whether they grew up to become movie stars, heavyweight champions of the world, steelworkers, or corner newsstand owners, they had come further than their parents and they trusted their children would do even better.

When, through the later 1940s, 1950s, and early 1960s, scores of intellectuals, politicians, and economists celebrated the "end of ideology" and the rising "age of affluence," they were codifying the faith in capitalism and the American political system that the street children had held all along. What Godfrey Hodgson has identified as "the ideology of the liberal consensus" was not imposed from the top down.[27] The former street traders did not need Daniel Bell, Arthur Schlesinger, Jr., Peter Drucker, W. W. Rostow, John Kenneth Galbraith, or the editors of *Fortune* magazine to tell them that capitalism worked, "and since World War II [as Galbraith had put it], quite brilliantly."[28] It was not "false consciousness" or the hegemonic powers of the corporate state that had convinced them that this was the case; it was, rather, their particular experience as children reconfirmed in adult life.

The former street traders suffered from tunnel vision through their lifetimes. Their good fortune—and the celebration of it by mid-century ideologists and politicians—blinded them to the fate of the millions, here and abroad, who were not about to enter the age of affluence. The closure of ideological debate (a phenomenon described from opposite ends of the political spectrum by Daniel Bell and Herbert Marcuse) locked them into a one-dimensional universe of discourse where anticapitalist (equated with anti-American) arguments could be neither presented nor considered. When, in the late 1960s and early 1970s, oppositional, critical ideologies resurfaced with the civil rights and anti-war movements, they could be easily dismissed by the former street traders who, having hustled for pennies as children, could not accept the claim that America was not and had not always been the land of opportunity and beacon of freedom for the poor and oppressed.

The street children's good fortune stayed with them through the years. They were born in cities expanding in economic opportunities for young white males. They grew old amidst the economic euphoria and unprecedented supremacy this nation enjoyed in the aftermath of World War II. They retired when the Social Security system was still a marvel of solvency. By the time a prolonged economic downturn set in, in the 1970s and 1980s, their time was running out.

The street traders are no longer with us, but their influence on our culture remains as strong today as it was thirty and forty years ago. Their faith in America and in capitalism was so comforting, so proudly proclaimed, so in tune with the ideological currents of the mid-century liberal consensus, so often confirmed by their personal experience, and so vividly presented to the public that it exerted an influence far greater than it should have.

From the vantage point of the middle 1980s—with jobs disappearing from these shores, infrastructures collapsing, credit tightened, and overall unemployment locked at record-high levels—it would be sheer folly to retain much faith in the social and economic order the street traders trusted. And yet their optimism, their Americanism, their trust in the ability of the economy to right itself remain with us—as a barrier to the rethinking and restructuring that must take place if we are to proceed toward a more productive and more just future. The "American Century," so labeled and celebrated by Henry Luce in the 1940s, was coterminous with the street children's lifetime. But it has ended. And will not return.

While we must consign to political oblivion those who continue to espouse the old platitudes about the good life in America, we can and should remember the children of the city and the cities they grew up in. Those cities were probably as dangerous, as dirty, and as depraved as ours, but they were places of promise, of hope, of trust in the future. When we talk to our parents, grandparents, and relatives who grew up on the streets or see before us the image of James Cagney singing "I'm a Yankee Doodle Dandy," or the Marx brothers outwitting villans, or George Burns crooning "Take Me Out to the Ball Game" at the 1983 All-Star Game, we are momentarily brought back to that world and enriched by it.

Appendix:
A Note on Sources:
The Newsboy Studies

An invaluable source for this work have been the "newsboy studies" completed between 1902 and 1922. The child labor and child welfare reform groups and, in some states, departments of labor and industrial statistics, collected as much data as possible about working children, convinced that the data put into proper form would convert an otherwise apathetic public to their cause. Much of the material was never published. Some remains in note form or as rough drafts, interview schedules, case studies, or internal memoranda.

In the course of my research, I was able to locate and consult reports on newsboy conditions in the following cities and states (full references to these reports can be found in the Notes):

New York City (1902–3, 1906, 1911, 1912, 1915, 1915–18), Buffalo (1903), Syracuse (1911), Mount Vernon (1912), Albany (1920), and Yonkers (1920), New York; Chicago, Illinois (1905, 1918); Milwaukee, Wisconsin (1911); Des Moines, Iowa (1920); Cincinnati (1908, 1917), Cleveland (1908–9), and Toledo (1920), Ohio; Seattle, Washington (1915–16); Dallas, Texas (1921); Birmingham, Alabama (1920); Philadelphia, Pennsylvania (1910); Detroit, Michigan (1914); Boston, Massachusetts (1920); Baltimore, Maryland (1913, 1915, 1916); Bennington, Rutland, and Burlington, Vermont (1910); St. Louis (1910) and Kansas City (1914–15), Missouri; Newark, Hoboken, Paterson, Jersey City, Bayonne, Trenton, and Elizabeth, New Jersey (1912).

Statewide reports on child laborers with specific sections on newsboys were available for New Jersey (1907), Alabama (1922), Tennessee (1920),

Kentucky (1919), North Carolina (1918), Oklahoma (1918), Iowa (1922), Ohio (1919), and Pennsylvania (1922).

A guide to the published reports is *Children in Street Trades in the United States: A List of References*, compiled by Laura A. Thompson, U.S. Department of Labor (Washington, D.C., 1925).

Unpublished reports were located in the papers of the New York Child Labor Committee, New York State Library, Albany, New York; papers of the National Child Labor Committee, Manuscript Division, Library of Congress, Washington, D.C.; Jane Addams Memorial Collection and the papers of the Juvenile Protective Association, University of Illinois at Chicago, Chicago, Illinois; and Jane Addams Papers, Swarthmore College Peace Collection, Swarthmore, Pennsylvania.

Abbreviations

Abbreviations for Manuscript and Oral History Collections

AJC   William E. Wiener Oral History Library of the American Jewish Committee, New York, New York.

CP   Oral History of Chicago-Polonia, Chicago Historical Society, Chicago, Illinois.

CSS   Community Service Society Papers, Rare Book and Manuscript Library, Butler Library, Columbia University, New York, New York.

FLPS   Chicago Foreign Language Press Survey, Works Projects Administration, 1942, Department of Special Collections, University of Chicago Library, Chicago, Illinois.

IC   Italians in Chicago Project, Manuscript Department, University of Illinois at Chicago Library, Chicago, Illinois.

ICMA   International Circulation Managers Association, Reston, Virginia.

IHS   Illinois Humane Society Papers, Special Collections, University of Illinois at Chicago Library, Chicago, Illinois.

JAMC   Jane Addams Memorial Collection, Special Collections, University of Illinois at Chicago Library, Chicago, Illinois.

JAP   Jane Addams Papers, Swarthmore College Peace Collection, Swarthmore College, Swarthmore, Pennsylvania.

JPA   Juvenile Protective Association Papers, Special Collections, University of Illlinois at Chicago Library, Chicago, Illinois.

LC   Library of Congress, Washington, D.C.

LDT   Lea Demarest Taylor Papers, Special Collections, University of Illinois at Chicago Library, Chicago, Illinois.

LW   Lillian Wald Papers, Rare Book and Manuscript Library, Butler Library, Columbia University, New York, New York.

NCLC   National Child Labor Committee Papers, Manuscript Division, Library of Congress, Washington, D.C.

NYCLC   New York Child Labor Committee Papers, New York State Library, Albany, New York.

NYWP   New York World Papers, Rare Book and Manuscript Library, Butler Library, Columbia University, New York, New York.

YIVO   Oral History Collection, YIVO Institute for Jewish Research, New York, New York.

Notes

Chapter One

1. David Ward, *Cities and Immigrants: A Geography of Change in Nineteenth Century America* (New York, 1971), 51–150; Sam Bass Warner, *Urban Wilderness* (New York, 1972), 85–112.

2. On Chicago: Harold M. Mayer and Richard C. Wade, *Chicago: The Growth of a Metropolis* (Chicago, 1969), 214; on Boston: Sam Bass Warner, *Streetcar Suburbs* (New York, 1976), 46–116; on Cincinnati: Zane L. Miller, *Boss Cox's Cincinnati: Urban Politics in the Progressive Era* (New York, 1968), 25–29; on Columbus, Ohio: Roderick Duncan McKenzie, *The Neighborhood: A Study of Local Life in the City of Columbus, Ohio* (Chicago, 1923), 360–62; on Pittsburgh: John Bodnar, Roger Simon, and Michael P. Weber, *Lives of Their Own: Blacks, Italians, and Poles in Pittsburgh, 1900–1960* (Urbana, 1982), 21–25; on Manhattan: Theodore Dreiser, *The Color of a Great City* (New York, 1923), 6–7.

3. Gerard R. Wolfe, *New York: A Guide to the Metropolis* (New York, 1975), 163–85.

4. Ibid.

5. Glen E. Holt and Dominic A. Pacyga, *Chicago: A Historical Guide to the Neighborhoods* (Chicago, 1979), 17–18; Mayer and Wade, *Chicago*, 218–20.

6. William Leach, "Department Stores and Consumer Culture: The Transformation of Women in an Age of Abundance, 1890–1920" (unpublished paper, 1982); Susan Porter Benson, "Palace of Consumption and Machine for Selling: The American Department Store," *Radical History Review*, no. 21 (Fall 1979), 208–11.

7. Leach, "Department Stores," 1.

8. Theodore Dreiser, *Sister Carrie* (New York, 1932), 24.

9. Leach, "Department Stores," 8–10.

10. Lloyd Morris, *Incredible New York: High Life and Low Life of the Last 100 Years* (New York, 1951), 259–72.

11. On the new nightlife, see Lewis A. Erenberg, *Steppin' Out: New York Nightlife and the Transformation of American Culture, 1890–1930* (Westport, Conn. 1981).

12. Erenberg, *Steppin' Out*, 67. Also, on vaudeville, see Russel Nye, *The Unembarrassed Muse: The Popular Arts in America* (New York, 1970), 167–72; Gunther Barth, *City People: The Rise of Modern City Culture in Nineteenth-Century America* (New York, 1980), 192–228.

13. Nye, *Unembarrassed Muse*, 168.

14. Barth, *City People*, 211.

15. Arnold Bennett, *Your United States: Impressions of a First Visit* (New York, 1912), 137.

16. Erenberg, *Steppin' Out*, 40–41.

17. Ibid., 45.

18. Ibid., 49–50; Morris, *Incredible New York*, 243.

19. Erenberg, *Steppin' Out*, 148–71; Nye, *Unembarrassed Muse*, 327.

20. Morris, *Incredible New York*, 273.

21. H. G. Wells, *The Future in America* (New York, 1906), 135.

22. Robert Shackleton, *The Book of Chicago* (Philadelphia, 1920), 177–78.

23. See, for example, Oscar Handlin, *The Uprooted*, 2nd ed. (Boston, 1973); and, in rebuttal to Handlin, Rudolph J. Vecoli, "Contadini in Chicago: A Critique of the Uprooted," *Journal of American History* 51, no. 3 (December 1964), 404–17.

24. M. E. Ravage, *An American in the Making: The Life Story of an Immigrant* (1917; reprint, New York, 1971), 72–73.

25. James Borchert, *Alley Life in Washington: Family, Community, Religion, and Folklife in the City, 1850–1970* (Urbana, 1980); Paul Underwood Kellogg, ed., *The Pittsburgh Survey*, vol. 5: *The Pittsburgh District: Civic Frontage* (New York, 1914), 92–114; Thomas Lee Philpott, *The Slum and the Ghetto: Neighborhood Deterioration and Middle-Class Reform, Chicago, 1880–1930* (New York, 1978), 6–41.

26. Dreiser, *Color of a City*, 86.

27. Robert W. DeForest and Lawrence Veiller, eds., *The Tenement House Problem*, 2 vols. (New York, 1903), I:8.

28. Ibid., 436.

29. Ibid., 425.

30. Edith Abbott, *The Tenements of Chicago, 1908–1935* (Chicago, 1936), 213.

31. Mike Gold, *Jews Without Money* (1930; reprint, New York, 1965), 100.

32. Ibid., 88–89.

33. Ravage, *American in the Making*, 60, 66–77.

34. Harry Roskolenko, *The Time That Was Then: The Lower East Side: 1900–1913—An Intimate Chronicle* (New York, 1971), 97; see also Katherine Anthony, *Mothers Who Must Earn* (New York, 1914), 9.

35. Roskolenko, *Time That Was*, 91–107; Anthony Sorrentino, *Organizing Against Crime: Redeveloping the Neighborhood* (New York, 1977), 38.

36. Simon Patten, *The New Basis of Civilization* (New York, 1913), 23; Waverley Lewis Root, *Eating in America: A History* (New York, 1976), 234.

37. Root, *Eating in America*, 234–35.

38. Ibid., U. S. Department of Agriculture, *Consumption of Food in the United States, 1909–52* (Washington, D.C., 1953), 109.

39. Susan Strasser, *Never Done: A History of American Housework* (New York, 1982), 27–29; Daniel Boorstin, *The Americans: The Democratic Experience* (New York, 1974), 315–16.

40. Strasser, *Never Done*, 16–23; Boorstin, *The Americans*, 322–24; Root, *Eating in America*, 188; Patten, *New Basis*, 20.

41. Patten, *New Basis*, 19; U. S. Department of Labor, "Women in the Candy Industry in Chicago and St. Louis," in *Bulletin of the Women's Bureau*, no. 25 (Washington, D.C., 1923), 1; Root, *Eating in America*, 421.

42. Michael and Ariane Batterberry, *On the Town in New York: From 1776 to the Present* (New York, 1973), 168; Al Hirshberg and Sammy Aaronson, *As High as My Heart: The Sammy Aaronson Story* (New York, 1957), 19.

43. Moss Hart, *Act One: An Autobiography* (New York, 1959), 8.

44. Hy Kraft, *On My Way to the Theater* (New York, 1971), 13.

45. Charles Zueblin, *American Municipal Progress*, rev. ed. (New York, 1916), 3–4.

Chapter Two

1. Theodore Dreiser, *The Color of a Great City* (New York, 1923), 44–45.

2. Henry James, *The American Scene* (New York, 1946), 131–34; Dreiser, *Color of a City*, 44; Robert Woods, ed., *The City Wilderness: A Settlement Study* (Boston, 1898), 235.

3. See, for example, Homer Hoyt, *One Hundred Years of Land Values in Chicago* (Chicago, 1933).

4. Madison (Wis.) Board of Commerce, *Madison Recreation Survey* (Madison, 1915), 7; see also Roderick Duncan McKenzie, *The Neighborhood: A Study of Local Life in the City of Columbus, Ohio* (Chicago, 1923), 604.

5. Oral history of Frank Broska, IC, 19.

6. See, for example, "The Pre-Adolescent Girl in Her Home," LDT, box 7, folder 4, 11.

7. Catharine Brody, "A New York Childhood," *The American Mercury* XIV (1928), 57.

8. Mike Gold, *Jews Without Money* (1930; reprint, New York, 1965), 38 39.

9. Iona and Peter Opie, *Children's Games in Street and Playground* (London, 1969), 11; Colin Ward, *The Child in the City* (New York, 1978), 97.

10. Johan Huizinga, *Homo Ludens: A Study of the Play Element in Culture* (Boston, 1955), 10.

11. Harry Roskolenko, *The Time That Was Then: The Lower East Side: 1900–1913—An Intimate Chronicle* (New York, 1971), 24; Gold, *Jews Without Money*, 31.

12. Opie, *Children's Games*, 10.

13. Gold, *Jews Without Money*, 28.

14. Harpo Marx with Rowland Barber, *Harpo Speaks* (New York, 1974), 36.

15. John Collier and Edward M. Barrows, *The City Where Crime Is Play: A Report by the People's Institute* (New York, 1914), 14–18.

16. Jane Addams, *The Spirit of Youth and the City Streets* (1909; reprint, New York, 1972), 55–57; on "juvenile justice," see also Anthony M. Platt, *The Child Savers: The Invention of Delinquency* (Chicago, 1969); Ellen Ryerson, *The Best-Laid Plans: America's Juvenile Court Experiment* (New York, 1978), 35–77.

17. Collier and Barrows, *The City*, 18; Alan Levy, *The Bluebird of Happiness: The Memoirs of Jan Peerce* (New York, 1976), 46.

18. Gold, *Jews Without Money*, 28.

19. Eddie Cantor, as told to David Freeman, *My Life Is in Your Hands* (New York, 1928), 50; Charles Angoff, *When I Was a Boy in Boston* (New York, 1947), 97–98.

20. Philip Davis, *Street-land: Its Little People and Big Problems* (Boston, 1915), 28; Woods, *City Wilderness*, 235.

21. Marx, *Harpo*, 17–18, 27–28.

22. Samuel Ornitz, *Haunch, Paunch, and Jowl: An Anonymous Autobiography* (New York, 1923), 30–31.

23. Frederick Thrasher, *The Gang: A Study of 1,313 Gangs in Chicago*, 2nd rev. ed. (Chicago, 1936), 288.

24. Huizinga, *Homo Ludens*, 11–12; Opie, *Children's Games*, 2–4.

25. Kate Simon, *Bronx Primitive* (New York, 1982), 140–42, 152–53; Brody, "New York Childhood," 57–60; Sophie Ruskay, *Horsecars and Cobblestones* (New York, 1973), 41–44.

26. Collier and Barrows, *The City*, 27, 42–44; John Chase, "Street Games of New York City," *Pedagogical Seminary* XII (1905), 503–4; Joseph E. Lee, "Play and Congestion," *Charities and the Commons* XX (April 4, 1908), 43–45; Samuel Chotzinoff, *A Lost Paradise* (New York, 1955), 84–90.

27. George Burns, *The Third Time Around* (New York, 1980), 9–10.

28. Gold, *Jews Without Money*, 32–36; Chotzinoff, *Lost Paradise*, 84–90.

29. Burns, *Third Time Around*, 11.

30. Brody, "New York Childhood," 57; Oral history of Celia Blazek, CP, 10–11; Jerre Mangione, *Mount Allegro* (New York, 1972), 2–3; Milton Berle with Haskel Frankel, *Milton Berle* (New York, 1974), 25–26.

31. Thrasher, *The Gang*, 28, 215.

32. Ibid., 35–36.

33. Oral history of William Gropper, AJC, tape 1, 15–16.

34. See, for example, Ornitz, *Haunch, Paunch*, 18, 35–37, 48–51.

35. Thrasher, *The Gang*, 194.

36. Chotzinoff, *Lost Paradise*, 86; Marx, *Harpo*, 35–36.

37. J. Alvin Kugelmass, *Ralph J. Bunche: Fighter for Peace* (New York, 1962), 27–30; Harry Golden, *The Right Time: An Autobiography* (New York, 1969), 49.

38. Marx, *Harpo*, 35–36; Burns, *Third Time Around*, 31.

39. For Cleveland, see Henry W. Thurston, *Delinquency and Spare Time* (Cleveland, 1918), 34–35; for New York City, see Chotzinoff, *Lost Paradise*, 84.

40. Thurston, *Delinquency*, 24–25.

41. David I. Macleod, *Building Character in the American Boy: The Boy Scouts, YMCA, and Their Forerunners, 1870–1920* (Madison, Wis., 1983), 35–36.

42. Simon Patten, *The New Basis of Civilization* (New York, 1913), 52.

43. Otto T. Mallery, "The Social Significance of Play," *Annals* XXXV (January–June 1910), 156; Macleod, *Building Character*, 66–71.

44. Roy Rosenzweig, *Eight Hours for What We Will: Workers and Leisure in an Industrial City, 1870–1920* (Cambridge, England, 1983), 150–51.

45. Rosenzweig, *Eight Hours*, 149; Henry S. Curtis, "Provision and Responsibility for Playgrounds," *Annals* XXXV (January–June 1910), 342.

46. See special issue of *Annals* on "parks movement": *Annals* XXXV (January–June 1910), 304–70.

47. City Club, *Amusements and Recreation in Milwaukee* (Milwaukee, 1914), 10; Rowland Haynes and Stanley Davies, *Public Provision for Recreation* (Cleveland, 1920), 23–24; Collier and Barrows, *The City*, 11.

48. Huizinga, *Homo Ludens*, 12.

Chapter Three

1. J. C. Kennedy, *Wages and Family Budgets in the Chicago Stockyards District* (Chicago, 1914), 63–68; Louise Bolard More, *Wage-Earners' Budgets: A Study of Standards and Cost of Living in New York City* (New York, 1907); Louise C. Odencrantz, *Italian Women in Industry* (New York, 1919), 18–21; Louise C. Odencrantz and Zenas L. Potter, *Industrial Conditions in Springfield, Illinois* (Department of Surveys and Exhibits, Russell Sage Foundation, New York, 1916), VIII:120; Robert Coit Chapin, *The Standard of Living Among Working Men's Families in New York City* (New York, 1909), 55; Virginia Yans-McLaughlin, *Family and Community: Italian Immigrants in Buffalo, 1880–1930* (Ithaca, 1977), 161.

2. Odencrantz and Potter, *Springfield*, 120; Kennedy, *Wages and Budgets*, 68.

3. Odencrantz, *Italian Women*, 18–19; Yans-McLaughlin, *Family and Community*, 38–43.

4. U. S. Congress, Senate, *Reports of the Immigration Commission* (Washington, D.C., 1911), 11:388.

5. David Montgomery, *Workers' Control in America* (Cambridge, England, 1979), 41.

6. John Bodnar, Roger Simon, and Michael P. Weber, *Lives of Their Own: Blacks, Italians, and Poles in Pittsburgh, 1900–1960* (Urbana, 1982), 89–108; Elizabeth H. Pleck, "A Mother's Wages: Income Earning Among Married Italian and Black Women, 1896–1911," in Michael Gordon, ed., *The American Family in Social-Historical Perspective*, 2nd ed. (New York, 1978), 490–510.

7. John Gillis, *Youth and History: Tradition and Change in European Age Relations, 1770–Present*, Expanded Student Edition (New York, 1981), 57–61.

8. Paul Boyer, *Urban Masses and Moral Order in America, 1820–1920* (Cambridge, Mass., 1978), 96; Thomas Bender, *Toward an Urban Vision: Ideas and Institutions in Nineteenth-Century America* (Baltimore, 1982), 140.

9. Bender, *Urban Vision*, 147–149.

10. U. S. Department of Commerce, Bureau of the Census, *Children in Gainful Occupations at the Fourteenth Census of the United States* (Washington, D.C., 1924), 18–28; U. S. Department of Commerce, Bureau of the Census, *Comparative Occupation Statistics for the United States, 1870–1940*," by Alba Edwards (Washington, D.C., 1943), 91–92; Paul Osterman, "Education and Labor Markets at the Turn of the Century," *Politics and Society* IX, no. 1 (1979), 103–22; Selwyn Troen, "The Discovery of the Adolescent by American Educational Reformers, 1900–1920: An Economic Perspective," in Lawrence Stone, ed., *Schooling and Society* (Baltimore, 1976), 239–51.

11. Troen, in Stone, *Schooling and Society,* 241–42; New York Factory Investigating Commission, *Second Report of the Factory Investigating Commission* (1913), I:266.

12. Robert S. and Helen Merrell Lynd, *Middletown: A Study in American Culture* (1929; reprint, New York, 1956), 40–42; Osterman, *Education and Labor,* 113–15.

13. See, for example, National Industrial Conference Board, *The Employment of Young Persons in the United States* (New York, 1925); Massachusetts Commission on Industrial and Technical Education, *Report* (Boston, 1906), 46.

14. Committee on Industrial Welfare of the Cleveland Chamber of Commerce, *A Report on the Problem of the Substitution of Women for Man Power in Industry* (Cleveland, 1918), 25, 29; Isaac A. Hourwich, *Immigration and Labor. The Economic Aspects of European Immigration to the United States* (New York, 1912), 318–24.

15. U. S. Bureau of the Census, "Children in Gainful Occupations,"19.

16. Lynd and Lynd, *Middletown,* 30.

17. U. S. Department of Commerce, Bureau of the Census, *School Attendance in 1920,* by Frank Alexander Ross (Washington, D.C., 1924), 189, 190, 181; National Center for Educational Statistics, *Digest of Educational Statistics* (Washington, D.C., 1980), 44; David Hogan, "Education and the Making of the Chicago Working Class, 1880–1930," *History of Education Quarterly* XVIII (Fall 1978), 228.

Chapter Four

1. Alan Levy, *The Bluebird of Happiness: The Memoirs of Jan Peerce* (New York, 1976), 34.

2. Harry Golden, *The Right Time: An Autobiography* (New York, 1969), 55.

3. Hy Kraft, *On My Way to the Theater* (New York, 1971), 18.

4. Investigator's report on Theodore Waterman, NYCLC, box 31, folder 9; Milton Berle with Haskel Frankel, *Milton Berle* (New York, 1974), 66; Eddie Cantor with Jane Kesner Ardmore, *Take My Life* (Garden City, 1957), 15.

5. Harry Roskolenko, *The Time That Was Then: The Lower East Side: 1900–1913—An Intimate Chronicle* (New York, 1971), 32; James Cagney, *Cagney by Cagney* (New York, 1977), 31; George Burns, *The Third Time Around* (New York, 1980), 23.

6. Investigator's report on Nicholas Giordano, NYCLC, box 31, folder 9.

7. Edward Clopper, "Children on the Streets of Cincinnati," *Proceedings of the Fourth Annual Meeting of the National Child Labor Committee* (Supplement to the *Annals,* 1908), 117–18.

8. M. E. Ravage, *An American in the Making: The Life Story of an Immigrant* (1917; reprint, New York, 1971), 97–99.

9. Mark Sullivan, *Our Times, 1900–1925,* vol. IV: *The War Begins, 1909–1914* (1932; reprint, New York, 1972), 88.

10. Bessie Turner Kriesberg, "Autobiography," YIVO, 286.

11. Kraft, *On My Way,* 17.

12. Burns, *Third Time,* 39–40.

13. Harry Jolson, as told to Alban Emley, *Mistah Jolson* (Hollywood, 1952), 43–50.

14. Irving Howe, *World of Our Fathers: The Journey of the East European Jews to America and the Life They Found and Made* (New York, 1976), 556.

15. Ibid., 558.

16. Eddie Cantor, as told to David Freedman, *My Life Is in Your Hands* (New York, 1928), 22.

17. Norman Katkov, *The Fabulous Fanny: The Story of Fanny Brice* (New York, 1953), 8–9.

18. Jolson, *Mistah Jolson,* 43–50.

19. Burns, *Third Time,* 23–26.

20. Ibid., 27; Cantor, *My Life,* 22–23; Jolson, *Mistah Jolson,* 43–50.

21. Katkov, *Fabulous Fanny,* 8.

22. Berle, *Milton Berle,* 50–51.

23. National Child Labor Committee, *Child Welfare in North Carolina* (New York, 1918), 220.

24. Ibid.

25. Harpo Marx with Rowland Barber, *Harpo Speaks* (New York, 1974), 32–33.

26. See, for example, Samuel Chotzinoff, *A Lost Paradise* (New York, 1955), 204–6.

Chapter Five

1. Jacob A. Riis, "The New York Newsboy," *Century Magazine* LXXXV (December 1912), 240–48.

2. Frank Luther Mott, *American Journalism, A History: 1690–1960,* 3rd ed. (New York, 1962), 447; Gunther Barth, *City People: The Rise of Modern City Culture in Nineteenth Century America* (New York, 1980), 79.

3. William R. Scott, *Scientific Circulation Management* (New York, 1915), 108.

4. Alan Trachtenberg, *The Incorporation of America: Culture and Society in the Gilded Age* (New York, 1982), 123–24; Barth, *City People,* 90–92; Edwin

Emery, *The Press and America: An Interpretative History of Journalism*, 2nd ed. (New York, 1962), 404.

5. Barth, *City People*, 88–90; *Editor and Publisher*, December 21, 1907, 4; Alfred McClung Lee, *The Daily Newspaper in America: The Evolution of a Social Instrument* (New York, 1937), 289–90; Maurice Hexter, "The Newsboys of Cincinnati," *Studies from the Helen S. Trounstine Foundation* I, no. 4 (January 15, 1919), 120–21.

6. Emery, *The Press*, 516.

7. *Editor and Publisher*, December 21, 1907, 4.

8. *Editor and Publisher*, May 24, 1902, 2.

9. Hexter, "Newsboys," 148–49.

10. See "Circulation Manager's Column" in *Editor and Publisher*, March 25, April 13 and 20, May 6 and 27, June 3, July 1, and October 21, 1916.

11. *Editor and Publisher*, June 30, 1917, part II, 13.

12. Edward Clopper, "Children on the Streets of Cincinnati," *Proceedings of the Fourth Annual Meeting of the National Child Labor Committee* (Supplement to the *Annals*, 1908), 115.

13. Hexter, "Newsboys," 148–49.

14. Joseph Gies, *The Colonel of Chicago* (New York, 1979), 32–37; Wayne Andrews, *Battle for Chicago* (New York, 1946), 232–35; Lloyd Wendt, *Chicago Tribune: The Rise of a Great American Newspaper* (Chicago, 1979), 352–53; John Cooney, *The Annenbergs: The Salvaging of a Tainted Dynasty* (New York, 1982), 31–39.

15. Lee, *Daily Newspaper*, 266.

16. For New York City, see "Memo to George Hall from C. Aronovici, Special Investigator, September 26, 1906," NYCLC, box 31, folder 13, 5; Harry Bremer, "Report of Investigation: New York Newsboy," NCLC, box 4, 2; for Chicago, see [Myron Adams], "Newsboy Conditions in Chicago" JAP, 27; for Baltimore, see Lettie Johnston, "Street Trades and Their Regulation," *Proceedings of the National Conference of Charities and Correction* (1915), 520; for Cincinnati, see Clopper, "Children of Cincinnati," 116; for Dallas, see Civic Federation of Dallas, *The Newsboys of Dallas* (Dallas, 1921), 3.

17. Research Department, School of Social Economy of Washington University, "The Newsboy of Saint Louis" (St. Louis, n.d.), 10.

18. U. S. Department of Commerce, Bureau of the Census, *Children in Gainful Occupations at the Fourteenth Census of the United States* (Washington, D.C., 1924).

19. U. S. Department of Labor, Children's Bureau, *Child Labor Legislation in the United States* (Washington, D.C., 1915), 12–13 (Summary Chart No. 1, Table 6).

20. "Saving the Barren Years," in *The Child in the City: A Handbook of the Child Welfare Exhibit*, 1911, JAMC.

21. Edward Clopper, *Child Labor in City Streets* (New York, 1912), 35.

22. Hexter, "Newsboys," 122.

23. Anna Reed, *Newsboy Service: A Study in Educational and Vocational Guidance* (Yonkers, 1917), 27–44. Figures for the percentage of newsboys per grade were computed by dividing the number of newsboys per grade by the total number of males per grade.

24. Memo from George Hall, November 15, 1911, NYCLC, box 31, folder 13, 4.

25. Justice Harvey Baker to C. Watson, March 13, 1911, NYCLC, box 31, folder 15.

26. Hexter, "Newsboys," 118–19.

27. William Le Roy Zabel, "Street Trades and Juvenile Delinquency" (M.A. dissertation, University of Chicago, 1918), 46; Alexander Fleisher, "The Newsboys of Milwaukee," *Fifteenth Biennial Report of the Bureau of Labor and Industrial Statistics*, State of Wisconsin (1911–12), 77; Charles Storey, "Report of Newsboy Investigation in Syracuse," NYCLC, box 31, folder 13, 5.

28. Investigator's report, December 29, 1916, NYCLC, box 31, folder 22.

29. Loraine B. Bush, "Street Trades in Alabama," *American Child* IV, no. 2 (August 1922), 109.

30. Leonard Benedict, *Waifs of the Slums and Their Way Out* (New York, 1907), 106–7; Mary Aydelott, "Children in Street Trades" (M.A. dissertation, University of Chicago, 1924), 24–26; Elsa Wertheim, "Chicago Children in the Street Trades" (1917), JAMC, 5–9.

31. Fleisher, "Newsboys of Milwaukee," 67.

32. Grace W. Cottrell, "Investigation of the Newsboys of Mount Vernon" (May 14, 1912), NYCLC, box 31, folder 13, 7.

33. Harry Bremer, "Street Trades Investigation" (October 9, 1912), NCLC, box 4, 1–3, 9.

34. Margaret Kent Beard, "A Study of Newsboys in Yonkers—1920," NYCLC, box 31, folder 27, 7.

35. Lewis W. Hine, "Conditions in Vermont Street Trades, etc.," (December 1916), NCLC.

36. Clopper, *Child Labor*, 55–56.

37. Ibid., 55; Reed, *Newsboy Service*, 130.

38. Joe E. Brown, as told to Ralph Hancock, *Laughter Is a Wonderful Thing* (New York, 1956), 12–13.

39. Harry Golden, *The Right Time: An Autobiography* (New York, 1969), 39–40.

40. George Burns, *The Third Time Around* (New York, 1980), 30.

41. *Editor and Publisher*, July 20, 1918, 37; New York *Times*, October 4, 1917, 18.

42. *Editor and Publisher*, June 1, 1918, 21; *The Hustler*, April 1918, 8.

43. New York *Times*, August 23, 1912, 8.

44. *Editor and Publisher*, October 7, 1916, 26.

45. New York *Times*, May 31, 1911, 10; New York *Times*, May 26, 1911, 12; *Editor and Publisher*, June 3, 1916, 16, and October 27, 1917, 27.

46. *The Hustler*, February 1918, 4.

47. Reed, *Newsboy Service*, 135–36; Fleisher, "Newsboys of Milwaukee," 71.

48. Harry Bremer, "Report of Investigation: New York Newsboy" (1913), NCLC, box 4, 8–9; see also Fleisher, "Newsboys of Milwaukee," 91.

49. Golden, *The Right Time*, 55; Chicago Vice Commission, *The Social Evil in Chicago* (Chicago, 1912), 238–39.

50. Mrs. W. J. Norton, "A Study of the Newsboys of Cleveland" (Winter 1908–9), NYCLC, box 31, folder 15, 5; Florence Kelley, "The Street Trader Under Illinois Law," in Sophonisba P. Breckinridge, ed., *The Child in the City* (Chicago, 1912), 291.

51. Mott, *American Journalism*, 480–82, 524–26, 584–85.

52. Bremer, "Street Trades Investigation," 1; Scott Nearing, "The Newsboy at Night in Philadelphia," *Charities and Commons* XVII (February 2, 1906), 778.

53. Johnston, "Street Trades," 523; William Hard, "De kid wot works at night," *Everybody's Magazine* XVIII (January 1908), 35; Bremer, "Street Trades Investigation," 12–13.

54. Nearing, "Newsboy at Night," 779.

55. Bremer, "New York Newsboy," 20–21; see also Storey, "Newsboy in Syracuse," 6–7.

56. Clopper, *Child Labor*, 64.

57. Wertheim, "Chicago Children," 4; Bremer, "New York Newsboy," 20.

58. See, e.g., Clopper, *Child Labor*, 63–64.

59. Names and phrases borrowed from the titles of Horatio Alger novels.

Chapter Six

1. Betty Smith, *A Tree Grows in Brooklyn* (New York, 1943), 8–9.

2. Ibid.

3. Bosley Crowther, *Hollywood Rajah: The Life and Times of Louis B. Mayer* (New York, 1970), 17–20.

4. Juvenile Protective Association, *Junk Dealing and Juvenile Delinquency* (Chicago, n.d.), JAMC, 5.

5. Massachusetts Child Labor Committee, *Child Scavengers* (Boston, n.d.), 2.

6. Martin V. Melosi, *Garbage in the Cities: Refuse, Reform, and the Environment, 1880–1980* (College Station, Texas, 1981), 159–60, 153.

7. Charles Zueblin, *American Municipal Progress*, rev. ed. (New York, 1916), 73–83; Melosi, *Garbage in Cities*, 143.

8. Zueblin, *Municipal Progress*, 77–81.

9. Melosi, *Garbage in Cities*, 170–75.

10. Ibid., 161–62.

11. Sophonisba P. Breckinridge and Edith Abbott, "Housing Conditions in Chicago, Illinois: Back of the Yards," *American Journal of Sociology* XVI, no. 4 (January 1911), 464–65; Howard E. Wilson, *Mary McDowell, Neighbor* (Chicago, 1928), 143–44.

12. Upton Sinclair, *The Jungle* (1905; reprint, New York, 1960), 29–30.

13. Breckinridge and Abbott, "Back of the Yards," 466.

14. See, e.g., Leonard Covello, *The Heart Is the Teacher* (New York, 1958), 34; Massachusetts Child Labor Committee, *Child Scavengers*, 1–2.

15. The Children's Aid Society, *New York Street Kids* (New York, 1978), 44.

16. Perry Duis, "The Saloon and the Public City: Chicago and Boston, 1880–1920" (Ph.D. dissertation, University of Chicago, 1975), 132.

17. Clifford Shaw, *The Jack-Roller: A Delinquent Boy's Own Story* (1930; reprint, Chicago, 1966), 50–53.

18. Detroit *Free Press*, August 8, 1914, 5.

19. Henry W. Thurston, *Delinquency and Spare Time* (Cleveland, 1918), 26.

20. Covello, *Heart Is Teacher*, 28.

21. Ibid., 34.

22. Hy Kraft, *On My Way to the Theater* (New York, 1971), 13–14.

23. Oral history of John Madro, CP, 10.

24. Oral history of Marie Arendt, CP, 3–4.

25. Katherine Anthony, *Mothers Who Must Earn* (New York, 1914), 9–10.

26. Ibid., 146.

27. Charles Chapin, *Municipal Sanitation in the United States* (Providence, 1902), 316.

28. Philip Davis, *Street-land: Its Little People and Big Problems* (Boston, 1915), 73.

29. Juvenile Protective Association, *Junk Dealing,* 17; Massachusetts Child Labor Committee, *Child Scavengers,* 2.

30. Juvenile Protective Association, *Junk Dealing,* 13, 11, 58–60.

31. Harpo Marx with Rowland Barber, *Harpo Speaks* (New York, 1974), 38, 58.

Chapter Seven

1. National Child Labor Committee, *Child Workers in Kentucky* (New York, 1919), 185.

2. "Hearing Upon the Various So-Called Labor Bills Before the Judiciary of the Senate at the Senate Chamber," Albany, N.Y., March 4, 1903, NYCLC, box 2, folder 9, 10.

3. "Memo" on Chicago *Daily News* letterhead, JAMC, 6.

4. U.S. Department of Labor, Children's Bureau, *Child Labor Legislation in the United States* (Washington, D.C., 1915), 382–417.

5. [Myron Adams] "Newsboy Conditions in Chicago," JAP, 23; *Proceedings of the Fifth Annual Conference of the National Child Labor Committee* (Supplement to the *Annals,* March 1909), 230–31, 228–29.

6. "Hartford Regulates Child Street-Trades," *Survey* XXV (December 31, 1910), 511–12.

7. Lewis W. Hine, "Conditions in Vermont Street Trades, etc." (December 1916), NCLC.

8. On household chores, see Leslie Woodcock Tentler, *Wage-Earning Women: Industrial Work and Family Life in the United States, 1900–1930* (New York, 1979), 147–49; Sophonisba B. Breckinridge, *New Homes for Old* (New York, 1921), 54–65, 122–28; Susan Strasser, *Never Done: A History of American Housework* (New York, 1982).

9. Oral history of Adelia Marsik, IC, 4; E. G. Stern, *My Mother and I* (New York, 1917), 29–30; "The Pre-Adolescent Girl . . . Gads Hill Center," LDT, box 7, folder 4, 13; "The Pre-Adolescent Girl in Her Home," LDT, box 7, folder 4, 11; Breckinridge, *New Homes,* 124–27.

10. Stern, *Mother and I,* 55–56; Catharine Brody, "A New York Childhood," *The American Mercury* XIV (1928), 60.

11. "The Pre-Adolescent Girl in Her Home," 3, 5.

12. Greenwich House, *Thirteenth Annual Report* (New York, 1913–14), 18.

13. New York *Times,* April 9, 1909, 11.

14. John Modell and Tamara K. Hareven, "Urbanization and the Malleable Household: An Examination of Boarding and Lodging in American Families," in Tamara K. Hareven, ed., *Family and Kin in Urban Communities, 1900– 1930* (New York, 1977), 164–66; Gunther Barth, *City People: The Rise of Modern City Culture in Nineteenth-Century America* (New York, 1980), 47– 50.

15. U.S. Congress, Senate, *Reports of the Immigration Commission* (Washington, D.C., 1911), 26:139, 85, 92; J. C. Kennedy, *Wages and Family Budgets in the Chicago Stockyards District* (Chicago, 1914), 63.

16. On variations among different ethnic groups, see, e.g., John Bodnar, Roger Simon, and Michael P. Weber, *Lives of Their Own: Blacks, Italians, and Poles in Pittsburgh, 1900–1960* (Urbana, 1982), 102–8; Elizabeth H. Pleck, "A Mother's Wages: Income Earning Among Married Italian and Black Women, 1896–1911," in Michael Gordon, ed., *The American Family in Social-Historical Perspective,* 2nd ed. (New York, 1978), 490–510.

17. Tentler, *Wage-Earning Women,* 141; Thomas Bell, *Out of This Furnace* (1949; reprint, Pittsburgh, 1976), 149–53.

18. Charlotte Baum, Paula Hyman, and Sonya Michel, *The Jewish Woman in America* (New York, 1976), 108–9; Virginia Yans-McLaughlin, *Family and Community: Italian Immigrants in Buffalo, 1880–1930* (Ithaca, 1977), 214– 15.

19. State of New York, *Preliminary Report of the Factory Investigating Committee* (March 1, 1912), Appendix VII; Jeremy Felt, *Hostages of Fortune: Child Labor Reform in New York State* (Syracuse, 1965), 140–45; Mary Van Kleeck, *Child Labor in Home Industries* (New York, 1910).

20. *Reports of the Immigration Commission,* 26:94, 295, 643, 202, 295.

21. See *Preliminary Report of Factory Investigating Committee* for copies of these photographs.

22. Marie Ganz, in collaboration with Nat J. Ferber, *Rebels: Into Anarchy and Out Again* (New York, 1919), 40.

23. Brody, "New York Childhood," 61–62.

24. Greenwich House, *Thirteenth Report,* 18. I have rearranged the first and third paragraphs for clarity.

25. Kate Simon, *Bronx Primitive* (New York, 1982), 70.

26. Oral history of Marietta H. Interlandi, IC, 37.

Chapter Eight

1. David I. Macleod, *Building Character in the American Boy: The Boy Scouts, YMCA, and Their Forerunners, 1870–1920* (Madison, Wis., 1983), 112.

2. Michael M. Davis, Jr., *The Exploitation of Pleasure: A Study of Commercial Recreations in New York City* (New York, 1912), 8–9.

3. Juvenile Protective Association, "First Lessons in Gambling" (1911), JPA, folder 118; see also Betty Smith, *A Tree Grows in Brooklyn* (New York, 1943), 10–12.

4. Smith, *A Tree Grows,* 12–13.

5. *The Hustler,* December 1917, 12, 14.

6. Davis, *Exploitation of Pleasure,* 10.

7. Lewis Jacobs, *The Rise of the American Film* (New York, 1939), 4–7.

8. On first nickelodeon: ibid., 55–56; on New York City: John Collier, "Cheap Amusements," *Charities and the Commons* XX (April 1908), 74; on Chicago: Lucy France Pierce, "The Nickelodeon," *World Today* XV (October 1908), 1052.

9. Milton Berle with Haskel Frankel, *Milton Berle* (New York, 1974), 55.

10. Barton Currie, "The Nickel Madness," *Harper's Weekly* LI (August 24, 1907), 1246.

11. Roy Rosenzweig, *Eight Hours for What We Will: Workers and Leisure in an Industrial City, 1870–1920* (Cambridge, England, 1983), 197.

12. Edward Wagenknecht, *The Movies in an Age of Innocence* (Norman, Okla., 1962), 15, 20–21.

13. Wagenknecht, *The Movies,* 26; Jacobs, *Rise of Film,* 57, 68–71; Stuart and Elizabeth Ewen, *Channels of Desire: Mass Images and the Shaping of American Consciousness* (New York, 1982), 88–91.

14. Jacobs, *Rise of Film,* 67–76.

15. Robert Sklar, *Movie-made America: A Social History of American Movies* (New York, 1975), 45; Cleveland Recreation Survey, *Commercial Recreation* (Cleveland, 1920), 21; Wagenknecht, *The Movies,* 15; Sam Levenson, *Everything but Money* (New York, 1966), 109.

16. Cleveland Recreation Survey, 33; Jane Addams, *The Spirit of Youth and the City Streets* (1909; reprint, New York, 1972), 86–87; Levenson, *Everything but Money,* 108–11.

17. Rosenzweig, *Eight Hours,* 199–204; Phil Silvers with Robert Saffron, *The Laugh Is on Me* (New York, 1973), 10–11.

18. Esther Lee Rider, "Newsboys in Birmingham," *American Child* III, no. 4 (February 1922), 318; William Hard, "De kid wot works at night," *Everybody's Magazine* XVIII (January 1908), 35.

19. Madison Board of Commerce, *Madison Recreational Survey* (Madison, 1915), 78–80; Davis, *Exploitation of Pleasure,* 34; Research Department, School of Social Economy of Washington University, "The Newsboy of Saint Louis"

(St. Louis, n.d.), 9. See also Edward Chandler, "How Much Children Attend the Theater, the Quality of the Entertainment They Choose, and Its Effect Upon Them," *Proceedings of the Child Conference for Research and Welfare* (New York, 1909), 50.

20. Russell Sage Foundation, *Boyhood and Lawlessness* (New York, 1914), 67–68, 142–43; Addams, *Spirit of Youth*, 80.

21. William Saroyan, *The Bicycle Rider in Beverly Hills* (New York, 1952), 176.

22. Davis, *Exploitation of Pleasure*, 25, 35–36; Irving Howe, *World of Our Fathers: The Journey of the East European Jews to America and the Life They Found and Made* (New York, 1976), 213.

23. Davis, *Exploitation of Pleasure*, 32–33; Juvenile Protection Association, "Junk Dealing and Juvenile Delinquency," JAMC, 17; Harry Bremer, "Street Trades Investigation" (October 9, 1912), NCLC, 9.

Chapter Nine

1. Sophonisba Breckinridge, *New Homes for Old* (New York, 1921), 45.

2. Investigator's report on Charles Goldowsky, NYCLC, box 31, folder 9.

3. Investigator's report on Joseph Bosco, NYCLC, box 31, folder 9.

4. See NYCLC, box 1, folder 9. I manually computed the number of investigators' reports which mentioned that the boys were cheating their parents in this way.

5. Investigator's report on Dominick Abbruzzese, NYCLC, box 31, folder 9. See also reports on John Kovack and Frank Konfalo.

6. Investigator's report on Frank Brusco, NYCLC, box 31, folder 9.

7. Investigator's report on Dominick La Polla, NYCLC, box 31, folder 9.

8. Louise Montgomery, *The American Girl in the Stockyards District* (Chicago, 1913), 57–58.

9. Perry Duis, "The Saloon and the Public City: Chicago and Boston, 1880–1920" (Ph.D. dissertation, University of Chicago, 1975), I:167–68.

10. Marlin A. Gorsch and Richard Hammer, *The Last Testament of Lucky Luciano* (Boston, 1974), 9–11; Charles Angoff, *When I Was a Boy in Boston* (New York, 1947), 95–96; Harry Roskolenko, *The Time That Was Then: East Side 1900–1913—An Intimate Chronicle* (New York, 1971), 1.

11. "The Circle of Error," *Dziennik Związkowyi Zgoda* (March 15, 1910), FLPS.

12. Montgomery, *American Girl*, 60; Ruth True, *The Neglected Girl* (New York, 1914), 60.

13. *Narod Polski* V, no. 13 (March 27, 1901), FLPS. See also *Narod Polski* XVI, no. 43 (October 23, 1912), FLPS.

14. Mary Kingsbury Simkhovitch, *The City Worker's World in America* (New York, 1917), 130–31.

15. Katherine Anthony, *Mothers Who Must Earn* (New York, 1914), 51.

16. Simkhovitch, *City Worker*, 130–31.

17. Montgomery, *American Girl*, 57–58; True, *Neglected Girl*, 49.

18. Harry Bremer, "Report of Investigation: New York Newsboy" (1913), NCLC, box 4, chart #4; Maurice Hexter, "The Newsboys of Cincinnati," *Studies from the Helen S. Trounstine Foundation* I, no. 4 (January 15, 1919), 127; Alexander Fleisher, "The Newsboys of Milwaukee," *Fifteenth Biennial Report of the Bureau of Labor and Industrial Statistics*, State of Wisconsin (1911–12), 76; Herbert Maynard Diamond, "Street Trading Among Connecticut Grammar School Children," *Report of the Commission on Child Welfare to the Governor*, Supplementary Number (1921), 20.

Chapter Ten

1. Samuel Ornitz, *Haunch, Paunch, and Jowl: Anonymous Autobiography* (New York, 1923), 30.

2. See, e.g., National Child Labor Committee, "Street-workers," Pamphlet no. 246 (July 1915), 3; George Hall, "The Newsboys," *Proceedings of the Seventh Annual Meeting of the National Child Labor Committee* (Supplement to the *Annals*, 1911), 100–2.

3. "Sex O'Clock in America," *Current Opinion* LV (August 1913), 113; Lewis Erenberg, *Steppin' Out: New York Nightlife and the Transformation of America Culture, 1890–1930* (Westport, Connecticut, 1981), 76; James R. McGovern, "The American Woman's Pre-World War I Freedom in Manners and Morals," *Journal of American History* LV (September 1968), 27; Linda Gordon, *Woman's Body, Woman's Right: A Social History of Birth Control in America* (New York, 1976), 136–72.

4. Chicago Vice Commission, *The Social Evil in Chicago* (Chicago, 1912), 247–51.

5. Ibid., 237; Mike Gold, *Jews Without Money* (1930; reprint, New York, 1965), 6.

6. Chicago Vice Commission, *Social Evil*, 6.

7. Edward Clopper, *Child Labor in City Streets* (New York, 1912), 111–13.

8. Ruth True, *The Neglected Girl* (New York, 1914), 19.

9. "The Pre-Adolescent Girl . . . Gads Hill Center," LDT, box 7, folder 4, 13.

10. Mark Thomas Connelly, *The Response to Prostitution in the Progressive Era* (Chapel Hill, North Carolina, 1980), 114–35.

11. Ruth Rosen, *The Lost Sisterhood: Prostitution in America, 1900–1918* (Baltimore, 1982), 20.

12. Betty Smith, *A Tree Grows in Brooklyn* (New York, 1943), 218; Kate Simon, *Bronx Primitive* (New York, 1982), 138–42.

13. See, e.g., "Minutes" of NYCLC Executive Committee, October 17, 1904, August 30 and December 20, 1905, and January 20, February 24, and May 8, 1906, NYCLC, box 11, folder 1, part 2, 3; Elsa Wertheim, "Chicago Children in the Street Trades" (1917), JAMC, 9; Bruce Watson, "Street Trades in Pennsylvania," *American Child* IV (August 1922), 121.

14. U. S. Department of Labor, Children's Bureau, *Child Labor Legislation in the United States* (Washington, D.C., 1915), 382–417.

15. Lillian Wald, *The House on Henry Street* (1915; reprint, New York, 1971), 71–72.

16. See, e.g., on controversy over "stage children" in Chicago, S. H. Clark, "The Artist Child," in *The Child in the City,* ed. Sophonisba P. Breckinridge (Chicago, 1912), 302–9.

17. Milton Berle with Haskel Frankel, *Milton Berle* (New York, 1974), 67–71.

18. New York *Times,* May 20, 1913, 1.

19. SPCC folders, LW, box 42.

20. James Paulding, "Enforcing the Newsboy Law in New York and Newark," *Charities* XIV (June 10, 1905), 836.

21. John Commons et al., *History of Labor in the United States* (New York, 1935), III:435; U. S. Department of Labor, *Child Labor Legislation,* 382–417.

22. Paulding, "Enforcing Newsboy Law," 836–37; Elizabeth C. Watson, "Report of Investigation Conducted for the NYCLC" (1911), NYCLC, box 3, folder 4, 3–8; see also "Report of Committee on Newsboys to the Board of Directors," February 15, 1909, November 18, 1910, and March 2, 1917, in "Minutes" of NYCLC Executive Board, NYCLC, box 11, book 2; letters dated November 8, 1911, from superintendents of schools in Utica and Yonkers to George Hall on "enforcement of laws," NYCLC, box 31, folder 12; "View of Situation—2/13/17—E. H. Sullivan," memo, NYCLC, box 31, folder 22.

23. Paulding, "Enforcing Newsboy Law," 836–37; Esther Lee Rider, "Newsboys in Birmingham," *American Child* III (February 1922), 316; Alexander Fleisher, "The Newsboys of Milwaukee," *Fifteenth Biennial Report of the Bureau of Labor and Industrial Statistics,* State of Wisconsin (1911–12), 61–62; Wilma Ball, "Street Trading in Ohio," *American Child* I (August 1919), 126; Edward Clopper, "Children on the Streets of Cincinnati," *Proceedings of the Fourth Annual Meeting of the National Child Labor Committee* (Supplement to the *Annals,* 1908, 116; Maurice Hexter, "The Newsboys of Cincinnati," *Studies from the Helen S. Trounstine Foundation* I, no. 4, (January 15, 1919), 165.

24. "Extracts from School Superintendents' Letters Regarding Newsboy Law," NYCLC, box 11, book 2; letters sent to George Hall on the enforcement of the newsboy law, NYCLC, box 31, folder 6.

25. Report by Ethel Hanks, NYCLC, box 15, folder 12.

26. "View of Situation," NYCLC, box 31, folder 22.

27. Philip Davis, *Street-land: Its Little People and Big Problems* (Boston, 1915), 199–201.

28. Davis, *Street-land*, 202–11, 217–18; Lewis E. Palmer, "Horatio Alger, Then and Now," *Survey* XXVII (December 2, 1911), 1276.

29. Davis, *Street-land*, 202–5; Boston School Committee, "Superintendent's Report, Appendix D," in *School Documents* (1910), 137.

30. Boston School Committee, *School Documents*, 135–37; Lyman Beecher Stowe, "Boy Judges in a Boys Court," *Outlook* CIII (March 1, 1913), 495–96.

31. Stowe, in *Outlook*, 496.

32. Palmer, in *Survey*, 1276.

33. Stowe, in *Outlook*, 496.

34. Davis, *Street-land*, 221; Perry O. Powell, "Getting Hold of Milwaukee's Newsboys," *Playground* X (November 1910), 296–300; B. E. Kuechle, "Newsboys' Republic," *Survey* XIX (March 22, 1913), 859; Fleisher, "Newsboys of Milwaukee," 61–62.

35. "Milwaukee Newsboys' Republic," *Outlook* CIII (April 5, 1913), 743–44.

36. Madeleine Appel, "Enforcement of the Street Trades Law in Boston," *American Child* IV (August 1922), 104–6.

Chapter Eleven

1. *Editor and Publisher*, May 17, 1902, 7.

2. Maurice Hexter, "The Newsboys of Cincinnati," *Studies from the Helen S. Trounstine Foundation* I, no. 4 (January 15, 1919), 120; Alexander Fleisher, "The Newsboys of Milwaukee," *Fifteenth Biennial Report of the Bureau of Labor and Industrial Statistics*, State of Wisconsin (1911–12), 69.

3. Anna Reed, *Newsboy Service: A Study in Educational and Vocational Guidance* (Yonkers, 1917), 16–17; Hexter, "Newsboys," 120.

4. Harry Bremer, "Street Trades Investigation" (October 9, 1912), NCLC, box 4, 12–13.

5. David I. Macleod, *Building Character in the American Boy: The Boy Scouts, YMCA, and Their Forerunners, 1870–1920* (Madison, Wis., 1983), 282, 292.

6. Charity Organization Society papers. CSS. (To preserve confidentiality, further citation prohibited by rules governing use of this collection.)

7. Illinois Humane Society, case no. 548 (February 25, 1910), IHS, record 60.

8. William Hard, "De kid wot works at night," *Everybody's Magazine* XVIII (January 1908), 35.

9. Jacob Riis, "The New York Newsboy," *Century Magazine* LXXXV (December 1912), 252.

10. Fleisher, "Newsboys of Milwaukee," 69–70; Riis, "New York Newsboy," 253; [Myron Adams] "Newsboy Conditions in Chicago," JAP, 8.

11. Investigators' reports on Dominic Pavano and Harry Browne, NYCLC, box 31, folder 9.

12. Mervyn LeRoy, as told to Dick Kleiner, *Mervin LeRoy: Take One* (New York, 1974), 20.

13. "What a member of the Newsboy Law enforcing squad thinks about newspaper selling for young boys" (1914), NYCLC, box 33, folder 20.

14. Seattle *Post-Intelligencer,* October 6, 1917, 1.

15. See, e.g., Joe E. Brown, as told to Ralph Hancock, *Laughter Is a Wonderful Thing* (New York, 1956), 4.

16. *The Hustler* I, no. 4 (November 1917), 3.

17. Hexter "Newsboys," 147.

18. Robert Bruère, "Industrial Democracy: A Newsboys' Labor Union and What It Thinks of a College Education," *Outlook* LXXXI (1906), 879–83.

19. Johan Huizinga, *Homo Ludens: A Study of the Play Element in Culture* (Boston, 1955), 12.

20. G. Stanley Hall, *Adolescence: Its Psychology and Its Relations to Physiology, Anthropology, Sociology, Sex, Crime, Religion and Education,* 2 vols. (New York, 1905).

21. Allen F. Davis, "Introduction," in Jane Addams, *The Spirit of Youth and the City Streets* (1909; reprint, New York, 1972), xii–xiii; Macleod, *Building Character,* 112–13.

Chapter 12

1. W. A. Swanberg, *Pulitzer* (New York, 1967), 144–45.

2. Memos for Mr. Pulitzer on the newsboys' strike (July 21, 22, 24, 1899), NYWP.

3. Frank Luther Mott, *American Journalism, A History: 1690–1960,* 3rd. ed. (New York, 1962), 598.

4. Edwin Emery, *The Press and America,* 2nd ed. (Englewood Cliffs, N.J., 1962), 444.

5. Memo to Pulitzer, July 27, NYWP, 3.

6. New York *Times,* July 21, 1899, 2; New York *Sun,* July 21, 1899, 3.

7. *Times*, July 22, 4; *Sun*, July 22, 3.

8. *Sun*, July 22, 3.

9. *Times*, July 22, 4; *Sun*, July 22, 3.

10. Brooklyn *Daily Eagle*, July 21, 2.

11. *Sun*, July 21, 3.

12. New York *Daily Tribune*, July 26, 2.

13. *Sun*, July 21, 3.

14. Memo to Pulitzer, July 25, NYWP, 1–2.

15. Memo to Pulitzer, July 27, NYWP, 2.

16. *Sun*, July 21, 3, July 24, 3, July 25, 2, and July 31, 2; *Tribune*, July 26, 2, July 28, 2, and August 1, 3.

17. *Times*, July 23, 3; *Sun*, July 23, 2, and July 24, 3.

18. *Sun*, July 23, 2.

19. Memo to Pulitzer, NYWP, July 24, 2, and July 25, 2.

20. *Sun*, July 23, 2.

21. *Tribune*, July 26, 2.

22. *Sun*, July 23, 2.

23. *Sun*, July 25, 2; *Times*, July 25, 3; *Tribune*, July 24, 1.

24. Memo to Pulitzer, July 27, NYWP, 2.

25. *Tribune*, August 2, 3.

26. Mott, *American Journalism*, 598.

27. *Sun*, July 27, 3, and July 28, 2; *Tribune*, July 31, 3.

28. *Tribune*, July 26, 2.

29. *Times*, July 22, 4, and July 23, 3.

30. *Sun*, July 28, 2.

31. *Sun*, July 25, 2.

32. *Times*, July 25, 3.

33. *Sun*, July 25, 2; *Times*, July 25, 3.

34. *Tribune*, July 27, 2.

35. *Sun*, July 25, 2, July 27, 3, and July 28, 2.

36. *Times*, (1910), February 6, 16, July 22, 7, July 27, 5, November 24, 4, and November 25, 3; H. H. J. Porter, "The Strike of the Messenger Boys," *Survey* XXV (December 1910), 431–32; Detroit *Free Press*, June 11, 1914, 8.

37. Emery, *The Press*, 521.

38. *Editor and Publisher,* December 9, 1916, 34, and February 24, 1917, 10.

39. David Montgomery, *Workers' Control in America* (Cambridge, England, 1979), 95, 97.

40. *The Hustler* I, no. 4 (November 1917), 9; Seattle *Post-Intelligencer,* October 6, 1917, 1.

41. *Times,* July 3, 1918, 8; *Editor and Publisher,* July 20, 1918, 37.

42. Letter to editor, Minneapolis *Journal,* July 11, 1918, NYCLC, box 31, folder 15.

43. *Editor and Publisher,* January 26, 1918, 1; *Times,* January 28, 1918, 7; *Tribune,* January 29, 1918, 11.

44. *Tribune,* January 29, 1918, 11.

45. James M. Hardin, "The History of the Little Merchant System," ICMA, 22.

46. *Tribune,* January 29, 1918, 1.

47. *Editor and Publisher,* February 2, 1918, 5; *Times,* February 1, 18, February 2, 9, February 3, 4, February 4, 14, and February 8, 1; *Tribune,* February 3, 9.

48. *Editor and Publisher,* July 20, 1918, 36; *Tribune,* August 24, 1918, 6.

49. *Tribune,* (1918), August 17, 1, August 18, 1, August 20, 1, August 22, 1, and August 23, 1; see continuing coverage by the *Tribune* through January 25, 1919.

Chapter Thirteen

1. Confidential Report, "The Bootblack Industry of the City of New York," prepared by Francis H. Nichols, special agent of the Child Labor Committee (February 2, 1903), NYCLC, box 33, file 20.

2. Edward A. Steiner, *On the Trail of the Immigrant* (New York, 1906), 289–90; U.S. Immigration Commission, "The Greek padrone system in the United States," *Reports* (1911), II: 387–408; North American Civic League for Immigrants, "Report of New York–New Jersey Committee, December 1909–March 1911," 33–34; Leola Benedict Terhune, "The Greek Bootblack," *Survey* XXVI, 852–54.

3. Terhune, in *Survey,* 852–54; June Namias, *First Generation: In the Words of Twentieth Century American Immigrants* (Boston, 1978), 20–25.

4. Philip Davis, *Street-land: Its Little People and Big Problems* (Boston, 1915), 156.

5. National Child Labor Committee, *Child Welfare in Tennessee* (New York, 1920), 381; National Child Labor Committee, *Child Welfare in North Carolina* (New York, 1918), 217–18, 230.

6. Ernest Poole, *Child Labor—The Street* (New York, n.d.), 24; Harry Bremer, "Street Trades Investigation" (October 9, 1912), NCLC, box 4, 14; Nichols,

"Bootblack Industry," 3; Anthony Sorrentino, *Organizing Against Crime: Redeveloping the Neighborhood* (New York, 1977), 50–51.

7. Harpo Marx with Rowland Barber, *Harpo Speaks* (New York, 1974), 56; Joe E. Brown, as told to Ralph Hancock, *Laughter Is a Wonderful Thing* (New York, 1956), 13; George Burns, *The Third Time Around* (New York, 1980), 30.

8. Herbert Newton Casson, *The History of the Telephone* (Chicago, 1910), 178–82; Sam Levenson, *Everything but Money* (New York, 1966), 84.

9. *Editor and Publisher*, July 14, 1917, 12, and December 8, 1917, 26.

10. James M. Hardin, "The History of the Little Merchant System," ICMA, 21; William R. Scott, *Scientific Circulation Management* (New York, 1915), 90–96; *Editor and Publisher*, April 20, 1918, 4; Frank Luther Mott, *American Journalism, A History: 1690–1960*, 3rd ed. (New York, 1962), 597–98.

11 Scott, *Circulation*, 136–37; *Editor and Publisher*, October 13, 1917, part II, 5, and December 22, 1917, 25; Anna Reed, *Newsboy Service: A Study in Educational and Vocational Guidance* (Yonkers, 1917), 73; Margaret Kent Beard, "A Study of Newsboys in Yonkers—1920," NYCLC, box 31, folder 27, tables 9, 10, 14, 15.

12. Scott, *Circulation*, 98.

13. Harry Shulman, *Newsboys of New York: A Study of Their Legal and Illegal Work Activities During 1931* (New York, 1931), 6.

Epilogue

1. Daniel Bell, *Work and Its Discontents* (Boston, 1956), 31.

2. Jerre Mangione, *Mount Allegro* (New York, 1972), 223.

3. Harry Golden, *Only in America* (Cleveland, 1948), 53.

4. Leonard Covello, *The Heart Is the Teacher* (New York, 1958), 41. See also, for attitudes of Italian immigrants on the education of their children, John Briggs, *An Italian Passage: Immigrants to Three American Cities, 1890–1930* (New Haven, 1978), 191–244.

5. Jean-Paul Sartre, *Search for a Method*, translated by Hazel Barnes (New York, 1963), 85–89.

6. See Chapter 4.

7. Gilbert Seldes, *The Movies Come from America* (New York, 1937).

8. Philip French, *The Movie Moguls* (Chicago, 1971), 21–49.

9. Edward G. Robinson with Leonard Spigelgass, *All My Yesterdays* (New York, 1973), 112.

10. Bosley Crowther, *Hollywood Rajah: The Life and Times of Louis B. Mayer* (New York, 1960), 235–41; French, *Movie Moguls*, 40.

11. Robert Sklar, *Movie-made America: A Cultural History of American Movies* (New York, 1975), 161.

12. Ibid., 179–80.

13. Jack B. Warner, *My First Hundred Years in Hollywood* (New York, 1964), 199–201; Hal Wallis and Charles Higham, *Star Maker: The Autobiography of Hal Wallis* (New York, 1980), 23; Mervyn LeRoy, as told to Dick Kleiner, *Mervyn LeRoy: Take One* (New York, 1974), 93–94.

14. Robinson, *Yesterdays*, 116–17.

15. Robert Warshow, *The Immediate Experience: Movies, Comics, Theater, and Other Aspects of Popular Culture* (Garden City, N.Y., 1962), 131.

16. Sidney Kingsley, *Dead End: A Play in Three Acts* (New York, 1936), 150.

17. Sklar, *Movie-made America*, 196–97.

18. Andrew Bergman, "Frank Capra and Screwball Comedy," in Richard Glatzer and John Raeburn, eds., *Frank Capra: The Man and His Films* (Ann Arbor, Mich. 1975), 75.

19. John Raeburn, "Introduction," ibid., ix.

20. Joe Adamson, *Groucho, Harpo, Chico, and Sometimes Zeppo* (New York, 1973), 285.

21. Ibid., 90–91.

22. Seldes, quoted in Irving Howe, *World of Our Fathers: The Journey of the East European Jews to America and the Life They Found and Made* (New York, 1976), 566.

23. Howe, ibid., 566.

24. Patrick McGilligan, "Introduction: The Life Daddy Would Have Liked to Live," *Yankee Doodle Dandy*, screenplay (Madison, Wis., 1981), 16.

25. June Namias, *First Generation: In the Words of Twentieth Century American Immigrants* (Boston, 1978), 27.

26. Jerre Mangione, *An Ethnic at Large* (New York, 1978), 175–76.

27. Godfrey Hodgson, *America in Our Time* (New York, 1978), 67–98.

28. John Kenneth Galbraith, *The Affluent Society* (New York, 1957), 1.

Index